CHRISTIAN PEACEMAKING & INTERNATIONAL CONFLICT

CHRISTIAN PEACEMAKING & INTERNATIONAL CONFLICT

A REALIST PACIFIST PERSPECTIVE

DUANE K. FRIESEN

FOREWORD BY STANLEY HAUERWAS

A CHRISTIAN PEACE SHELF SELECTION

HERALD PRESS
SCOTTDALE, PENNSYLVANIA
KITCHENER, ONTARIO

Library of Congress Cataloging-in-Publication Data

Friesen, Duane K.
    Christian peacemaking and international conflict.

    "A Christian peace shelf selection."
    Bibliography: p.
    Includes indexes.
    1. Peace—Religious aspects—Christianity.
2. Christianity and international affairs.   I. Title.
BT736.4.F74   1986   261.8'73   85-24803
ISBN 0-8361-1273-3 (pbk.)

Unless otherwise indicated, Scripture quotations are from the Revised
Standard Version of the Bible, copyrighted 1946, 1952, © 1971, 1973.

Scripture quotations marked NEB are from *The New English Bible*. © The
Delegates of the Oxford University Press and The Syndics of the
Cambridge University Press 1961, 1970. Reprinted by permission.

Scripture quotations marked NIV are from the HOLY BIBLE: NEW
INTERNATIONAL VERSION. Copyright © 1973, 1978, 1984 by the
International Bible Society. Used by permission of Zondervan Bible Publishers.

To ELIZABETH, ANNE, AND SARA

TABLE OF CONTENTS

Foreword

Anyone reading this book will know it needs no foreword by me. The book commends itself as it obviously is the work of a serious and mature thinker. Though Professor Friesen covers many different issues, he does so with a directness, simplicity, and economy of style that is characteristic of people who are in command of their subject. The only reason, therefore, for me to write a foreword is that, as a Mennonite camp follower, I remain closely enough identified with the Protestant mainstream that my name on the book may encourage some to overcome their prejudice against avowed pacifists and read it.

I do not mean to sound overly critical of such prejudice as it is one I long shared. Brought up on the thought of Reinhold Niebuhr, I simply assumed that pacifism, even if it could be justified theologically, could never sustain an intelligible social and political ethic. That prejudice unfortunately was too often confirmed by pacifists who tried in various ways to turn their political irrelevance into a virtue; they could help to keep those of us who chose to be politically responsible "honest." As a result, most of us in the Protestant (and Catholic) mainstream praised the pacifists for their vocational purity but felt justified in ignoring those who wrote in the pacifist tradition since they lacked "intellectual seriousness." Pacifists were assigned to the ghetto only to be noticed when we needed an example of an "ideal type."

Friesen's book is nothing less than a declaration of war against the pretentious arrogance of the mainstream's dismissal of pacifists. Calling himself a "realist pacifist" Friesen refuses to be relegated to a ghetto. He forcefully argues that his pacifist commitments make him no less able to provide political analysis or to be a political actor. Noting that pacifists have too often failed to provide a link between their theological and ethical stance with the world of international politics, he sets out to do exactly that. Thus the book begins with a well-formed critique of some of the dominant presumptions about international relations. Relying on theories that stress the cooperative nature of relations between nations, Friesen is able to show how the balance of power model distorts our understanding of the nature of international relations.

With unusual facility Friesen draws on both theological and social scientific literature to suggest that living in a more peaceful world is no utopian dream but a realistic alternative. The problem is not that living in a more peaceful world is not attainable, but that our imaginations have long been schooled out of such a hope by a false "realism."

Friesen's book, therefore, is an extended exercise in freeing our imaginations from the "necessity" of violent alternatives. By suggesting ways we can delegitimate war as an institution, he starts us on the path of finding ways to make wars less likely. He knows this will not be accomplished quickly, but he suggests that that does not mean we should not begin.

Friesen also attacks head-on the oft-made claim that justice and peace are finally incompatible since attempts to secure justice will inextricably require us to resort to violence. By challenging assumptions about what a "justice" achieved through violence might mean, Friesen helps us gain a new perspective on the nature of just communities. Rather than peace and justice being antithetical, he shows that peace offers the way to justice by reminding us that no theory of justice can be substituted for a community's practice of aiding the disadvantaged.

I have emphasized the "realistic" side of Friesen's book because that is the aspect of the pacifist perspective that is usually missing. However, it would be a mistake to overlook Friesen's equally compelling account of the theological basis for his pacifism. Indeed, the power of his book derives from his skillful interweaving of the theological and social analysis. In doing so, his book is no less a challenge to the pacifist as to those who have accepted war as an alternative for Christians. Friesen will give no comfort to those pacifists who think their very commitment to pacifism is enough. Rather, he forces us who would be pacifists to recognize the many ways we may, inspite of our explicit avowal of pacifism, lead lives that implicitly accept violence as acceptable for others.

It is my hope that Friesen has written the book that will finally begin the discussion that we have long needed between the so-called "peace churches" and the mainstream of Christianity. He has done what pacifists have constantly been challenged to do—namely, show how the pacifist commitment can make realistic political sense. If he is ignored, as pacifist thinkers of the past have been unfairly ignored, it will only be because so many of us continue to have our imaginations captured by the self-imposed necessity of violence.

—Stanley Hauerwas
Durham, North Carolina

CHRISTIAN PEACE SHELF PREFACE

This book represents a new direction for the Christian Peace Shelf. The list to date has consisted largely of expositions of biblical pacifism, exhortations and theologizing about peacemaking, examples of the peace witness in history, and treatises on the implications of the peace ethic for issues such as the military draft and war taxes. These have been necessary and useful contributions to our stated purpose: "the promotion of Christian peace principles and their applications." For the most part, the suggested "applications" have been limited in scope to individual ethical decisions, or to recommendations for the life of the church community.

Now, however, we are publishing a book that enters the realm of international politics and dares to propose the relevance of a pacifist ethic for the formidable problem of world order. *Christian Peacemaking and International Conflict* attempts provocative new linkages between theological foundations, ethical principles, and social institutions.

In this book, Duane Friesen brings together authentic faith and considerable scientific knowledge. His academic credentials recommend him for the task; he is conversant in theology, ethics, and the social sciences. He can move ably from theoretical analysis to concrete cases to a concern for spiritual empowerment.

Friesen is well aware of the risks he is taking in presenting this book to the public. He can anticipate the barrage of counter-arguments. The politically oriented critics will accuse him of being simplistic, naive, utopian. Many persons grounded in traditional sectarian pacifism will claim that he has no business trying to rid the world of war.

But the times demand a book like this. Conventional "realism," whether political or theological, has brought the globe to the brink of catastrophe. Perhaps we are now ready to acknowledge "realist pacifism" as an example of the new kind of thinking that Albert Einstein called for at the dawn of the atomic age.

As a longtime member of the Christian Peace Shelf editorial board, I'm delighted that we can now recommend Duane Friesen's work to our readers. It represents a new stage in the application of basic theological convictions to the public agenda of our times. It is ambitious, prophetic, rooted in Christian wisdom, appropriate for serious study by anyone who cares about the well-being of our global village.

—J. R. Burkholder
Goshen, Indiana

AUTHOR'S PREFACE

I wish to express my appreciation to many persons and institutions who have helped to make this book possible. Though the flaws and shortcomings of this book are my own, I am now more aware than ever of the corporate nature of the human enterprise as I reflect on the process that gave birth to and nurtured this project.

The original stimulus for my research came as a result of being charged in 1973 with the responsibility of developing a Peace Studies Program at Bethel College in North Newton, Kansas. That process involved the inauguration of a Peace Lecture Series. I was part of a team of persons that helped to make peacemaking a central theme of the college as a whole. To help support this goal the college received a grant from the "Fund for the Improvement of Post-Secondary Education" (FIPE) of the United States government. The Peace Lecture Series and the FIPE grant brought many scholars and activists to campus who have been important to my own thinking: Dorothy Day, Paul Wehr, Elise Boulding, Karl Deutsch, Tom Stonier, Philip Berrigan, Kenneth Boulding, Lloyd Dumas, Hanna Newcombe, Richard McSorley, Danilo Dolci, and many others.

At the same time I became active in the Consortium of Peace Research, Education, and Development (COPRED), where I came into contact with scholars, teachers, and activists concerned with peace. Many of the ideas for this book came as a result of conversations with (and reading the books of) this community of scholars.

I particularly want to express appreciation to William Keeney, who was academic dean at Bethel College when the Peace Studies Program was begun. He was a colleague of mine in the Peace Studies Program, served with me on the committee to help administer the FIPE grant, and for a number of years was executive director of COPRED, including several years when the headquarters of COPRED was located at Bethel College. Bill has been a conversation partner of mine for many years about issues of peace and justice. He also read the entire manuscript and gave numerous suggestions on how to improve it.

I began writing the book in 1976-77 while on sabbatical leave from Bethel College at the Ecumenical Institute for Theological and Cultural Research in Collegeville, Minnesota. I appreciated this relaxed and stimulating atmosphere where I first tested ideas with fellow scholars. Also during that year I had the opportunity to share with students and faculty at the Associated Mennonite Biblical Seminaries in Elkhart, Indiana. John H. Yoder gave valuable suggestions after reading an earlier draft of the manuscript. I wish also to thank the group of persons appointed by Peace Section of the Mennonite Central Committee to review books for the Peace Shelf series of Herald Press. Ted Koontz, John R. Burkholder, and John Stoner read the manuscript and gave numerous suggestions for improvement. My editor, Richard Kauffman, has worked with me diligently in helping to improve the manuscript.

Over the years, many of my faculty colleagues at Bethel College have been conversation partners and have served as a stimulus and inspiration. My students at Bethel College have had to endure hearing me lecture and discuss with them the ideas in this book. I appreciate their patience and the many conversations with them I have been privileged to enjoy. Two students have had a very direct hand in this book. I thank Duane Goossen (currently a legislator in the Kansas House of Representatives), who helped write chapter eight, and Elizabeth Schmidt (currently a graduate student in theology at Iliff School of Theology), who wrote much of chapter nine.

I want to thank a number of other persons who have had an important hand in this project at one stage or another: Robin Craig Reimer, who helped type the manuscript and prepare the bibliography; Barry Bartel, who made corrections in the manuscript and prepared the index; and Mary Regier, Debbie Flickinger, and Cynthia Goerzen, who also typed the manuscript as it went through its various stages of development.

Above all, my family has been a source of encouragement, inspiration, and joy over the many years this project has been in process. I wish to acknowledge both that larger extended family that we have been privileged to be near the past fifteen years and my wife and daughters. My wife, Elizabeth, has listened many hours to the ideas in the book. She also read the entire manuscript and provided her gentle critique. I am grateful to our daughter, Anne, who contributed the design of the cover of the book. Our daughters, Anne and Sara, have grown up to be young adults while this project has been in process. It is my prayer that our generation may leave to our children a world not closer to the brink of destruction but one that is more peaceful and just.   O

PART I
THE PERSPECTIVE

1 INTRODUCTION

A. THE PROBLEM STATED

How does a Christian perspective on life help us to interpret and respond to international conflict? What does it mean to be a peacemaker in a world in which war and injustice are dominant realities? How do Christians relate to the fact that war is accepted by most persons as a permanent feature of the human condition, is legitimated and prepared for by most governments, and is one of the major preoccupations of statesmen in their development of foreign policy? Must we acquiesce to conditions of inequality and oppression which divide the human race into rich and poor as permanent features of the social environment?

B. A REALIST PACIFIST PERSPECTIVE

I have defined my approach as a "realist" and "pacifist" perspective. Some persons regard these two terms as inherently contradictory. A pacifist perspective—the rejection of violence as a means to preserve or bring about peace and justice—is regarded by many as utopian and unrealistic. True, some kinds of pacifism fit the stereotype of utopianism, lacking realism because of their naive and optimistic assumptions about human nature and human institutions. I want, however, to argue for a type of pacifism that is applicable to the world in which we live, a pacifism that is not only ethical but one that is practical as well, an approach that is essential if we are to survive as a human race. "Realist" means two things: (1) a pacifism that takes seriously the nature of human sinfulness as it expresses itself in the egoistic self-interest and exploitation of political and economic systems; and (2) a pacifism that is political, that seeks to apply its ethic to resolution of practical, economic, and political issues within human institutions.

My position has grown out of three traditions of human thought that have deeply influenced me the past 20 years: (1) the pacifist tradition of the Bible, the historic peace churches, and the political nonviolence movement exemplified by such persons as Mohandas K. Gandhi and Martin L. King; (2) the just war tradition from St. Augustine through Paul Ramsey and Ralph Potter; and (3) the peace research tradition of the past thirty years, particularly the study and research done by a growing number of social

19

scientists on human conflict and how it has been and can be resolved peacefully. All three streams of thought have influenced me deeply; all three
traditions provide insight into the problem and solution of international
conflict. Though obviously major conflicts exist between and within these
three streams of thought, this book draws from all three traditions in
proposing an approach to international conflict.

C. CONFLICTING APPROACHES TO PEACEMAKING: HOLDING JUSTICE AND NONVIOLENCE TOGETHER

The word "peace" is an extremely ambiguous concept. It is used by
the United States Air Force in its motto, "Peace is our profession." Most
military strategists would claim that peace is the aim of their policies. Pacifists have understood peace in a fundamentally different way—as an
ideology in which the threat of use of violence is completely rejected.
Marxists use the term to refer to the social and economic conditions of a
classless society. Henry Kissinger, Le Duc Tho, Anwar Sadat, and
Menachem Begin have all been awarded a Nobel Peace Prize.

We can broadly define two contrasting views of peace, views which do
not necessarily contradict each other, but place the emphasis upon different
considerations. The one view—a view that Roland Bainton describes as the
Pax Romana—is the concept of peace as the absence of war, the absence of
overt hostility between groups or persons. This is probably the most common concept of peace. It is said, for instance, that peace has been restored
between Israel and Egypt in the Middle East, in Vietnam, or in an urban
ghetto, meaning that overt violent conflict has ceased. Persons like Henry
Kissinger and Le Duc Tho are awarded the Nobel Peace Prize for bringing
about this kind of peace.

Bainton characterizes another kind of peace with the Hebrew concept
of *shalom*. Shalom refers to a situation in which justice and righteousness
exist.[1] The contrast between the concepts of the Pax Romana and shalom
are evident in Martin Luther King's popular statement: "Peace is not
merely the absence of tension but the presence of justice and broth-
erhood."[2] This distinction between pax and shalom illuminates the nature
of racial tension in the United States. One could have argued that in the
fifties a peaceful (pax) relationship existed between blacks and whites, since
there was relatively little overt direct violence between individuals and
groups. Yet we know that behind the so-called peaceful relationships of the
fifties was a system of exploitive relationships that failed to meet the test of
shalom.

The positive definition of peace is the dominant perspective in the Bible. For the Old Testament prophets shalom is a social-environmental con-

dition in which righteousness and justice prevail, not just the absence of war or violence. Peace is a condition of general social welfare, as reflected in Jeremiah's statement to the exiles in Babylon to seek the welfare (shalom) of the city in which they are living: "You shall not see the sword, nor shall you have famine, but I will give you assured peace in this place" (Jeremiah 14:13). Hosea, too, envisions a situation of shalom, one which includes even the birds and the beasts.

> Then I will make a covenant on behalf of Israel with the wild beasts, the birds of the air, and the things that creep on the earth, and I will break bow and sword and weapon of war and sweep them off the earth, so that all living creatures may lie down without fear. (Hosea 2:18-19, NEB)

The New Testament continues a similar vision in which peace is both a present reality and a future hope. The book of Revelation envisions a new Jerusalem in which the "old order has passed away." For the writer of Ephesians the new order is realized in a new community.

> For he is himself our peace. Gentiles and Jews, he has made the two one, and in his own body of flesh and blood has broken down the enmity which stood like a dividing wall between them; for he annulled the law with its rules and regulations, so as to create out of the two a single new humanity in himself, thereby making peace. This was his purpose, to reconcile the two in a single body to God through the cross, on which he killed the enmity. (Ephesians 2:14-16, NEB)

For Paul, "God has reconciled us men to himself through Christ, and he has enlisted us in this service of reconciliation" (2 Corinthians 5:18, NEB). In the Sermon on the Mount Jesus says, "Blessed are the peacemakers for they shall be called the children of God" (Matthew 5:9). In this biblical vision, peace is both a hope, a vision for the future, and a present task, a ministry of peacemaking and reconciliation.

The absence of a holistic view of peace is the leading cause of failures and illusions in the pursuit of peace. Peace is both a means of reconciliation through nonviolent processes of conflict resolution and a goal or end in which conditions of social justice and environmental wholeness have been achieved. When the emphasis is upon negative peace as the absence of overt physical violence to the exclusion of social justice, then one may pursue policies of pacification or repression that force persons to accept unjust social conditions. Sometimes pacifists have been so dominated by the concern to prevent overt physical violence or abstain from war that they have failed to support as vigorously the conditions and processes that lead to justice. On the other hand, to stress the goal of justice and liberation from oppression at the expense of the search for nonviolent means of social change fails to acknowledge the important connection of means and ends. "Peace by peace" became the motto of Betty Williams and Mairead Corrigan's peace people in Ireland, to distinguish themselves from those who also claim that peace can be obtained through violent means.

Peace, then, must be defined in terms of both (1) the goal of justice and (2) nonviolence as the means to achieve justice. Justice should define the goal of the peacemaker rather than the assumption that order is more peaceful than the disruption that comes about through change. People who are relatively secure and comfortable tend to have a stake in preserving order. Justice, rather than one's position in society, should determine the course of action. We choose a course of action in the imperfect world in which we live. When two courses of action are measured against a concept of justice, it may be necessary to seek to change a social system even though that may be disruptive. Sometimes the preservation of order is preferable. Much depends, of course, upon our understanding of social justice, which we will discuss in chapter five. We can diagram this relationship as follows:

JUSTICE
determines the
direction in which
one goes

system maintenance

system change

Peace = a situation
in which order
must be maintained
to preserve justice

Peace = a situation where
social arrangements must
be fundamentally altered
so that full human
development is possible.

The other variable in the definition of peace is the *means* used to obtain the goal of peace. Here we can make the simple distinction between violent and nonviolent actions, terms which will be further clarified in chapter six. I am using the term "violence" to refer to intentional, overt physical harm or injury that is directed against another individual or group. If we relate the goal variable and the means variable to each other, we can then define four possible conceptions of the nature of peacemaking. I have placed the term "justice" in the middle of the diagram to indicate that justice is the basic ethical norm which determines whether one should work to change a social system or seek to maintain order in a social system.

GOAL ORIENTATION

	System Maintenance	System Change
Violent Action	(1) The use of violent action to bring about an end to overt conflict, or to preserve or restore some kind of just order in a society or between nations.	(2) The use of violent action to bring about fundamental structural change that changes the relationship between groups or nations so that the relationship is just or nonexploitive.
	————————— JUSTICE —————————	
Non-violent Action	(3) The use of nonviolent action means to bring about a cessation of hostilities, or restore the original situation of a just social order.	(4) The use of nonviolent action to bring about fundamental structural change in a society that changes the relationship between groups or nations so that the relationship is just or nonexploitive.

(Left axis label: MEANS ORIENTATION)

Each of the above positions defines typical approaches to the nature of peace and how it is to be brought about. Most people assume that the way to peace is through types 1 and 2, the use of violence or the threat of violence either to maintain or change a social system. I intend to show in the chapters that follow that these two positions are not only ethically and theologically inadequate, but they are unrealistic and politically dangerous. More creative and imaginative resolutions of conflict and injustice must be explored if the human race is going to have a future on this planet.

Type 1: System Maintenance Through Violent Means

The assumption of this position is that the international system as it has now evolved must be basically accepted as the framework for a secure peace. Modifications of the system may occur, but only so long as one keeps in mind the basic givens of national sovereignty and national self-interest. Because war is generally not in the self-interest of nations, much effort is spent in determining how, given the international system, overt hostilities can be avoided. What are the minimal conditions necessary for peace? Since it is assumed that nations operate out of their own self-interest, a danger or threat from other nations or blocks of nations always exists. Therefore, the maintenance of peace is based upon a strong military defense system which can deter other nations from taking advantage of others. Military weakness is viewed with alarm, because it is believed that weakness will invite aggression. This approach undergirds and sustains the current arms race among the superpowers and encourages arms sales to smaller nations in order to "secure" the peace.

Those who work within these assumptions seek to train professional scholars and practitioners who are capable of a "realistic" appraisal of the international system and their own nation's place within it. The majority of educational programs in international studies at American universities and colleges operate from these assumptions. Most politicians and diplomats also accept these assumptions. If war does break out, these professionals need to be skilled at bringing an end to hostilities in such a way that the nation's self-interest is protected.

The ethical tradition of "just war" theory basically operates within the framework of these assumptions.[3] The world has been corrupted by sin. These sinful realities are particularly expressed in human political and economic institutions. Just war theory is a system of ethical thought which is relevant to these conditions of sin. The use of violent force is a regrettable and unfortunate necessity in a world governed by egoistic self-interest. Just war theory is a system of ethical guidelines to define the conditions under which violent force may be used to bring about peace with justice.

Type 2: System Change Through Violent Means

This type proposes to make fundamental changes in the system, but to accomplish that goal sees the necessity of using violence to deal with the entrenched political and economic power which resists social and systemic change. For the most part no one advocates type 2 on an international scale (though traditional Marxist-Leninist theory was international in scale), so peacemaking is directed primarily to internal situations within countries, especially so-called developing nations. Today this revolutionary tradition undergirds various liberation movements in Africa, Asia, and Latin America. In some of these settings Christians and Marxists have joined together in the liberation struggle. As far as the church is concerned, the ethical tradition of just revolution is predominantly a post-Reformation phenomenon, reflected in the Calvinist theocratic vision, especially in the left wing of Puritanism, and most recently in some forms of liberation theology.[4]

In addition to the theological and ethical difficulties with types 1 and 2, in the light of a Christian perspective, these perspectives fail to assess adequately the inherent and necessary connection of means and ends. It is assumed that violence can lead to "good" ends without acknowledging sufficiently that violence, once used, is perpetuated in the social system. Both types 1 and 2 have good intentions: an outcome that is peaceful. Instead, both perpetuate systems of violence that have led to the precarious predicament of the human race today.

It is time to think more creatively and imaginatively about a different approach to peace than is represented by types 1 and 2. Such a tradition of thought and action does exist. However, it has only been perpetuated by a minority throughout history. Most people are unaware of this history. Most politicians and diplomats do not even consider these alternatives when pursuing peace. The general public, including most Christians who should be aware of this peacemaking tradition, are woefully ignorant of its potential. The chapters that follow elaborate and defend ethically, theologically, and practically an approach to peacemaking reflected by types 3 and 4.

Type 3: Nonviolent Means to Maintain a System of Order

This type utilizes nonviolent means in such a way as to maintain a system of order with justice. Nonviolent means of conflict resolution can be used to end hostilities and their causes in such a way which takes into account the self-interest of the persons or groups involved in the conflict. A growing body of research and action models are available for consideration by reconcilers or third-party intervenors who can help to bring about resolution of tension.

Variations of this type are nonviolent strategies and techniques of national defense. Gene Sharp and Adam Roberts, among others, have written books which discuss the role of nonviolence as a defense mechanism.[5] Some Scandanavian countries are allocating part of their defense budget for such research. Norway employed nonviolent techniques very effectively against the Nazis in the Second World War. Czechoslovakia's use of nonviolent tactics against the Russian invasion in 1968 is another interesting case study. In these cases nonviolent means are employed to preserve a system against aggressors who are seeking to disrupt, exploit, or take over one's country.

The sixteenth-century Anabaptist tradition of Christian pacifism is also a variation of type 3. This position generally accepts the assumptions of type 1 about the sinful nature of human institutions. Pacifists in this tradition, however, believe that they are called to witness to a different kind of ethic which practices love and compassion and refuses to harm any human being in any way. This peacemaking position refuses to cooperate with violence (through conscientious objection to war or war taxes) and seeks to find alternative forms of human service which express compassion. Because the Anabaptists believed that their pacifist ethic would be practiced only by a small minority who would likely suffer for their convictions, the position has often been labeled as a "withdrawal" position. In fact, by acts of omission and commission, the Anabaptists engaged in sharp conflict with the dominant institutions of medieval society. These actions contributed to the development of a pluralistic society and the rise of democracy.

Type 3 pacifism is also reflected in many so-called utopian or communal groups which develop a social lifestyle and context set apart from society. Sometimes this separation is deliberately sought so as to avoid conflict with society. But even such deliberate withdrawal from society may have long-term effects upon the larger social order because of the witness or model that is exemplified.

Type 4: Nonviolent Means Toward System Change

A fourth type of peacemaking aims to bring about fundamental systemic change toward social justice with nonviolent forms of action. Variations in this position range along a continuum from gradualist long-range change, using orderly established procedures with a minimum of conflict with the system, to a kind of change which more sharply conflicts with the social system and uses extraordinary and extralegal forms of action to bring about change.

Disarmament plans, or the development of some kind of international or global system of world order, usually envision a long-range program of gradualist change. So-called liberal pacifism of the early twentieth century, with its various shades of interpretation, would probably fit in this category. Usually liberal pacifism is criticized for its optimistic assumptions about the possibilities of educating nations to have more altruistic attitudes towards others. However, a much more realistic view of the problem of changing the international system can be taken.

Tom Stonier and Kenneth Boulding see war as a human social institution which has been created by human beings given certain social conditions. Stonier says that just as slavery as an institution has practically disappeared, so it is possible that war as an institution will gradually become unacceptable as a means of resolving conflict. This does not mean that nations can be educated to be more altruistic, as conflicts between groups will continue to occur and other means of resolving these conflicts will need to be found. Rather, the survival of the human race and thus national self-interest requires us to eradicate war itself. Kenneth Boulding says:

> Man is now faced with the problem of getting rid of war, and this is a unique and unprecedented problem peculiar to the twentieth century. In the age of civilization war was a stable social institution, and for mankind as a whole, a tolerable one. In the twentieth century the system of international relations which was based on unilateral national defense has broken down because of the change in the fundamental parameters of the system, and war has therefore become intolerable.[6]

Boulding acknowledges that some serious thinkers believe that humanity is not capable of solving this problem. He himself is modestly optimistic. The solution will come, however, not because nations will suddenly become more altruistic, but because they will need to solve the problem out of their own self-interest.

Gradualist change can be aided by voluntary associations and the professions. Through voluntary organizations, power is organized into some kind of socially cohesive force to bring pressure to bear upon social institutions. Through the professions human beings can apply their creative energies to envision and create alternative institutions of conflict resolution.[7] Nonviolent direct action, as employed by such persons as Mohandas K. Gandhi and Martin L. King, is the most widely known method of nonviolent social change as an alternative to violent revolution. Much research is being done on the role of this kind of action in achieving social change. Historians have tended to focus upon the role of violence in social change, but persons such as Gene Sharp and George Lakey argue that nonviolent strategies have often played a predominant role in bringing about fundamental social change.[8] Sometimes nonviolent action theory is regarded by critics as naively optimistic about the possibilities for change. Both Gandhi and King, however, were prepared to suffer and engage in a long struggle because of the intransigence of evil institutions. Thus they said nonviolent activists need to prepare themselves spiritually for a long and hard struggle.

When types 3 and 4 are viewed from a Christian perspective, the eschatological vision of shalom reflected in the Old Testament prophets and in the Gospels of the New Testament is a crucial resource. Peace for the whole earth is the goal, though Christians must still recognize that they live within an imperfect world. Nevertheless, the Christian is to live as if the future were already here and to seek to translate that future into practical social and political action. The problem is not unlike that which Paul faced on the role of women. The vision of equality between the sexes is reflected in Paul's statement in Galatians 3:28: "There is neither male nor female." Yet Paul had to relate this vision to a patriarchal social situation. How can a new vision of freedom be expressed within a fallen social order? On another issue, slavery, Paul urges that Onesimus, the runaway slave, return to his master, also that his master treat him with equality as a brother in Christ. In recent history the church seems to have understood the biblical vision on slavery as rejection of the institution entirely. Likewise, the church is in the process of developing more fully the vision of Galatians 3:28 on the role of women. But it hardly has begun to attempt to apply the eschatological vision of shalom to the problem of war.

Christians have found themselves defending all four types of peacemaking. The purpose of this book, however, is not just to describe and analyze how and why Christians have thought and acted the way they have. Rather, its purpose is to show how and why the approach reflected in types 3 and 4 is the appropriate peacemaking vocation for Christians living in the twentieth century. It is the calling of the church in the twentieth century to utilize its spiritual and intellectual resources to take the eschatological vision of shalom as both a means and a goal and to apply this vision to the problem of war and injustice. This vision must be applied in such a way as to avoid a naive optimism and to take into account the realistic situation of human sin that is especially lifted up by type 1. It must also take seriously unjust social structures and the need for fundamental change emphasized by type 2. Both of these concerns, however, must be approached from the standpoint of the nonviolent way of life of types 3 and 4. Toward this end the church can learn from the biblical and Christian heritage of pacifism as well as from the social science research which has recently developed helpful models for the peaceful resolution of conflict.

D. AN OUTLINE OF THE ARGUMENT

An adequate position on Christian peacemaking requires thinking through the interlocking relationship of theological, ethical, empirical, spiritual, practical, and strategic factors. The weakness of pacifist literature is that a "systematic" and thorough statement of the position does not exist. Some books provide a good theological and ethical foundation for the position, but do not show how pacifism applies to the world of international politics. Other books argue for particular political strategies but do not give the theological and ethical rationale. The most serious weakness in pacifist literature is its failure to connect a theological and ethical framework with an empirical understanding of the world of international politics. This book is a special effort to be interdisciplinary by attending to relevant research from the social sciences concerning international politics and by reflecting upon the theological and ethical traditions of political thought.

Whenever we develop a political philosophy we operate on certain assumptions about who we are, to whom we are speaking, and what the nature of the context is within which our thinking is being done. How we view the international system is particularly critical. Chapter two demonstrates how a view of the international system as a transnational network of interconnections is both more descriptive of the world and more amenable to Christian values than the traditional balance of power view. A transnational network model involves long-range thinking as well as a global perspective. Both of these dimensions are more compatible with commitment to the church as a transnational community which speaks for universal values that transcend national loyalties.

These contextual judgments are closely connected with theological and philosophical views on humanity, history, and human institutions. Chapters three and four show how our observation of the world and interpretation of what is going on fit into a more overarching perspective about the meaning of history, of God's relationship to human affairs, and our vocation as creatures of God. Chapter three will describe the task of theology and look at the issue of peace and justice from the standpoint of the doctrines of creation and sin. Chapter four will look at these issues from the standpoint of the doctrines of redemption and eschatology.

Ethical judgments are made about means and ends, about what actions are right or wrong, and what goals or values are coming into being. These ethical judgments are closely tied to a theological perspective, but they also influence and are influenced by the empirical data regarded as ethically relevant. Chapter five will elaborate the concept of justice and chapter six the concept of nonviolence. Chapter six includes a critique of theories of justified violence.

Once having defined a general orientation in terms of these levels of analysis, we conclude with three chapters that are more practical. Chapter seven proposes what general policies must be pursued in order to prevent war. Chapter eight outlines specific types of action that can be taken in the light of these general recommendations. A final chapter describes the spiritual resources and communal structures that are necessary to sustain a Christian vocation of peacemaking amidst the obstacles it will encounter in this evil and conflict-ridden world. ○

2 ASSUMPTIONS AND PERSPECTIVE FOR A THEOLOGY OF PEACEMAKING

Our understanding about who we are, to whom we are speaking, and our definition of the temporal and geographical context of our thought determine to a large degree how we approach issues of international conflict. Traditional thinking about international conflict is shaped by four assumptions: one, that policymakers (presidents and secretaries of state, for example) are the primary actors in international affairs; two, that the nation-state is the dominant reality in the international system and its role is to protect the national self-interest (though perceptions of what constitutes self-interest may vary considerably); three, that a strong military is critical in maintaining national security; and four, that immediate and short-range policy considerations take precedence over long-range ones.

These four assumptions are integrally connected. These assumptions not only explain the world, but they also prescribe the options that are available to policymakers. If the world indeed works as traditionalists believe it does, certain definite patterns of action follow from this view of the world. If one perceives the locus of power to be in the heads of nation-states who are principally concerned with the threat of or use of military power to protect national self-interest, then foreign policy, for example, will be dominated by security interests.

Most Christian ethicists who have written about international affairs have assumed that their ethical reflection must be directed to policymakers—to presidents, secretaries of state, prime ministers, and other persons in positions of power who hold the views described above. This assumption itself determines to a great extent what can and will be said about international relations. This assumed orientation of the "court theologians" dictates that ethical reflection will be seen within a narrow time framework—the immediate policy considerations facing a particular nation-state at a particular time. Secondly, these court theologians must adjust their thinking to fit into the realistic assumptions of policymakers whose primary consideration is the national self-interest. Thus, ethical reflection is adjusted to fit into the more narrow particularism of various nationalisms or tribalisms in order to appear realistic to policymakers. Such an orientation lacks a more far-reaching internationalist or global perspective. Thirdly, this viewpoint begins by accepting the present structure of the international system since most statesmen operate within the givens of that structure. Questions about fundamental systemic change in the international system do not arise. Traditional nation-state structures, concepts of sovereignty, and balance of power relationships dominate the thinking. This so-called realist perspective has dominated most Protestant ethical thinking about international affairs throughout the 1950s and 1960s.

A. POLITICAL MODELS: TRANSNATIONAL NETWORK RATHER THAN BALANCE OF POWER

The realist school of thought is based upon a balance of power model of the international system where the dominant actors in international politics are a group of powerful and relatively balanced nation-states. This model views the international system as a plurality of nation-states who interact with each other out of concern to protect their own sovereignty and self-interests. On the one hand, nations seek to preserve their own relative power so as to remain secure in the face of threats and aggression from other states, and on the other hand seek to augment their own power to take advantage of the quarrels of others in order to aggrandize themselves. Quincy Wright says these two principles are the "two incompatible shibboleths of the game of world politics" that have dominated from the 1500s to the end of World War II.[1] Within such a system war has been prevalent.

In balance of power theory nation-states aim to maintain an equilibrium in the international system. No one state can then have so much more power than another as to disturb that equilibrium through armed force. To maintain the system of equilibrium, states either seek to maintain their own strength through armaments (leading opposing states, of course, to do the same, resulting in an arms race); form alliances against an opposing state (which leads usually to an opposing alliance so that, instead of a plurality of states, each checking the other's power, a bipolar system develops); or develop a system of collective security, in which all states agree to come to the aid of any other state that is attacked.

The system of collective security—the principle underlying the formation of the League of Nations—was in fact unstable since it attempted to impose the post-World War I status quo upon the defeated nations, especially upon Germany. It was inevitable that Germany, in alliance with other nations such as Italy and Japan, would refuse to accept the status quo and seek to augment its own power to change the status quo. Thus in just one decade after the founding of the League of Nations, the equilibrium of nations was again in jeopardy. A struggle for power developed between those nations seeking to maintain and those wanting to change the status quo. The preservation of power to further one's own interest, according to Quincy Wright, is "the inherent contradiction in the . . . balance of power" theory and the reason that "it did not give permanent stability."[2]

According to the balance of power model the roots of war are competing national interest, miscalculation by leaders about their relative power, and the overconcentration of power in any one nation-state or alliances of nation-states. Peace is, therefore, sought through military strength in order to check power with power. But instead of preventing war, the system is inherently unstable, as Quincy Wright has pointed out, and war frequently breaks out.

There are two general criticisms of the balance of power model of international relationships: one, it is inadequate as a model to describe the nature of international relationships; and two, its view of what makes for peace and prevents war is badly mistaken because the system generates arms races which increase insecurity and undermine peace.

The world can no longer be understood in terms of a relatively symmetrical relationship of power between a group of fairly similar nation-states engaged in policies of alliance and counter-alliance. Even if a balance of power image could be applied to the bipolar relationship of the United States and the Soviet Union this image does not as readily apply to China. China is primarily a regional power, not a world power like the United States and the Soviet Union. Nor does the image apply to Western Europe and Japan. Western Europe and Japan are powerful forces in the world largely in terms of competitive economic factors, not military power. Most countries in the world (over 150 now) are not in any kind of a balance of power strategy at all, but are genuinely nonaligned, and not even much affected by the bipolar American-Soviet relationship. Countries generally feel free to enter into economic relationships with either of the great powers without fear of jeopardizing their relationship with other powers. Countries of Eastern Europe still remain relatively under Soviet control, and countries in East Asia (Taiwan, South Korea, the Philippines, and Thailand) are seen in a limited way as part of the American balance of power in the Far East. However, the Vietnam War showed very clearly the limitations of the balance of power concept in the Far East. Though the United States might have entered Vietnam with notions of a balance of power vis-a-vis China, the Vietnam struggle was settled by local factions basically independent of the United States, China, or the Soviet Union. In many conflicts in the third world and in the Middle East, the danger is that the great powers might become involved, but the potential destructiveness of war has prevented them thus far from engaging in an all-out balance of power struggle as was characteristic of the European nation-states in the eighteenth, nineteenth, and first half of the twentieth centuries. That is why the bloody conflicts in the Congo, Indonesia, Nigeria, and India-Pakistan did not involve the big powers militarily as one might have expected under the old balance of power system.

The most vivid illustration of the basic changes that have occurred in the international system in the past four decades is in Western Europe. Although it was the locus of many major wars from the seventeenth to the first half of the twentieth century, Europe has now become so integrated economically that it is difficult to conceive that France, Germany, or England would make war on each other. Robert Keohane and Joseph Nye put it as follows:

> Particularly among industrialized, pluralist countries, the perceived margin of safety has widened: fears of attack in general have declined, and fears of attack by one another are virtually nonexistent. France has abandoned the *tous azimuts* (defense in all directions) strategy that President de Gaulle advocated (it was not taken seriously even at the time). Canada's last war plans for fighting the United States were abandoned half a century ago. Britain and Germany no longer feel threatened by each other. Intense relationships of mutual influence exist between these countries, but in most of them force is irrelevant or unimportant as an instrument of policy.[3]

These fundamental changes in the relations between nations have led another group of international theorists like Keohane and Nye to challenge the old balance of power model. These theorists view the world as a global system in which nation-states are only one set of actors. Many other forces of a transnational nature—cultural, economic, and political—challenge the view of nation-states as self-contained independent actors.[4]

So long as one continues to think in terms of the nation-state operating basically as a self-contained power unit in a world of self-contained nation-states, then war as an institution for solving disputes between these units seems inevitable. On the other hand, the more one begins to see the interconnectedness of transnational networks of trade, communication, transportation, technology, resources, reliance upon transnational institutions for monetary stability, and other factors, the more difficult it is to conceive of war as an appropriate and inevitable means by which disputes can or will be solved. Nations are becoming so interdependent for their own well-being and survival that to engage in war with an opposing nation may simply be too costly in terms of a nation's own self-interest. Richard Barnet points out how these entangling economic relationships have crossed ideological lines.

> One graphic illustration of the entangling economic relationships that now cross ideological lines is the pipeline system for the flow of oil and natural gas. Romanians are importing large quantities of oil from Iran through an Israeli pipeline that is the major conduit through which Iranian oil flows to Europe. It is not only to symbolize independence of the Soviet Union but to derive a crucial economic advantage that has made Romania the one country of Eastern Europe to maintain good relations with Israel. Knowledgeable European oil dealers claim that the Soviets have also received oil through Israel's pipeline. In the early 1960's the Soviets began to build a pipeline network of their own. The first pipeline was to Czechoslovakia, and the next, the Friendship Pipeline, linked Soviet oil fields to East Germany and the Baltic seaports. In the 1970's the Soviets have extended the Czech pipeline to make it possible to supply oil and natural gas to Western Europe. (Since the pipeline is entirely inside Czechoslovakia, East Germany does not have to be consulted about sales to West Germany.) A branch of the pipeline serves Northern Europe. The Friendship II Pipeline connects new fields in Siberia with West Europe. For many years Soviet oil sales to West Europe through the pipeline system . . . have become increasingly important for the West European economy.[5]

The clash between the two images of the world became evident in 1982 when President Ronald Reagan attempted to halt Western Europe's technological cooperation with the Soviet Union to build a natural gas pipeline from Siberia to Western Europe. Operating out of old images of the world which would erect barriers between nation-states based on ideological differences, Reagan failed to halt the flow of history toward greater technological and economic interdependence.

As interdependence increases, resorting to war becomes increasingly costly and less likely. In the former European balance of power system, war was a relatively acceptable alternative to peace. Nations were ready to go to war for what today would be regarded as relatively minor causes. War today between the United States, Japan, and the countries of Western Europe is simply out of the question. The reason is that war is too costly. The benefits likely to result from war are far outweighed by the costs—the destruction likely to come from even a so-called limited war. It is far better to try to pursue the national interest through relatively peaceful competitive strategies. Says Edwin Reischauer, former U.S. ambassador to Japan:

Unlike the European situation in the eighteenth and nineteenth centuries, war between the major military powers can no longer be considered by them to be a really acceptable alternative to peace and could be seriously contemplated only under the most dire and unusual circumstances. Thus, the balance of power between them is very solid, more like a great shift of forces—something very much out of the ordinary, comparable to a cataclysmic flood or earthquake—to destabilize the balance and set a great landslide or war in motion.[6]

Reischauer furthermore says that

military power and warfare . . . are dwindling aspects of international relations and other matters are beginning to loom as more crucial. Limited regional wars will no doubt continue to be fought in the less developed parts of the world, but wars between the great powers appear to be a receding threat. If this is true, then our present heavy concentration on military matters is a somewhat outdated response that runs the danger of diverting our attention and efforts from more serious problems.[7]

It is true that the Soviet Union and the United States or Israel and the Arab states operate very much according to traditional patterns of national self-interest and military power. In this sense the traditional balance of power model does account for some international behavior. The problem is that leaders of these nations will remain locked in to these images that can only produce instability and eventually war. The danger is that political leaders will continue to conduct foreign policy in terms of past images and balance of power patterns and fail to recognize other possible patterns of interdependence.

Political leaders act and respond to events based upon memory or images learned from teachers who lived in a very different world. One of the problems in foreign policy formation is how to integrate feedback into the system so that a social system can actually learn to respond to the changes in the world.

Unfortunately, United States foreign policy is still being conducted largely in terms of balance of power politics, in which military strength continues to be the primary measure of power. Western Europe, at one time the locus of most international wars, is now so interdependent economically that it is almost impossible to conceive of these nations engaging in war against each other. In effect transnational factors have become much more fundamental in the behavior of European states and national factors

have become relatively less important. This has happened without any deliberate transfer of sovereignty to the international level.

Bruce Russett points to the European Common Market as a case of
economic and cultural integration which makes

> traditional nation-state relationships obsolete. Regional organization
> has the positive value of substantially reducing the probability of con-
> flict within regions, while promoting social and economic integration
> within them.... In a world not yet ready or able to achieve integration
> at a global level, this regional integration can nevertheless be seen as a
> first step toward reducing the probability of war and encouraging cross-
> national political and economic ties.[8]

Though nation-states are still powerful actors in international politics,
economic factors are beginning to outweigh political factors in their operation. This is essentially Lester Brown's thesis in *World Without Borders*,
and what Richard Barnet and Ronald Mueller point out in *Global Reach:
the Power of Multinational Corporations*. The global corporation is dedicated to centralized planning on a world scale. Success is measured in terms
of growth of global profits and global market shares. A president of the IBM
World Trade Corporation said, "The boundaries that separate one nation
from another are no more real than the equator." According to George Ball,
the world corporation

> is planning and acting well in advance of the world's political ideas be-
> cause it is a modern concept designed to meet modern requirements.
> The nation-state is a very old-fashioned idea and badly adapted to our
> present complex world.[9]

Though these statements by Ball and the president of IBM can be exag-
gerated, they do convey an image of how our world is changing. Of course,
while the multinational corporation may inhibit wars between nations, it
creates other problems which we will discuss in chapter five.

Other transnational networks, including legal structures, voluntary associations, and supranational organizations such as religious bodies, also
transcend nation-state boundaries and are not necessarily governed by the
policies of national governments. The church is one such transnational
entity in international politics. The impact of papal views on birth control
and abortion may affect the behavior of Catholics on a worldwide basis independent of the policies of the particular nation-states within which
Catholics are citizens. To some extent during the Vietnam struggle a

minority of church members effectively represented a transnational perspective that may have had some effect on the actual outcome of the war. At least the opinions and behavior of a minority prevented the United States from pursuing its policy without considerable resistance from its own citizens, who also had support for their resistance from Christians and persons of many other persuasions around the world. Modern communication technology makes possible such a transnational network.

B. CONCEPTS OF POWER: CONSENT OF THE PEOPLE RATHER THAN MILITARY MIGHT

In the traditional balance of power model of world politics, power is measured primarily in military terms. Power is assumed to reside in the heads of states who can utilize this power to accomplish political ends. It is assumed that the heads of states ultimately determine what happens in international affairs. In order to be relevant, therefore, traditional Christian ethicists seek to think ethically in terms that are acceptable to the heads of states.

Though the leaders of nation-states do have power to affect the course of world affairs, this power is much more relative and limited than is usually supposed. The hidden power of every state, even the most totalitarian, resides to a great extent in the consent, either overt or passive, of the governed. Karl Deutsch points out that "the voluntary or habitual compliance of the mass of the population is the invisible but very real basis of the power of every government."[10]

The reality of "people" power is reflected in the recent changes in Iran. Despite the overwhelming military power of the Shah which included massive military support from the United States, the Shah was unable to remain in power because of massive, largely nonviolent, resistance to his power by the people. The Iranian situation is only one illustration of many other similar cases where people power has shaped political events. Gene Sharp, in *The Politics of Nonviolent Action*, describes a number of such uses of people power. Sharp contrasts two types of power. One view of power sees citizens as dependent upon the goodwill and decisions of the people at the top of the hierarchical systems to which they belong. In this view, power is monolithic, residing in the few at the top of the power structure. It is self-perpetuating and reinforcing. If rulers do not voluntarily decide to limit their power, it can only be checked or controlled by overwhelming physical might. War is based on this view of power.

A second view of power is that governments depend on people, that power is pluralistic and fragile because it depends on many groups for its reinforcement. In this view governments are limited by the consent of the people they govern. People can limit, control, and change their governments either by refusing to give consent to what they are commanded to do, or by doing things they are not expected to do. When large numbers of people exercise this kind of power, they can have a tremendous effect on changing the behavior of rulers or in even overthrowing them. Since power is, in this case, the unwillingness to obey or to act contrary to expectations, such power can achieve results in nonviolent ways.[11]

The assumption of this study is that power resides in people, not just statesmen, and that, furthermore, a large number of actors affect the direction of international affairs, not primarily heads of state. Thus the intended audience of this study is ordinary people who can have an effect on international affairs, not primarily because they can influence statesmen (though that is one form of action) but because they are actors themselves, especially as members of economic institutions and other nongovernmental organizations. President Ronald Reagan, for example, was essentially powerless to prevent the technological and economic integration of natural gas supplies across ideological lines because economic and technological factors were more determining factors. President Jimmy Carter's grain embargo was largely ineffective and represented only a brief interlude in an ongoing trade relationship between wheat farmers and the Soviet Union. The Kansas wheat farmer is an actor in international politics. Hosts of similar economic actors who represent a powerful interest may so shape the course of world events that the heads of nation-states will no longer be able to pursue outmoded power politics.

C. TIME AND SPACE:
THE LONG-RANGE, GLOBAL VIEW
RATHER THAN THE SHORT-RANGE, NATIONAL VIEW

Those who hold to the balance of power model think in terms of a short span of time and primarily from a national perspective. Persons with a transnational network model view the solutions to the problems of war and economic injustice from a long-range perspective and in a global framework. It is only in terms of this model that it is possible to think creatively about alternatives to arms races and war.

The search for an alternative to war is only a meaningful question, if we look at the issue from a long-range global perspective. If one takes the long view, it is more difficult to conceive of modern war as a useful policy. Political leaders are often caught in the trap of knowing a better long-range approach while being locked into more immediate short-range responses. Modern warfare is so destructive that the very pursuit of war as an instrument of national policy defeats the very self-interest of the nation which utilizes war. Yet it is a tempting short-range solution. Kenneth Boulding has said that "the missile and the nuclear warhead have potentially made the conventional national states as obsolete as gunpowder made the feudal baron and the walled city."[12] Long-range thinking is the only way we can get out of the present traps which bind us to destructive violence and injustice.

Balance of power thinking assumes that its view of the world has been true from the beginning of time and will be true in the future. The paradox of the balance of power view is that it generalizes from how the system works now to what reality is like, as if the current system has a kind of cosmic necessity about it. Because it fails to take a historical view of the way the international system has changed over time, it views the recent era of the domination of the nation-state as the way international politics has always worked and will always work in the future.

Sometimes balance of power thinking is legitimated by supporting short-range thinking about the international system with general theories of human nature which define war as inevitable. The current international system, which produces arms races that eventually result in war between states, is often explained by theologians in terms of a basic flaw in human nature. If this is the case, of course, then the human race is doomed to repeat the same sins over and over again. This point of view is evident in the thought of St. Augustine, Martin Luther, and continues in contemporary theology in Paul Ramsey. Theologians often interpret stories in the first part of Genesis as symbolically pointing to the fact that war is a result of the Fall. The consequence of the Fall was Cain's act of murder against his brother Abel. This act of violence is forever established in the city of humankind, and it will never be overcome until the city of God is ushered in at the end of time when God will act to establish his kingdom on earth. The Tower of Babel story symbolically points to the plurality of human languages, cultures, and political systems to which humanity is condemned. Fallen humanity is forever doomed to misunderstandings and conflicts. As Paul Ramsey put it, the state and the institution of war is ordained by God as an alien act of his mercy to check power with power.[13]

In this view, the only way the consequences of the Fall, such as war, can be overcome is through God's gracious intervention into human affairs to alter the human relationship to God and therefore also to each other. Luther held that true Christians would not need the state symbolized by the coercive power of the sword to order their lives because love would rule among them. However, as Augustine pointed out, the wheat and the tares always remain together on earth, and even though true Christians are reoriented in their attitude and behavior, Christians and unbelievers must cooperate together in the preservation of order in the earthly city where the coercive power of the sword will persist. Until all human beings are converted and lives are changed to a new fellowship of love, war will be an inevitable component of human history.

Some political theorists have adopted a similar view. Machiavelli argued that "all those who have written upon civil institutions demonstrate that whoever deserves to found a state and give it laws, must start with assuming that all men are bad and ever ready to display their vicious nature."[14] The relationship between political groups is a game involving a struggle for power, a game which will at some point most likely result in war. Similarly, Thomas Hobbes asserted that "there is a general inclination of all mankind, a perpetual and restless desire for power after power that ceaseth only in death."[15] Unless restrained by some superior authority, the natural state of humanity would be a "war of every man against every man."[16] The Hobbesian view leads to the problem that even though the natural violence of humans can be restrained within a particular state, there is no authority to which all states give their allegiance which can restrain violence between states. In the absence of this authority, states are doomed to war.

The necessity of group violence has also been legitimated by some psychologists and ethologists. Freud and his followers suggested that group violence derives from a simple extension of the death or destructive instinct. Some ethologists regard war as an extension of human biological nature. Human beings draw upon a genetic inheritance of aggressiveness and territoriality which can be observed throughout the animal kingdom.

This view was initially proposed by the well-known ethologist, Konrad Lorenz, developed by persons like Anthony Storr, and popularized by Robert Ardrey and Desmond Morris. According to this view, human beings differ from animals in two ways: first, since they have no natural weapons, humans use their intelligence to create weapons of destruction to express the fighting instinct; second, humans lack the inhibition of intra-specific killing which protects other animal species.

Some critics have accused Lorenz of legitimating violent conflict since he assumed it is an inevitable part of our biological nature. Lorenz himself, however, would argue that fighting among humans can be sublimated, displaced, and channeled into less destructive battling grounds. Lorenz speculated that games and athletic events are ways to ritualize the fighting instinct in humans. The popularizers of Lorenz, Ardrey and Morris, can be accused of giving a "cosmic legitimacy" to war. In 1968 Robert Ardrey popularized Lorenz with his book, *The Territorial Imperative*.

A Gallup Poll, conducted about the same time—during the height of the Vietnam War—found that "a large proportion of the respondents felt that war was an inevitable consequence of human nature and that efforts to do away with it are futile."[17] This is not to say that Ardrey's views had influenced many Americans to hold similar views, but rather to say that views which hold war to be an inevitable expression of human nature expressed during a war may in fact be ways in which people legitimate the war.

General explanations of war in terms of human nature, whether these are theological, biological, psychological, or political theories, are all problematic because of their generality and lack of historical perspective. These theories are not able to explain why human behavior sometimes expresses itself in war. These theories are not able to explain why some nations go to war with each other and others do not. The explanation of war in terms of human nature involves an a priori concept of human nature which leads persons holding the view to find always and everywhere forms of behavior supporting what was believed to be true in the first place.

The generalization from sin to war as a necessary and permanent component of the fabric of human history fails to ask whether the general condition of sinfulness must express itself in war. For example, crime and physical violence are expressions of human sinfulness. Although theologically we would say all humans are sinners, most persons do not express their sinfulness in a life of crime or physical violence. These expressions of sinfulness occur under certain conditions. The key question, then, is, what are the conditions under which human sinfulness expresses itself in the institution of warfare? Slavery, dueling, lynching, vigilantism, and war are expressions of human sin under certain conditions. The question, then, is whether these conditions are permanent or passing phases in human history. If war is resorted to only under certain conditions within the international system, then we ought to determine what those conditions are and seek to create such conditions that war cannot or will not occur.

The movement toward an international system or network of transnational economic forces seems to be creating conditions that make war less likely, at least in the European arena. John Bennett and Harvey Seifert summarize well what is also my argument:

> All static and deterministic views of human sin are wrong. We cannot deduce from doctrines particular conclusions about what is possible or impossible in international relations.[18]

Some analogies from other institutional expressions of human sinfulness, such as slavery and male dominance over women, help illuminate our criticism of the human nature explanation for war and the need for a long-range view. Under certain conditions the institution of slavery is an expression of human sinfulness. In the first century the institution of slavery within the Roman Empire appeared to be a permanent and inevitable institution. The apostle Paul and other early Christians did not propose the abolition of the institution of slavery. Paul sought to describe how it was possible for masters and slaves to relate to each other as Christians while remaining in their roles within the institution of slavery. Later the church fathers spoke of slavery as the law of man *(jus gentium)*, an adjustment of the natural law to the conditions of sin. Eventually, after many centuries, the abolition of slavery as an institution began to become a meaningful question.

This change in thinking happened for two primary reasons: gradually the economic conditions changed such that it was profitable to use machines rather than slave labor; and, secondly, the system of psychological and theological legitimation of the institution of slavery was challenged and undermined. We cannot go into the complex interaction of these two factors. Basically, slavery has been abolished. The institution of slavery is regarded as illegitimate by most human beings. Most humans no longer regard it as a permanent aspect of the fabric of history as once was the case. We are not arguing that human beings have made progress or that today they are less sinful. Human oppression has many expressions, perhaps some even worse than slavery, but nevertheless, the institution of slavery has been abolished. Slavery as an institution is a passing phase in human history. This particular institution was not an inevitable expression of human sinfulness.

We can also draw an analogy to the issue of male-female roles. In the past couple of centuries, many persons have become aware of the oppression of women. Traditionalists have argued that the patriarchal structure of the Old Testament is a permanent aspect of creation ordained by God. More recently many would hold that these patriarchal structures are temporally and geographically conditioned, and are not a permanent feature of human nature.

Our thinking about war has not yet changed. Paul Ramsey, a contemporary Protestant ethicist, argues that war is inevitable. Though he developes a just war theory in an attempt to limit war based on certain ethical criteria, war itself has been assumed as inevitable within the earthly city. Ramsey criticizes the World Council of Churches study document, *Christians and the Prevention of War in an Atomic Age*, for its "crypto pacifism." Ramsey says that this document mistakenly and unrealistically hopes for the prevention of war. For Ramsey the appropriate question is how to limit war so that it can be conducted justly.

[handwritten margin note: Justifications of Slavery + War]

Ramsey's position, as well as much of the just war tradition, is based upon certain theological convictions about the nature of man and political authority. Ramsey cites with approval the Lutheran position of Helmut Thielicke, who saw the establishment of government by God as an alien work of God's mercy, by means of which arbitrary and unlimited power of a nation is to be restrained by further power. The world's nations are fated to govern one another through an opposition system in which power is restrained by further power. This primordial division of humanity cannot and furthermore ought not be overcome by "good words in the institutional field."[19] For Ramsey, therefore, war itself can be viewed as ordained by God as an alien act of his mercy to check power with power.

Is war any more ordained by God than is male dominance of women? Are we not dealing in both cases with a religious legitimation of a particular human institution that appears at a particular time and place in human history? The legitimation of patriarchal social structures is a way of perpetuating these structures. The assertion that war is ordained by God serves the same function. As we are beginning to recognize that patriarchal structures have no cosmic necessity, so we can begin also to assert the same about war.

D. THE CITIZEN:
A PERSPECTIVE RECOGNIZING GOD'S COMPASSION

A view of international politics is a combination of empirical observations and value judgments. A "values" perspective is reflected especially in those with whom we identify. The balance of power model tends to identify primarily with the nation and with heads of state. I have already explained why this view is inadequate on an empirical basis. It is also inadequate from a Christian values perspective. I am attempting to write this book with three basic values in mind: one, the Christian identity with the church as a community called by God to fulfill a special mission in the world; two, the Christian identity as a world citizen rather than primarily as a citizen of the United States or some other nation; and three, the Christian concern with how policies and proposals affect the least advantaged in the world. All of these values are closely tied together. The church is a community called by God to transcend national boundaries and to speak and act in behalf of the poor and weak in the world.

The words "Christian" and "church" are ambiguous and misleading words. We will clarify later what these words mean. I do not mean by church an exclusive group of people who believe they are absolutely right and are seeking to convert others to their worldview and standard of morality. I do not mean by church the mainline denominations with their institutional bureaucracies and membership lists. I reflect a theological definition of the church, a normative view, in which the church serves God's purpose in the world to bring good news to human beings, good news of justice and peace to those in misery and to those suffering from ravages of exploitation and war. To be a member of the church means to speak and act on behalf of humanity, to speak and act with compassion to enable life to become more human. We have opportunities today to transcend purely nationalistic frameworks, thus making it possible for the church to bring to bear more universal values upon international politics. By being an active member of a genuinely international church body, one is forced to take into account the views of others and overcome the value bias primarily influenced by membership in one society. The church has the potential for operating from a more universal consciousness to overcome more narrowly nationalistic perspectives.

But being a Christian is not an exclusive identity. Christian identity overlaps with the concerns of humanism and many other religious perspectives. In this book I want to share what I understand the vision for peace and justice to be when looked at in terms of God's compassion for human beings in Jesus Christ. I hope that the humanist, the atheist, and persons of other religious persuasions will not feel excluded from this inquiry, but will view this book as a contribution to an ongoing dialogue about the meaning and purpose of human life, a dialogue in which we can share with each other and learn from each other.

To be a Christian, to be a follower of Jesus Christ, means to declare oneself in solidarity with all peoples. As Dietrich Bonhoeffer said, Jesus Christ is "the man for others." This action and declaration in behalf of others is the primary vocation of all Christians in all walks of life. The task before us is to define how Christians can more faithfully see themselves as citizens of the world who are called in a special way to speak and act on behalf of the poor, the sorrowful, the victims of oppression, the widow, and the orphan. ○

Part II
A THEOLOGICAL PERSPECTIVE FOR THE COMMUNITY OF FAITH

3 THEOLOGICAL PERSPECTIVE ONE: CREATION AND SIN

A. THE NATURE AND TASK OF THEOLOGY

The aim of this section of the book is to elaborate on how peacemaking is illuminated by Christian theology. How does a view of God's relationship to the world help us to orient ourselves in a world of injustice and violence? What does it mean to be peacemakers who understand the shape and direction for peacemaking from the standpoint of God's revelation in Jesus Christ?

Theology is a perspective, a way of looking at issues from a particular point of view. A Christian theology is one that looks at the world and what is happening to it by taking as ultimately decisive for life the reality of Jesus Christ. Christian theology takes Jesus Christ seriously in two respects: as the one through whom ultimate reality (God) is revealed, and as the one who expresses the human in its wholeness. In contrast to humanism or naturalism, which understands human life and responsibility in one-dimensional terms—from the perspective of the human or the natural, Christian theology insists upon viewing life in terms of the reality of God.

The Old Testament prophet Amos is a model of how to do theology. Amos was aware of what was happening in international politics. He reported the interactions between and within the nations in explicit detail: the deportation of exiles to Edom, the invasion of the farmlands of Gilead, the burning of cities, the burning of the bones of the king of Edom, cheating of the poor by the rich in Israel, violence against kinsmen in Edom, luxurious living and insensitivity to the poor in Israel. All of these political and social realities are not viewed, however, in one-dimensional terms, but are interpreted in light of God's requirements of justice, righteousness and mercy, and God's judgment upon the nations for their failure to obey him. Amos was an astute political observer and was deeply sensitive to the transcendent reality of God who is Lord over the nations and will judge them according to the standards of justice and righteousness.

Using Amos as a model, the theologian should bring to the Bible an awareness of what is happening in the world—revolutionary violence in Latin America, an arms race among the big powers, a drought and famine in Africa. At the same time the theologian should bring to bear upon current events the biblical story of God's judgment and gracious intervention in history. Authentic Christian theology is an ongoing conversation between these two worlds.

The Bible is important for Christian theology because the Bible is a witness to the key events of God's action in history. These events are the fundamental points of orientation for the community of faith. To be a "Christian" means to look at the Bible from the Christ event—that event through which reality (God) has been most supremely revealed. From a "Christian" perspective, the Christ event is the key to the interpretation of the whole of redemption history.

However, we must also add that this event cannot be understood properly without viewing it in terms of God's redemptive activity in history, beginning with Abraham. Nor does the emphasis upon the primacy of the Christ event mean we can ignore the other dimensions of the biblical canon, or the history of interpretation by the church of the Christ event.[1] Christian ethics deals with the drama of redemption which culminates for Christians in the Christ event as seen through the entire biblical canon, and as interpreted by the church tradition.

The Bible is authoritative for us because it enables us to interpret human experience today. The Bible provides a rich source of insight into our understanding of human political, economic, and social life. This ancient collection of writings is still important to us because biblical insights continue to help us interpret human experience. The God of Abraham and Jesus Christ, who created the world and seeks to overcome the evil of the world through his gracious intervention into human affairs, is the same God we experience today when we seek to make sense of our life together. If the Bible did not help us interpret our life today, then it could not and would not be an authoritative source of insight.

The role of the Bible in providing a perspective for understanding the world of politics and economics is often misunderstood. The Bible is authoritative because of the way it sheds light upon and also helps us interpret human experience, not because we commit ourselves to it as an authority apart from the insight it provides. Some Christians say that first one must believe in the absolute authority of the Bible and then take that biblical viewpoint and apply it to human experience. The Bible supposedly supplies the entire content for theological reflection. Contemporary human experience is completely discounted. In this view we are to fit our modern experience completely into a biblical worldview. This view requires us to sacrifice modern scientific theory or our understanding of human psychology or sociology if it does not fit the Bible.

This approach to the Bible fails to take into account that the Bible is an historical or contextual document. The books of the Bible reflect the culture, issues, and perspectives of the people who wrote them. We who live several thousand years later are not required to adopt precisely the same cultural attitudes or worldview. Our task as interpreters of the Bible is to try to discern what are the basic themes, values, or perspectives on life reflected in the Bible. We must then seek to understand how these values apply to the new and different situation in our historical and cultural context. Inevitably in this process, our own cultural experience influences how we read the Bible. Those who hold to the absolute authority of the Bible cannot avoid reading the Bible from a particular perspective of the present. We are all interpreters of the Bible. No one can claim to duplicate the biblical view in an absolutely pure form.

We can illustrate how the Bible is to be used appropriately in Christian theological ethics by analyzing briefly an ethical issue spoken to by the apostle Paul when he gives advice to masters and slaves about how they are to treat each other. He advises masters to love their slaves and slaves to serve their masters with respect. The relationship between the two is no longer to be one of domination and submission but is to be transformed by the love of Jesus Christ. In Christ "there is neither slave nor free" (Galatians 3:28). Paul says that in the church, in the new community, Christians should relate to each other as if the institution of slavery no longer exists. Nevertheless, he does not call for the abolition of the institution of slavery itself. The book of Colossians (in the Pauline tradition, if not authored by Paul) calls on slaves to "obey in everything those who are your earthly masters" (Colossians 3:22). The runaway slave, Onesimus, is urged to go back to his master, Philemon, and Philemon is urged to accept Onesimus with love. Paul does not urge Philemon to give Onesimus his freedom from slavery as such. He is, rather, to treat Onesimus *as if* he were no longer his slave and Onesimus is to serve Philemon voluntarily out of a spirit of love *as if* he were no longer a slave.

In interpreting the meaning of this passage for today, one must understand both the basic biblical message as it applies to slavery and the sociocultural context within which Paul's words are to be understood. The biblical message of justice is radically opposed to slavery. God created human beings to be in fellowship as equals with each other. Slavery is an institution that arises out of the Fall and human sin. God is active in history to liberate people from slavery, from the leading of his people from slavery in Egypt to the coming of Jesus Christ who has come "to let the broken victims go free" (Luke 4:18). In the context, then, of the total biblical message, the institution of slavery is one of the "principalities and powers" over which Christ has been victorious (Colossians 2:13-15).

In the sociocultural context of Paul's time, slavery was a pervasive institution. There were probably as many slaves as free in Rome at the time of Claudius (A.D. 41-54), according to estimates of the historian, Gibbon. In Rome the slave had no personal rights but was regarded as a thing who had no protection from his master's cruelty. The slave was liable to death at the master's slightest whim. In this context, Paul's appeals to Philemon about how to treat his slave Onesimus are rather remarkable. Onesimus had not only run away, but he had evidently robbed his master (Philemon 18-19). Under ordinary circumstances, Onesimus' life would have been in danger. But Onesimus and Philemon were brothers in the Lord and this called for an entirely different kind of relationship than was prevalent in the world at the time.

Yet nowhere does Paul call for the abolition of the institution of slavery. Why not? It becomes quite clear if we keep the context in mind. In the first place, such a statement would have been completely utopian and unrealistic in a situation of so many slaves. Secondly, abolition of slavery as an institution would have required a bloody revolution and complete social upheaval. Thirdly, it is unlikely that the early Christian community had enough access to power to have any effect on changing the social situation. The church was a very small minority community. Therefore, Paul urged a new type of relationship within the new community, the church. The church should live out a new vision of the possibilities of human community, and thereby serve as a light and a witness to the world around it.

Once we are clear what the biblical message is and how it fits within its sociocultural context, the task of biblical interpretation for our time can begin. It would be a serious misuse of the Bible to assume that we should make exactly the same application to our time as Paul did in his time. Our sociocultural setting is much different from Paul's. Paradoxically, it is possible that the seemingly most faithful application of Paul, for example, a literal application of Paul to our time, might be the most unfaithful or unbiblical application. We have to ask what the biblical message of God's liberating message of love and reconciliation means for our situation, not Paul's. We have to discern what faithfulness means in our context where the sociocultural situation is much different. In our setting, a world that regards slavery as an evil, a world in which many of us have access to institutional structures, it would probably not be very courageous or biblical simply to imitate Paul or condemn an institution everyone agrees is evil.

A proper reading of Paul for our day should lead us to look at the forms of institutional evil and oppression that have replaced slavery: economic exploitation, conspicuous consumption by the wealthy, racism, and the gap between rich and poor. The appropriate interpretation of Paul is for us to ask: What is the application of the biblical Gospel message in our setting where forms of oppression similar to slavery exist?

In other words, biblical interpretation involves the discernment by the church of the meaning of the Bible in the context of political and social analysis. This Spirit-guided community, as it reads the Bible in Paul's context and seeks to understand what Paul was saying to his day, simultaneously must seek to discern what God's message is in the present sociopolitical situation. Without this movement back and forth from present to past and past to present, from the Bible in its context to the Spirit-guided community in our context and from the Spirit-guided community in our context back to the Bible, no biblical interpretation can be faithful. Biblically speaking, the most literal application of the past may turn out to be the most unfaithful.[2]

In summary, then, though the Bible as understood from the perspective of the drama of redemption culminating in the Christ event is normative for faith and life, contemporary human experience is also relevant to an understanding of the Bible. As members of the human community in general, we also can gain much truth from secular and humanistic insights. A dialectical relationship exists between revelation and general human insight; there is an ongoing conversation between the biblical world and human wisdom. Revelation is regarded as revelational because of the way it illumines, opens up, and makes sense of human experience. It is revelational precisely because of its power to explain human experience.

B. THE BIBLICAL DRAMA

The Bible is most helpful in interpreting human experience when we look at the biblical story as a whole. Four basic biblical themes shape a Christian attitude to sociopolitical reality—the themes of creation, the Fall, God's redemptive process in history, and the new age to come.

Human social and institutional life is an outgrowth of the creation of human beings in God's image. Human institutions are not inherently evil, but are expressions of the image of God in humanity. On a second level, human institutions are corrupted by sin, to the point that sometimes these institutions are viewed as the manifestation of demonic powers. A third theme is God's compassion, God's intervention into human life to make it whole, to restore human life to the original purposes for which God created it. On a fourth level, the Bible has a vision of what the future will be like when God has restored everything and the kingdom of God is fulfilled. Creation, fall, redemption, and eschatological vision—these are the basic categories of biblical thinking.[3]

All of these perspectives have been stressed in one way or another in the history of the church. One perspective emphasizes God's creation of humans as social beings, created in God's image to have dominion over nature. Political organization is a natural outgrowth of what it means for humans to be social animals. For Aristotle, humans form and shape their environment through a social process of social cooperation. Only in this social process of environmental modification which requires social cooperation and social organization do humans realize their potential as rational beings. Thomas Aquinas and the Roman Catholic natural law tradition are informed by this perspective on politics. This framework is the fundamental orientation of the encyclical of Pope John XXIII, *Pacem in Terris*, and the 1966 speech of Pope Paul VI at the United Nations. This position assumes that a common moral reason given by God in creation is the basis for justice and peace.

A second perspective on politics begins with the fallen human condition and sees political authority as a remedial institution ordained by God to curb and control the power of sin in society. Romans 13:1-7 is the classical biblical text supporting this position. St. Augustine, one of the classic interpreters of this view, sees the state as the punisher of evil and the protector of the good within the earthly city. The church cooperates with the state for the sake of earthly peace, until the heavenly peace of the city of God is ushered in at the end of time. Martin Luther held that if everyone were a true Christian there would be no need for political authority, for the state is ordained for the sake of order in a fallen world. The Anabaptists held that the state is ordained by God for the sake of the world, for those outside the Christian community of disciples. This perspective also informs the views of Reinhold Niebuhr and Paul Ramsey, who see politics as dominated by the Fall and, therefore, as inherently and inevitably dominated by power and coercive force. These views generally draw upon pessimistic political theories such as those of Machiavelli and Hobbes to support their position.

A third perspective views politics from the standpoint of God's redemptive activity in history to establish a new social order or community. A new social order is established through events like the Exodus, the liberation of a group of slaves from Egypt, and the establishment of a new covenant community at Sinai. Jesus is a liberator of the poor and oppressed (Luke 4:18-19). The church is a new sociopolitical reality in which a visible reconciliation between peoples (slaves and free, men and women, Jew and Greek) has been accomplished. Christ is Lord over the "powers," the cosmic sociopolitical forces of the world. This perspective on politics has been reflected especially in the Calvinist-Puritan heritage. This perspective informs those who take a more revolutionary approach to social change, most notably today those movements informed by "liberation theology."

The fourth perspective views politics from the standpoint of the new age to come, a new order of peace and justice which will be established by God. This eschatological hope is reflected in the Old Testament prophets like Isaiah and Hosea whose vision of a new covenant of peace involves both human beings and animals (Hosea 2:18f.; Isaiah 2:2-4; 11:1-9). In the New Testament the book of Revelation envisions the future as a new political order, "the holy city, new Jerusalem, coming down out of heaven from God, prepared as a bride adorned for her husband" (Revelation 21:2). These visions of a new age are usually also associated with visions of judgment upon the old political order. Sometimes the vision of the new age dominates the political dreams of Christians, as in the seventeenth century, left-wing Puritan groups such as the Levellers, Diggers, and Quakers. At other times the sense of judgment upon the present order is dominant, as is reflected in the radical perspectives of William Stringfellow and Art Gish who see America as the "Babylon which is falling."

Each of these perspectives has a contribution to make to a theology of peacemaking. Any one of these views by itself can distort an appropriate Christian attitude to politics. All of them draw upon an aspect of the biblical tradition and provide insight into human experience. An adequate theology must provide a holistic view in which all of these themes are properly related to each other.

C. CREATION:
THE GOODNESS OF HUMAN INSTITUTIONAL LIFE

Institutions are good and useful, an aspect of God's created order. Institutions provide stability, order, and regularity for our lives. Political systems, for example, enable people to coordinate their lives together and achieve goals as a group. People must organize themselves and create institutions to meet common needs: transportation and communication (streets, highways, postal service), public services and utilities (water supplies, sewer, emergency services for fire, flood). Since only in the smallest of communities can these decisions be made by the entire citizenry, certain systems of authority and leadership must be recognized by the people so they know who decides what goals a group is to pursue, what tasks need to be performed, and the manner in which these tasks are to be accomplished.

To achieve common goals for the common good requires resources. Some system for the collection of resources (usually in the form of taxes) must be developed. People often do not agree about what tasks should be pursued or how the resources from taxes are to be distributed. A system of procedures and rules for settling disputes must be recognized by the community if it wants to avoid constant strife and violence. Also a system of rules and sanctions needs to be developed to coordinate the behavior of people of a community so that each performs his or her proper role in the pursuit of tasks and so they do not forever infringe upon each other in ways that cause hostility and violence. In the exchange of goods, resources, and services in a community, people need either a system of barter or some medium for the exchange of goods and labor. An economic system that is relatively stable and provides for orderly exchange is desirable.

We could go on to describe many more functions that political and economic institutions perform in our lives. We count on institutions to provide order and stability, functions that are essential to human life. Institutions are usually taken for granted until some major crisis disrupts these institutions and plunges a society into disorder and chaos.

Though the Bible does not emphasize these institutional structures, they are often presupposed and considered important by the biblical writers. The covenant community of Israel developed an elaborate system of rules and procedures to regulate and coordinate life together. Patterns of authority and leadership are crucial in the communities of the Old Testament as well as in the early Christian community. Joseph, Moses and Aaron, Joshua and the judges, the various kings of Israel, Nehemiah, Jesus and his small band of disciples, Peter, Paul and the other apostles, the first deacons in the church—all had authority and exercised leadership in human institutions.

The New Testament church also recognizes the positive role of the state (Romans 13) in the coordination of human behavior. The governing authority provides a system of order that is, from the apostle Paul's perspective, "not a terror to good conduct" but is "God's servant for your good" (Romans 13:3a-4a). Paul appealed to his Roman citizenship—a human institutional provision which provided order and stability—when he came into conflict with the authorities. The church itself develops various institutional structures. One of the most interesting structures was the apparent procedure for handling conflict and deviant behavior (Matthew 18:15-18). The New Testament also describes the appropriate roles for the relationships of slaves and masters, wives and husbands, parents and children, in the well-known household tables of Ephesians and Colossians.

Contemporary theology has considered the place of human institutional life within God's purposes in history under the rubric of Christ and the "powers" or "principalities." The powers have their origin in the creative purpose of God.

> He is the image of the invisible God, the firstborn over all creation. For
> by him all things were created: things in heaven and on earth, visible

and invisible, whether thrones or powers or rulers or authorities; all things were created by him and for him. He is before all things, and in him all things hold together (Colossians 1:15-17, NIV).

Though most of the references in the New Testament view the powers from the perspective of the Fall, they are originally part of the good creation of God. John H. Yoder puts it as follows:

> Society and history, even nature, would be impossible without regularity, system, order—and this need God provided for. The universe is not sustained arbitrarily, immediately and erratically by an unbroken succession of new divine interventions. It was made in so ordered form and "it was good." The creative power worked in a mediated form, by means of the Powers that regularized all visible reality.[4]

The positive role of human institutions in God's provision for the ordering of human life is evident in the Genesis account of creation.

Human beings are fundamentally social animals. God creates us not as solitary, isolated individuals but as man and woman (Genesis 1:28). Woman is not created as a tool for man's use, but as a coworker. "It is not good for the man to be alone. I will provide a partner for him" (Genesis 2:18, NEB). Adam recognizes Eve as "bone of my bones" and "flesh of my flesh" (Genesis 2:23). This sociality is the foundation for the unity of the two in marriage (Genesis 2:24). This sociality serves no mere instrumental purpose. The man and the woman are called upon to be partners, coworkers, both to depend upon and care for each other. Neither can fulfill their own individual humanity apart from their co-humanity.

This co-humanity is even linked with the image of God. "So God created man in his own image; in the image of God he created him; male and female he created them" (Genesis 1:27-28, NIV). We become who we are in social interaction, and it is this relational quality of human life that is itself a reflection of the nature of God.[5]

Human sociality is made possible by our capacity to create symbols and interact socially through speech. The human symbolic capacity is what above all gives us our special place in creation. God brings all the wild animals and birds "to the man to see what he would call them, and whatever the man called each living creature, that was its name" (Genesis 2:19, NEB). It is this distinctive feature of human being that is the basis for the psalmist's exclamation: "Thou hast made him little less than a god, crowning him with glory and honour" (Psalm 8:5, NEB).

This symbolic capacity enables humans to create culture with social institutions which enable human beings to give order to human life. Other animals do not create culture or institutions. The patterns of life they need to survive are either programmed into them genetically or learned directly from other animals they imitate. Human symbolic capacity enables us to delineate patterns of behavior into symbolic forms, in various forms of speech, writing, diagrams, plans, systems of rules that can be transferred from one geographical location to another and from one time period to the next without anyone ever directly observing the behavior. The symbol "represents" the behavior pattern.

This symbolic capacity enables human beings to be creators of culture, for symbols enable humans to bind time—to remember and be affected by a past we may not have even experienced and to project ourselves into the future by imagining alternatives not yet in existence. We have the capacity to "represent" to ourselves through symbols a plan for future behavior. This behavior, which we have not yet acted out, nor has it been acted out in the past, makes possible human culture and human institutional life. In coordination with other persons, human beings can visualize, plan, and then act to create something new in the universe. For example, an architect can represent a building on paper. The architectural plan is not the building itself, but it can tell a builder what to do, even though he has never seen a building like it before. A group of people can imagine or visualize a way to organize themselves in order to get a task accomplished. It is not necessary to have experienced such behavior before they can act on the basis of a mental model or image of the future.

As creators of culture and of human social institutions, human beings reflect the image of God in them. They are cocreators with God. They literally construct their world. They are placed by God in a world that is still in the process of formation. As beings created in the likeness of God, they are given the task of being cocreators with God.

This is all pronounced "good" by God. In the first account of the creation, "and God saw that it was good" is repeated again and again. After the creation of humans and the designation of their special place within creation, the account climaxes with the statement, "and God saw all that he had made, and it was very good" (Genesis 1:31, NEB).

The fundamental goodness of human sociality is expressed also in the second story of creation: "Now they were both naked, the man and his wife, but they had no feeling of shame towards one another" (Genesis 2:25, NEB). This contrasts with their attitude toward themselves after they had violated the command not to eat from the forbidden tree. "Then the eyes of both of them were opened and they discovered that they were naked" (Genesis 3:7, NEB). Later in the account Adam responds to God's question,

"Where are you?" with the reply: "I heard the sound as you were walking in the garden, and I was afraid because I was naked, and I hid myself" (Genesis 3:10, NEB). The Fall brings about estrangement and mistrust between both the man and the woman, and between them and God. But their co-humanity as created by God was originally fundamentally good. Mistrust and estrangement are not a necessary component of being social beings, or a necessary part of being cocreators with God of institutional and cultural life.

The Genesis stories of creation symbolically express a perspective that illuminates what we also know about human sociality from nonbiblical sources.[6] The social-symbolic nature of human beings, regarded by Genesis as good and a function of the divine image, provides a basic theological perspective from which to interpret human experience.

Human social and cultural life develops over the process of time. "As the forms of life grow more complex, the weight of the power to adapt to circumstances, which eventually becomes conscious thought, grows also, and eventually outweighs the power of instincts, until finally, in human beings, instincts count for little behavior if any, and thinking and learning for almost all of it."[7] Thinking and learning in human beings makes us distinctively historical and cultural beings.

The more we are defined by history and culture, the more necessary it is for us to cooperate and coordinate our efforts. It is reasonable to assume that rudimentary forms of political behavior emerge simultaneously or parallel with the development of human social behavior. To say that humans are created as social beings with language as their distinctive mark is at the same time to think of humans as political beings. As beings who create culture which becomes more and more complex over time, the planning, organization, and coordination of social behavior becomes more and more central to human life. Political behavior is, then, an essential component of God's creation of human beings. In other words, the coordination, structuring, and organization of human social life for the sake of survival and creativity is an essential component of what it means to be human.

Human sociality is expressed not simply through I-Thou relationships of two people or the *Gemeinschaftlich* relationships of small groups where people know each other face to face, but it is also expressed through and in the context of patterned institutional relationships. Persons perform functions and play roles as part of a larger cooperative human effort. The more complex this organized human effort becomes, the more explicit and self-conscious becomes the organization of social behavior. Eventually certain persons take on defined roles of leadership, coordination, and organization.

To be human, then, means to be acted upon by others, to be pressed to conform to patterns of behavior and speech. One takes on the patterns of others—their language, habits, attitudes, metaphors, rituals, and gestures. To become socialized means to have one's behavior ordered so that it is coordinated and patterned to fit into the group as a whole. In this sense, behavior is determined. From this perspective, coercion is an aspect of being a social animal, and is not entirely a negative or sinful aspect of social life. The word "coerce" comes from the Latin root "co" and "arcere," which means to shut up or to press together. To be social means to be pressed together, shaped, structured into behavior that coordinates with others.

The previous analysis provides a point of view that enables us to avoid misconceptions about peacemaking that have been held by pacifists and nonpacifists alike. One of these misconceptions has been to equate coercion and violence. Some forms of coercion are violent if they are harmful to people (we shall elaborate these distinctions more fully in chapter six), but there is also a coercive element in all social life which is not inherently evil. Coercion that "orders" human social behavior into patterns of cooperation that is not exploitive is essential to human social life. A theology of creation which has not thought through what it means for humans to be social animals believes that the ideal is an anarchist golden age of spontaneous harmony. This view fails to recognize that social life entails roles, structure, and organization. An anarchist view is anti-institutional, and can provide no real basis for a theology of peacemaking. To long for a golden age, where human social life is spontaneously harmonized, where all relationships between human beings can be face-to-face, I-Thou relationships is essentially an asocial view of human life.

We are called to the task of ordering our lives through institutions. This is absolutely essential to the task of the peacemaker who must create institutions which can solve human problems of conflict and injustice. This means that politics is not to be understood only as an institution of the Fall. If we take Karl Deutsch's definition of politics, "the more or less incomplete control of human behavior through voluntary habits of compliance in combination with threats of probable enforcement,"[8] we are not describing a more corrupt form of social behavior different in kind from other social behavior. Deutsch's definition simply recognizes both the voluntary and coercive element inherent in all social behavior.

Another source of confusion is a result of the dichotomy we draw between freedom and determinism, between autonomy and heteronomy, as if these were two realities fundamentally opposed and contradictory to each other. Consequently, if one is to be free (that is, completely uncoerced), one must conclude that all forms of coercion are bad and an indication of human sinfulness. Again this confusion arises because of the failure to understand ourselves as social, historical beings.

On the one hand, freedom involves predetermination: by decision we mean precisely a movement in the present moment through which the future course of events will be determined. . . . If a father's decision did not significantly shape the future of his son, in what sense would he be free with reference to his son? . . . On the other hand, predetermination involves freedom. To "determine" (cf. "terminate") means to set limits; to predetermine is to set limits prior to the event. Predetermination thus presupposes the power to anticipate an event and to set certain bounds within which it will occur. But such power significantly to bind the future is precisely what is meant by freedom.[9]

To be human then, also means to be free to make structural decisions. Politics which denies this side of human sociality violates what it means for humans to be created as social beings. When politics operates so as to destroy that human capacity, then we have a politics of the Fall. This coercion violates the meaning of being human, and politics becomes "violent." The doctrine of creation affirms the truth of the polarity that we are social beings pressed into (coerced) patterned, structured behavior, and at the same time free to create, shape, and modify this same environment.

When the "imago dei" is defined in terms of man's creating himself through history, the old question whether sin merely defaces or effectively destroys God's image . . . is bypassed. As long as man exists, he will be continuously creating himself, and will thus bear the image of God, his historicity.[10]

Our sociopolitical nature as such is not inherently evil. This sociopolitical behavior may become corrupted so seriously as to become very destructive and demonic. But life, including politics, is potentially good. Such a theology of creation affirms what we also know from human experience. Human institutional life is a good that provides order and gives stability to life. Without predictable cultural patterns, life would be chaotic and extremely difficult to bear.

D. SIN:
THE BROKENNESS OF HUMAN INSTITUTIONAL LIFE

There is no human institutional life that is not affected to its core by human sinfulness. Though an aspect of our experience is order and stability—an aspect that reflects the goodness of these institutions—another aspect of our experience is the violence, oppression, and corruption of these same institutions.

We experience bondage to human institutions. Individuals often do not intend to do evil and may even be quite benevolent and "Christian" in their personal behavior, yet the institutions within which they work often function to perpetuate evils such as racism, violence, oppression and exploitation.[11]

The institutions of human culture are the result of a long historical development. For example, the evil of racism as it expressed itself in the past in slavery and segregation continues to exercise its effect in human institutions today, even when the attitudes and values of many of the individual people in these institutions may have changed. Slavery cut people off from their African culture, tore people from their roots of family, language, and culture. Blacks were thrust into an alien language and culture and treated as property, not persons. The damage done to a people by these acts several hundred years ago continues to have a detrimental effect on black people to this day. Black people were cut off from their culture and language. For many years they were not educated to enable them to read the language of the new culture. The cumulative effect of this history has been that to this day black children and young people on the average start out with a disadvantage in speaking, reading, and writing the English language. This disadvantage is reinforced by segregated housing patterns and patterns of segregation in education.

These racial patterns may not necessarily be deliberately intended by persons, but they are the result of the long history of separate cultural development of blacks and whites. Blacks were unable to compete for the best jobs because of their education and linguistic disadvantage and ended up in the most vulnerable job areas such as agricultural labor. When these jobs disappeared, they went to the cities to find work. Because of their economic level they were forced to live in ghetto areas where they went to schools that were largely black, and where the educational disadvantages continued.

It is a vicious circle. It may be that nowhere in this entire cycle do individual employers, teachers, or realtors purposely discriminate against black persons. Yet the cumulative effect of the structural arrangement of American society fosters patterns which inhibit the development of the potential of black people. The continued effect in America is two separate unequal societies—one poorer, less educated, and with a higher unemployment rate.[12]

The same patterns of structural or institutional evil are evident in the arms race between the nations. The leaders of two nations may be quite peaceful and benevolent persons; they may have no evil intent toward each other. But in each country, though they verbalize their peaceful intentions, they continue to arm to try to stay ahead or equal to the other power. Once the institutions of militarism are begun they inevitably continue, even though these structures may in fact be unnecessary to a large extent. It is practically impossible for nations to reverse the trend of the arms race escalation because of fear the other side will take advantage of the situation. Both nations thus continue to arm even when each would rather not.

Furthermore, even if leaders could convince each other to turn the tide, the pressures of domestic politics in both countries force the continuation of the institutional momentum of the arms race. People become economically dependent on government expenditures for military development. Once convinced that high military expenditures are necessary to be secure, people are not easily changed when more arms are no longer necessary for security. It is easy for politicians to exploit people's fears. So the institutional momentum of the arms race continues, even when no real basis may exist for the fear and insecurity.

Institutions intended to serve humane ends no longer serve the creative purposes of God.

> We find them seeking to separate us from the love of God (Rom. 8:38); we find them ruling over the lives of those who live far from the love of God (Eph. 2:2); we find them holding man in servitude to their rules (Col. 2:20); we find them holding men subject under their tutelage (Gal. 4:3). These structures which were supposed to be our servants have become our masters and our guardians.[13]

The root problem is sin. Basically, sin is a breach in friendship with God and simultaneously with one's fellow humans. In the temptation narrative in Genesis 3, God is pictured by the serpent as a deceiver, and thus a despot, in that God makes unreasonable demands upon his creatures. The serpent says, "Of course you will not die. God knows that as soon as you eat it, your eyes will be opened and you will be like gods knowing both good and evil" (Genesis 3:4-5, NEB). This text has led some like Erich Fromm to interpret the Fall as the first genuinely human act, the first fundamental expression of human freedom.

> Acting against God's orders means freeing himself from coercion, emerging from the unconscious existence of pre-human life to the level of man. Acting against the command of authority, committing a sin, is

in its positive human aspect the first act of freedom, that is, the first human act. In the myth the sin in its formal aspect is the eating of the tree of knowledge. The act of disobedience as an act of freedom is the beginning of reason.[14]

Fromm's interpretation is persuasive, however, only if it is assumed that the original relationship of God and persons is the relationship between a despot and slaves. Genesis can be interpreted in a quite different sense. We have pointed out that God creates humans as sociohistorical beings with the capacity of language. This enables humans to transcend themselves (bind time) by imagining alternative futures which they are given power to bring into being. They do not need to rebel to be free, unless freedom is thought of as some totally autonomous act, an act which can only be free if it is totally self-initiated.[15] Such a view of freedom is a misunderstanding of how human creativity depends upon a historical-environmental context that makes freedom possible. We could say that God is the ultimate limit (environment) in terms of which finite reality expresses itself. To be created by culture (and by God) is the condition of our own creativity. The relationship between God and humans, therefore, is not originally a despot-slave relationship but one of companionship and friendship. Fromm's view that rebellion is necessary for human freedom to express itself is itself part of the human delusion that totally self-initiated action is possible. Such freedom is possible only for God who is not dependent upon culture to express freedom. To assume that one needs to rebel in order to be free is itself a demonstration of human fallenness, our desire to be like God.

God relates to humans not as a despot but as an affectional being, one who creates us for companionship. God portrays the fundamental divine attitude of companion or friend of humans toward us again and again throughout the biblical story. The establishment of a covenant with Israel as God's people, the message of the prophets that even God's judgment is ultimately an expression of God's longing to reestablish a relationship with Israel, and the New Testament affirmation that in Christ God reconciles human beings to Godself—all point to this love and affection for humanity, to a longing for companionship which God seeks to reestablish. The Fall consists precisely in the human illusion that God is a despot, that the only way we can be truly human is to go on our own, to try to become independent, to become autonomous, to operate as if we were a law unto ourselves no longer needing to act in the universe in terms of the ultimate limit upon us, the divine companion.

The human rebellion against God's friendship has significant consequences for human social relationships. Indeed, as the Genesis narrative reports, the tempter promised that if humans eat of the tree they will become like gods. They do, indeed. Since they regard God as a despot over them, they become like the gods they imagine. They begin to conform to their self-created idol. Richard Mouw expresses this well:

> Adam and Eve initiated a project by which they attempted to conform to this false model of what a deity is: "You will be a God." Here we can see an important facet of John Calvin's insistence, in the opening pages of his *Institutes*, that the knowledge of God and the knowledge of self are inseparable. A change in human perspectives on the nature and motives of the Creator immediately signaled a change in self-image. Having revised their concept of "Lordship" from the idea of a loving creator to that of a selfish despot, Adam and Eve aspired to this latter kind of lordship.[16]

This breach in their companionship with God (symbolized by their hiding from God, now conceived as a despot) simultaneously affects human social relationships. Adam and Eve no longer can trust each other. This is symbolized by their recognition of each other's nakedness. They cannot trust each other because their conformity to their idol of God as despot leads them to a relationship of lordship and submission with respect to each other. In their self-imposed judgment, man becomes the master over woman while she is condemned to her role as bearer of children (Genesis 3:16). Human social relationships are thus infected to the core. A relationship of friendship and companionship is turned into one of lordship and submission. The human creative power to transform culture becomes one of pain and sorrow, for even the human relationship to the earth is now fundamentally altered (Genesis 3:17-18).

The Fall is thus simultaneously an interior breach between humans and God and a social breach between human beings themselves. The Fall expresses itself within sociohistorical reality. Furthermore, this fallenness is expressed not simply in the personal I-Thou relationships of individual human beings in their relationship with each other, but in collective and institutional reality.

In his book, *The Sacred Canopy*, Peter Berger describes this creative-cultural process in a threefold way: externalization, objectification, and internalization. Human beings express themselves individually and collectively (externalization) in various ways by creating symbols, tools, institutions, and artifacts which then take on an objective status of their own (objectification). Once created, they become part of culture, objects standing over against humans. These, then, become forces or objects which create or affect human beings. We are born into a culture consisting of language, institutions, a technology, certain defined roles and customs, which we then internalize (internalization) or appropriate and take on as meaningful or useful to ourselves.

The Fall, however, means that human institutions are infected by the fundamental breach in the human relationship with God and of humans with each other. These flaws became infused in the institutional patterns and roles of the collectivity, and these flaws are then adopted or internalized within new generations of human beings. All institutional life is affected. Human relationships once intended as relationships of companionship and friendship are now infected with patterns of lordship and submission. This pattern of lordship and submission can be seen in family patterns in which males dominate women and parents lord it over children, political relationships of despotism and submission, and economic patterns of exploitation and oppression. Though the ultimate root of human sinfulness is rebellion against God, the consequences of this sinfulness can never be separated from its expression in human, sociohistorical collectives.

The meaning of salvation therefore cannot be separated from the transformation of sociohistorical structures.[17] Though we are individuals who need to be transformed, we also function within institutions. For example, children who grow up in families or environmental conditions in which their dignity and self-esteem have been fundamentally damaged due to the absence of love, or who experience socioenvironmental conditions that prevent them from developing as creative persons because of poor nutrition or lack of intellectual stimulation, suffer the consequences of human sinfulness that expresses itself in social structures. Such persons may grow up mistrustful or hateful, unable to relate socially or lacking sufficient confidence to express themselves creatively in work and play. To restore the fundamental breach in relationship to God and in human relationships involves not only a change in inner attitude, but also a fundamental change in the structures that originally produced the damage and that continue to be perpetuated.

This break of companionship is expressed in and through political institutions in several ways. Human political institutions are never universal. They are organized by the sheer requirements of geographical area. This in itself is not a consequence of human fallenness.[18] The problem is when these particular sociopolitical identities are absolutized such that they become the ultimate object of loyalty.

In our modern world this absolutizing of a particular community of human beings expresses itself in the preference of "my" people at the expense of another. Though we have special obligations to those near to us, that obligation should not become so important that we violate others more distant from us as a result. War between nations is one form in which this absolutization expresses itself. The protection of the economic self-interest of one group at the expense of others is another form of this sin. The absolutizing of an ethnic or narrow religious community (or an ideal community or family) such that this community can ignore the rest of the world and bask in comfort in the confines of its little community is still another form of this idolatry.

The idolization of the particular may express itself either in messianic pretensions or in egoistic self-gratification and self-righteous withdrawal. By "messianism" we mean the presumption that a particular individual or group has the final truth, with the right and obligation to impose it on others. Messianic presumption is characteristic of political institutions, especially when these institutions are legitimated by religious symbols or their equivalent. The Nazi myth of Aryan supremacy, the Marxist myth of the communist future age, or the American myth of the righteous empire under God are all messianic visions which are idolatrous. All justify the massive use of force and destruction in order to impose on others their own particular vision as if it were a universal vision.

The violence of all these systems is, first of all, a violation of the first article of the creed, "I believe in God." "I believe in God" for those with messianic pretentions means the god of "my" people and its institutions and way of life, not the one who is Lord over all the nations. In the eighteenth and nineteenth centuries, American self-righteous messianism resulted in the imposition of its "better" way on the native inhabitants of the land and the eventual destruction of the way of life of the American Indian. In the twentieth century, this messianic pride is expressed in the assumption that America is the defender of freedom across the globe, that it has the right and duty to impose its vision upon the world because America is right and good. Both Marxist and American forms of messianism are compelling because they believe they are in the pursuit of a righteous cause. That makes them especially dangerous. They mask under compelling moral arguments, their own self-interest, and the absolutizing of my people over another people.

Only by worshiping the universal God, the one in whom all of being is valued, can this danger be avoided. God is the universal being, the Creator of all human beings, the one who gives to all human beings the capacity to create culture. God is for everyone, desiring to restore the broken relationship which is a consequence of the Fall. When human beings cease to love God with heart, soul, and mind, they turn away from the one to an idol, a deity of their own creation which is less than universal. In the name of this idol they then no longer relate to other human beings or the natural world from the perspective of the one, but rather from a particular framework which results in an expression of hostility or enmity to some particular dimension of that creation or human community. Violence, the harm of another individual or group, which is usually justified in terms of a particular good or as a necessity (in order to preserve the good) is thus not only a socioethical problem at the human level, but it is primarily or fundamentally a sin of idolatry, the absolutizing of the particular.[19]

Above all, the depth of human sinfulness is expressed in the way in which human beings deceive themselves into believing that the defense of, or commitment to, their own people requires the harm of other people. Indeed, this form of self-justification is understandable since the nation, the family, ethnic group, or other human particularity is a good without which humans could not exist. But to defend this group or extend this particularity by justifying the harm of others as if that were a good or a necessity, is itself human deception, a result of the Fall. For such enmity is a function of sin, a result in the breach of relationship with God and with others.

Messianism deludes itself into thinking that evil can be overcome by violence, that it is within human power to bring in a new age with the use of coercive force. It is deluded because it fails to recognize how the very means that are used to accomplish the socalled "good ends" corrupt the ends. To put the issue another way, the means become institutionalized (objectified into structures) that do not simply go away, but take on a power and momentum of their own.

For example, World War I, the "war to end all wars," became through the unjust settlement after the war, the major cause of World War II. World War II, the "war of necessity," led to the terror of technological warfare culminating in the advent of the atomic age. The attitudes of the cold war and the military machine necessary to implement the cold war policies of the West provided the conditions and the background for the Vietnam War. Out of all of these wars an institutionalized objective structure (called by some a military-industrial complex) has grown to the point that we have become enmeshed in it politically and economically so that it tends to control us rather than vice versa.

Similarly, revolutionary groups which overthrow oppressors with violence become in the new age the new oppressor. The very patterns which permit a revolutionary elite to destroy the lives of their opponents become so institutionalized when the elite gains power that "new" patterns of structural violence are inevitable: lack of freedom of press and speech and the unwillingness to tolerate organized opposing political viewpoints. So Jacque Ellul says:

The first law of violence is continuity. . . . Once a man has begun to use violence he will never stop using it, for it is so much easier and more practical than any other method. . . . Once you choose the way of violence, it is impossible to say: "So far and no farther"; for you provoke the victim of your violence to use violence in turn, and that necessarily means using greater violence.[20]

In the face of the massive power of objective evil structures, human beings are tempted to indulge in the opposite of messianism, a sense of fate, hopelessness, and despair. This sense of fate expresses itself in escapist and egoistic forms of self-gratification, in sloth and indolence, or in the sense of powerlessness that results from being locked into one's situation with no chance of escape. A symbolic relationship exists between the objective structural forms of evil and the internalized attitudes of those who feel enmeshed in these structures. The passivity, false dependence, and hopelessness of the oppressed is just as much a form of sin as the dominating power of the oppressor.

Another form of this despair is violence viewed as a necessity, a fact of life from which there is no escape and to which there is no alternative. Violence as "necessity" is another kind of self-justification and self-deception. The justification for violence on the grounds of necessity is, like messianism, another form of idolatry. In messianism the idol is our trust in ourselves and our own communities which we try to universalize. In pessimism we lack trust in God's power to break into history and transform human structures. This is idolatry because we still primarily look to ourselves as god, except instead of having great expectations about our possibilities we now look at our situation with a feeling of despair. The pessimism of despair does not worship the God who is Lord, the one who brings resurrection power, but its orientation is the human condition and the human possibility. Its view is based on human possibility, not God's possibility.

Sometimes a sense of fate, despair, and hopelessness about political institutions (often called apathy) leads to indolence and various kinds of religious, psychological, and hedonistic escapism. In the first several decades of this century it was necessary to expose the weakness of false optimism and expectation of human progress through human effort. Some of the despair of today may rest upon an earlier naive hope in progress that has been dashed to pieces. One certainly must take a realistic look at human institutions and the limited possibilities for renewal of these institutions. We must distinguish, however, between realism and a pessimism which leads to despair. Today the problem may be just the opposite of what Reinhold Niebuhr condemned, a prevailing sickness that pervades our institutions and our life that grows out of hopelessness and despair. The pessimism that results from our experience of the fruits of Western technological culture has made us wonder whether life on this planet is doomed. This is the diet on which children born since World War II have been reared.

In this setting the church only contributes to the prevailing sickness if it does not have a message of hope. When the doctrine of sin predominates at the expense of a theology of redemption and eschatological hope, the church only contributes to the predicament. The church must foster hope, a hope that can be creatively expressed in alternative forms of institutional life that solve the problems of human conflict and injustice. In part this can happen by helping people view the world in terms that offer hope for change. Traditional balance of power thinking reinforced by traditional doctrines of sin inhibit that process. We cannot evade the reality of sin, but sin must be balanced with a view of the world and a vision of life that offers hope.   O

4 THEOLOGICAL PERSPECTIVE TWO: REDEMPTION AND ESCHATOLOGICAL HOPE

The motivation to change human institutions to better fulfill their intended purposes is integrally linked with a concept of hope. What can human beings hope for? How are these hopes related to the actual institutions of human culture, institutions which are experienced ambiguously as both serving necessary functions for the human good and as corrupted by egoistic self-interest and pride? Every human enterprise which aims to change human institutions is driven by some hope that it is possible to make these institutions better serve the common good. Marxism is a secular humanism that is driven by a vision of the future to transform the world according to that vision. The various theologies of liberation that are popular today similarly reflect the human hope for the transformation and change of human institutions. This drive for transformation and change is based upon a vision of the future which springs from a deep human longing for structures that can fulfill what humans believe themselves to be.

The biblical themes of hope and redemption thus relate to a deeply rooted aspect of the common human experience. The key questions the Bible poses are: What is the nature of this hope? How is it linked to cultural life? What is the nature of redemption and how does redemption in history come about? What is the relationship of these redemptive forces to the ambiguous nature of human institutions which are experienced as both necessary and good and as corrupted by human sin?

The major theme of the Bible is the affirmation by God's people that they have been saved from the brokenness of the human condition. The enmity between God and humanity, as well as that between human beings has been broken down and a new relationship of friendship has been established. This redemption is celebrated as God's gift. It does not come about primarily by human effort, nor does it arise out of the inherent goodness of humanity. This makes the biblical concept of the redemption of human institutional life very different from various forms of secular humanism which have neither a view of human sin nor consequently a concept of grace. It is in the context of this gracious activity of God that human ethical responsibility for human institutional transformation should be understood.

A. REDEMPTION: THE TRANSFORMATION OF HUMAN INSTITUTIONAL LIFE

1. The Old Testament Perspective

The Old Testament makes it very clear that God's redemption of human beings includes the transformation of human cultural and institutional life. Salvation is not primarily the salvation of individuals (certainly not their souls) but rather the salvation of people and their institutions, of their political, economic, and social life. Salvation means to make whole, to restore cultural and social reality to its intended purposes in the creative order of God.

In the Old Testament the concept of peace (shalom) is integrally linked with the meaning of salvation. Basically the word shalom means a state of well-being, with a strong emphasis on the material side. It is often used as a greeting to convey a wish for the well-being of others. It often refers to the well-being of a group, particularly a nation which is enjoying prosperity.[1] The Old Testament contains no dualism which separates a spiritual or inward peace from an earthly or material peace. Gerhard von Rad says that

> when we consider the rich possibilities of "shalom" in the Old Testament we are struck by the negative fact that there is no specific text in which it denotes the specifically spiritual attitude of inward peace. There are, indeed, more passages in which it is used of groups rather than individuals.... In the majority of examples, in which the reference is to a group, the term "shalom" clearly denotes something which may be seen. When we remember the way in which it is linked with law, with justice (Zech. 8:16) or with righteousness (Is. 60:17), we are forced to say that in its most common use "shalom" is an emphatically social concept.[2]

Shalom is also closely linked with the concept of covenant, the root metaphor in the Old Testament for understanding the relationship between God and the people. Von Rad says that "the connection between the two words is so strong that 'shalom' seems to have become a kind of official term.... A relationship of 'shalom' is sealed by both parties in a covenant ... or conversely ... the covenant inaugurates a relationship of 'shalom.' "[3]

A widely held view among Old Testament scholars is that the concept of covenant is to be understood in the political context of the relationship of a great king and his vassals.[4] Yahweh is identified as the great king who has been gracious in his act of freeing his people from slavery in Egypt, and who expects certain obligations from his people (the Ten Commandments). The covenant united under the rulership of Yahweh a diverse group of people who otherwise had no basis for a relationship. According to George E. Mendenhall:

> If, as Israelite tradition maintained, there were only descendents of Abraham, Isaac, and Jacob, in short a group bound together by blood-ties or a clan, then it is not so likely that a covenant would have been necessary to bind them together as a religious group. . . . It is, however, becoming increasingly difficult to maintain that there were blood ties close enough to bind Israel together or to produce the feeling of solidarity. . . . If those blood-ties, kinship, as the basis of Israelite solidarity be given up, it is inconceivable, at least to the present writer, that there could have been, at that time, any other basis of solidarity than a covenant relationship.[5]

Covenant establishes both a new relationship with God and a new society of people—a condition of shalom. Shalom is God's gift since God initiates a new covenant relationship with his people. God's deliverance provides justice and peace for the land (Psalm 85). In the holiness code of Leviticus, God promises peace to his people if they will be obedient (Leviticus 26:6). The relationship of covenant and shalom is particularly clear in the prophet Ezekiel, who wrote during the time the Jews were in exile in Babylon. The covenant of peace which God will establish will mean that they no longer need to worry about being ravished by war. They will live in prosperity on the land. They will be able to depend on rain. The land will be fertile and bring forth fruit and produce. They will be able to live in security and not worry about being enslaved. They need not even worry about being attacked by wild beasts (Ezekiel 34:25-31).

In the Old Testament peace is a holistic spiritual-material condition in which well-being presupposes human spiritual-somatic (bodily) unity. Redemption presupposes creation, which disallows a dualism of matter and spirit and a false spiritualization of human life. Salvation is a transformation of the total person in his or her social environment. The Old Testament does not separate personal peace or peace between individuals and social or political peace. The basis for this holistic view is the Hebrew experience of redemption. God is the liberator of Israel as a people (a community), a liberation which renews the covenant relationship with God and at the same time brings about political and social freedom.

The establishment of this new covenant relationship is a highly significant event in political ethics.

The covenant was Israel's acceptance of the overlordship of Yahweh. And it is just here that that notion of the rule of God over his people, the kingdom of God, so central to the thought of both testaments, had its start.[6]

Allegiance is withdrawn from the dominant patterns of ancient Near Eastern kingship and a new loyalty is formed around Yahweh as King. Yahweh is different from the other kings in his basic identification with the oppressed and downtrodden. Yahweh is the one who freed the people from their hard labor and misery under the Pharaoh.

It may well be that a number of groups who were alienated from the kingship patterns of the ancient Near East were drawn together by this new covenant. This explains why Israel had a debate (see 1 Samuel 8) when the people wanted to change the political structure from a tribal confederacy to a kingship pattern. This debate probably reflects patterns of behavior at the height of Israel's political power under King Solomon when some experienced a patriotic exhilaration and others disillusionment.

And the Lord said to Samuel ... "They have rejected me from being king over them. . . . Now then, hearken to their voice; only, you shall solemnly warn them, and show them the ways of the king who shall reign over them. . . ." He [Samuel] said, "These will be the ways of the king who will reign over you: he will take your sons and appoint them to his chariots and to be his horsemen, and to run before his chariots; and he will appoint for himself commanders of thousands and commanders of fifties, and some to plow his ground and to reap his harvest, and to make his implements of war and the equipment of his chariots. He will take your daughters to be perfumers and cooks and bakers. He will take the best of your fields and vineyards and give it to his officers and to his servants. He will take your menservants and maidservants, and the best of your cattle and your asses, and put them to his work. He will take the tenth of your flocks, and you shall be his slaves" (1 Samuel 8:7-17).

The law which was grounded in the original Sinai covenant, since it viewed Yahweh as a liberator of the oppressed, stipulated that Israel must have a special concern for the poor, for slaves, and for strangers (see Exodus 22:21-27).

You shall not oppress a stranger; you know the heart of a stranger, for you were strangers in the land of Egypt (Exodus 23:9).

You shall not oppress the alien, for you know how it feels to be an alien; you were aliens yourselves in Egypt (Exodus 23:9, NEB).

Under the new patterns of kingship, oppression and injustice became commonplace in Israel. For example, under the Sinai covenant law it was stipulated that "if you lend money to any of my people with you who is poor, you shall not be to him as a creditor, and you shall not exact interest from him" (Exodus 22:25). According to Mendenhall, under the old system the loan was secured by a piece of property which went to the creditor in case of default.

But already by the time of Saul the situation had changed such that the person of the debtor was security for a loan. Upon default the creditor could seize the person (or family) as a slave. The only alternative for the debtor was flight. Evidently those who gathered about David as outlaws consisted of those who were in debt (1 Samuel 22:2). "This doctrine is identical to that of Babylonian law and no doubt of the Canaanites as well . . . but it is a legal tradition in total contradiction to the customs and morality of early Israel."[7] It is such practices that are so severely condemned by the prophets.

> For crime after crime of Israel
>   I will grant them no reprieve,
> because they sell the innocent for silver
>   and the destitute for a pair of shoes.
> They grind the heads of the poor into the earth
>   and thrust the humble out of their way (Amos 2:6-7, NEB).

> Ephraim says, "Surely I have become a rich man,
>   I have made my fortune";
> but all his gains will not pay
>   for the guilt of his sins.
> Yet I have been the Lord your God since your days in Egypt;
> I will make you live in tents yet again, as in the old days (Hosea 12:8-9, NEB).

> Shame on those who lie in bed planning evil and wicked deeds
>   and rise at daybreak to do them,
>   knowing that they have the power!

> They covet land and take it by force;
>> if they want a house they seize it;
> they rob a man of his home
>> and steal every man's inheritance (Micah 2:1-2, NEB).

The development of the prophetic role in Israel is highly significant for political ethics. In the ancient Near Eastern pattern of political authority the king was viewed as the representative of the gods and was not subject to criticism and judgment by any other group in society.[8] In contrast, the prophets in Israel represented a social reality distinct from the king. The prophet appealed to transcendent norms based upon a vision of Yahweh's lordship that is the basis for social criticism. So the prophet, Nathan, for instance, came to King David in order to point out his sin and to pronounce a word of judgment from God (2 Samuel 12). This prophetic perspective even led the prophet Jeremiah to counsel surrender to Babylonia (Jeremiah 34:1-5; 21:3-7), a demand that could only be perceived as outrageous and traitorous by both the devout and the zealots of Jerusalem.[9]

Though God breaks into history to make a new people, the fact is that Israel never perfectly lived out their new relationship with God. They constantly fell back into the sin of idolatry, of denying their ultimate ground of being, and simultaneously breaking their social relationships with other human beings by acting unjustly and unmercifully. Although the central theme of the Bible is God's redemptive activity in history, this redemptive activity often takes the form of judgment upon human sin. This theme is particularly evident in the Hebrew prophets who became the vehicle for God's word of judgment.

Out of this sense of the incompleteness of liberation and salvation emerges the hope for a new age when God will intervene again to restore his people to a new covenant relationship. Eschatological hope is implicit in the historical act of redemption. The word "shalom," then, is also an eschatological concept. One of the most familiar visions of peace is found in both Micah 4:1-7 and Isaiah 2:4. In this vision all the nations of the earth will come to the mountain of the Lord for instruction in the way of peace. The Lord will be the judge between the nations, the arbiter among peoples.

> They shall beat their sword into plowshares
>> and their spears into pruning hooks;
> nation shall not lift sword against nation
>> nor ever again be trained for war
> (Isaiah 2:4, RSV, NEB combined).

Some passages hope for a humble king who will bring peace to begin the messianic age. This vision is particularly striking in Isaiah 9:5f.:

All the boots of trampling soldiers
and the garments fouled with blood
shall become a burning mass, a fuel for fire.
For a boy has been born for us, a son given to us
    to bear the symbol of dominion on his shoulder;
    and he shall be called
    in purpose wonderful, in battle God-like,
    Father for all time, Prince of Peace.
Great shall the dominion be,
    and boundless the peace
bestowed on David's throne and on his kingdom,
to establish it and sustain it
    with justice and righteousness
    from now and for evermore (NEB).

The liberation of God's people is an ongoing process. Salvation is never complete. Sin persists, and with each new breakthrough, hopes are spawned of an even more complete shalom in an age to come. The Liberation or redemption of Israel is a re-creation, the redirection of Israel toward a righteous purpose. The goal of redemption is not to return to the garden of Eden, but to journey toward the Promised Land, there to become a holy nation. According to Gustavo Gutierrez: "Yahweh liberates the Jewish people politically in order to make them a holy nation. . . . The eschatological horizon is present in the heart of the Exodus."[10] The link between God as Creator and Redeemer is made clear in Isaiah:

Thus speaks the Lord who is God,
    he who created the skies and stretched them out,
    who fashioned the earth and all that grows in it,
who gave birth to its people;
    the breath of life to all who walk upon it:
I, the Lord, have called you with righteous purpose
    and taken you by the hand;
    I have formed you, and appointed you
    to be a light to all peoples,
    a beacon for the nations,
    to open eyes that are blind,
    to bring captives out of prison,
    out of dungeons where they lie in darkness (Isaiah 42:5-7, NEB).

At each stage of cultural and institutional development in Israel the meaning of being a people of God is reformulated. The stages of institutional development are recognized and the vision of being God's people is then related anew to these institutional developments. The concept of the Jubilee and the advice of the prophet Jeremiah to the people in exile illustrate this process of development. Mendenhall says that "the later law codes illustrate beautifully the way in which the early traditions and the needs of business were brought into harmony."[11] Under the commercial economy of the kingdom period, debtors who could not pay their debts were often forced back into slavery. This was so contrary to the early traditions of Israel that the prophets brought a harsh word of judgment. In this situation Israel needed to protect the debtor, preventing the development of a system of gross inequality, and at the same time to protect the rights of a creditor in a new and more complex economy. The Holiness code (Leviticus 17—26) reflects the attempt to adjust the principle of justice to the situation of a commercial economy.

> When your brother is reduced to poverty and sells himself to you, you shall not use him to work for you as a slave. His status shall be that of a hired man or a stranger living with you; he shall work for you until the year of jubilee. He shall then leave your service, with his children, and go back to his family and to his ancestral property: because they are my slaves whom I brought out of Egypt, they shall not be sold as slaves are sold. You shall not drive him with ruthless severity, but you shall fear your God (Leviticus 25:39-43, NEB).

This passage recognizes the obligation toward the creditor and yet maintains the original vision of complete freedom from slavery. The year of Jubilee is an attempt in Israel to institutionalize the normative principles of justice experienced earlier in the redemptive action of God in the Exodus.

The exile was a major crisis in Israel's history. The national life came to an end, including the institutions through which Israel had expressed her corporate life. Nevertheless, her history did not end, for out of the wreckage of the old she resumed her life as the people of God. The exile produced a real crisis of faith for Israel. How could she serve and worship God in a strange land without the institutions she had been used to? Some of the false prophets predicted that the solution would come quickly, that the yoke of Nebuchadnezzar would soon be broken (Jeremiah 28:10-11). But Jeremiah recognized that this false optimism could not sustain the faith. Instead, Jeremiah in a remarkable piece of political advice, counseled the people to relate the faith of their forebears to their new setting in Babylon:

Build houses and live in them; plant gardens and eat their produce.
Marry wives and beget sons and daughters; take wives for your sons
and give your daughters to husbands, so that they may bear sons and
daughters and you may increase there and not dwindle away. Seek the
welfare of any city to which I have carried you off, and pray to the Lord
for it; on its welfare your welfare will depend (Jeremiah 29:5-7, NEB).[12]

The word "welfare" is a translation of the word "shalom." In other words,
even in alien Babylon the people of God are to contribute to peace through
cultural and institutional renewal.

In this context of exile the hope for a new fulfillment again emerges (in
this case for a remnant of Israel—Jeremiah 31:7), and also for a new
covenant that will be within them, one written on their hearts (Jeremiah
31:33). The same prophet who counseled surrender also speaks of hope for a
new age. New situations create new opportunities.

According to Gustavo Gutierrez, "The promise unfolds—becoming
richer and more definitive—in the promises made by God throughout history."[13] The promise unfolds in Israel's history—in the Sinai covenant, in
the kingdom of Israel, and in the remnant. But each of these partial fulfillments anticipates an age in which the promise will be *fully* realized.

This dynamic of promise and fulfillment is a continuation of themes
we developed in the previous chapter. God gives human beings the power
to be creators of culture. This is an ongoing, developing process. Looked at
from the perspective of the Fall, this cultural process is always corrupted by
evil. But from the standpoint of God's redemptive history, there is hope.
God intervenes into human culture to restore the people to Godself and to
relationship with each other. In that historical process there are partial
breakthroughs, partial fulfillments of hope. The people experience God's redemptive activity in the midst of their broken communities. They
experience a breakthrough to a new creativity even in the sociopolitical
realm. The Exodus and the creation of the new covenant community, the
establishment of the Davidic kingdom, the life of the exile community, the
return of the exiles, and the building of the new Zion with its temple, and
eventually the coming into being of the church—a new society in the midst
of the old structures—are all manifestations of the breakthrough of God into
history. Each of these breakthroughs are concrete and historical, and thus
each also reveals the partial nature of the realization of God's rule. Each of
these breakthroughs thus gives rise to new hopes. According to Gutierrez,
"There exists a dialectical relationship between the promise and its partial
fulfillments. The resurrection itself is the fulfillment of something promised
and likewise the anticipation of a future."[14]

2. The New Testament Perspective

Though it is relatively convincing to read the Old Testament in terms of its social and political content, many scholars view the New Testament quite differently. In large part this different reading of the New Testament is the result of the failure to understand the New Testament from the perspective of the Old. I refer, for example, to Rudolf Bultmann's interpretation of the New Testament in individualistic, existentialist categories, the preoccupation of evangelical Protestantism with individual sin and guilt and salvation for eternal life, or the focus by orthodox Protestantism and Catholicism upon Christ's atoning death and resurrection divorced from the life and prophetic teaching of the Jesus of history.

However, when we read the New Testament in the light of the Old, a very different emphasis emerges. This New Testament perspective can be stated in seven theses: (1) Jesus' life and teachings are a continuation of the ethic of the prophetic tradition, a tradition concerned with justice, righteousness, and peace. (2) This ethic can be focused in the concept of the kingdom of God, a reality that is both present and future. (3) The death of Jesus and the meaning of the cross are to be interpreted in the context of Jesus' life struggle to inaugurate this kingdom of righteousness. (4) Jesus chose the role of servant to inaugurate his kingdom, rather than exercise his messiahship through holy war in the Zealot tradition. (5) Christ's servant role and acceptance of the cross is the most fundamental and also widely held ethical model in all the various strands of the early church tradition. (6) This servant Christ is Lord and is victorious over the powers and principalities, terminology which should be understood in sociopolitical terms. (7) The church is the institutional focus in history of the new ethical reality of the kingdom of God.

We must start with the concept of the kingdom of God, since this is central to Jesus' teaching as reflected in all three synoptic Gospels. Though the term "kingdom of God" is obviously a political metaphor, it has not been clear among New Testament scholars if the term has any sociopolitical content, and if it does, what that political content means. According to Norman Perrin, three major questions have surrounded the scholarly debates about the meaning of the concept: (1) Is the kingdom of God an apocalyptic concept, and if so, what is its meaning in the teaching of Jesus? (2) Is the kingdom present or future? or both? and how are we to understand the relationship between present and future if it is both? (3) What is the relationship between eschatology and ethics in the teaching of Jesus?[15]

The second question has basically been resolved by New Testament scholars. Since Schweitzer, some scholars have held that the kingdom of God is entirely future—that the concept is to be understood apocalyptically in terms of a dramatic and final break in historical continuity when the Son of man will come on the clouds to usher in the final age. Others, like C. H. Dodd, held just the opposite view—that the kingdom is wholly present. Perrin says that the conclusion now of New Testament scholarship is that

> it may be said to be established that the kingdom is both present and future in the teaching of Jesus. The discussion has reached this point; Weiss and Schweitzer were not able to convince the world of scholarship that it was wholly future. Dodd was not able to maintain his original view that it was wholly present and subsequently modified it, and Bultmann's wholly futuristic interpretation was modified at this essential point by his *Schüler* [his disciples].[16]

The mature position of Dodd probably states the relationship of the present and future most accurately. The kingdom is present in the life and ministry of Jesus, and in the church in a partial way, but it is also still beyond history, a reality yet to be fulfilled.[17] To put it another way, Jesus' life and ministry are lived out in the present in anticipation of a future which is still to come. This interpretation ties in well with what we just said about the Old Testament. The promise is to some extent fulfilled in history, but in such a way as to anticipate a greater fulfillment.[18]

Perrin says that most scholars also agree that the kingdom of God is an apocalyptic concept, but on the meaning of this apocalyptic concept, they do not agree.[19] If by apocalyptic we mean a dramatic event at the end of time that represents a complete break in the continuity of time, such an interpretation is difficult to harmonize with the fact that the kingdom of God is both present and future. It seems best to interpret the kingdom as future in the sense that God's rule in a final and total sense is still coming, but we can also expect the kingdom to break into our present history in new ways that will surprise us. The kingdom of God is a fulfillment of history, and at the same time, an event that occurs in the sinful condition of history, a breaking in of God's rule into the lives of people, both by bringing judgment upon and by transforming human institutions.

If the kingdom is both present and future, then Jesus' ethic is not simply an interim ethic, an ethic irrelevant to ongoing history. For if the kingdom is in some sense present, then the ethic of Jesus is relevant to the continuities of history, not just an ethic anticipating a future age beyond history.

Amos Wilder, who accepts the view that the kingdom is both present and future, sees the relationship of eschatology and ethics in the teaching of Jesus in three ways. (1) Insofar as the kingdom is future, "the coming event is ... motive for repentance and for urgency in doing righteousness, and the particular demands are looked on as conditions of entrances to the future kingdom."[20] (2) Insofar as the kingdom is present, the ethical teaching of Jesus reflects a way of life that is relevant to, and made possible by, the kingdom as a present experience. Wilder calls this an "ethic of the time of salvation of new-covenant ethics."[21] (3) Insofar as the coming of the kingdom is a crisis, a period of conflict, Jesus calls upon his followers to be disciples. "In particular the most exigent requirements of Jesus have to do with following him in the crisis of the kingdom."[22]

In the light of this clarification of the concept of the kingdom of God, we can return to our first thesis: Jesus is an agent of radical social change in the tradition of the prophets. This claim is made in the poetry of the early chapters of Luke's Gospel. The Magnificat of Mary, the words of Zechariah proclaiming the birth of John the Baptist, the words of John the Baptist, and the angelic announcement of the meaning of Jesus' birth are filled with sociopolitical content. The good news of the gospel is the fulfillment of a promise. Monarchs will be brought down from their thrones, the hungry will be satisfied, the people will be delivered from their enemies, and peace on earth and goodwill among people will happen. John H. Yoder says, "Too hastily we have passed all this language of annunciation through the filter of the assumption that, of course, it is all to be taken 'spiritually.' "[23]

Both Matthew and Mark report that Jesus began his ministry by preaching the kingdom of God, a message of good news. The word "kingdom" is a political term. If understood in terms of the Old Testament background and in terms of Jewish messianic expectations, it is filled with political meaning. The word "gospel" means "not just any old welcome report but the kind of publicly important proclamation that is worth sending with a runner and holding a celebration when it is received."[24]

This "good news" is expressed by Luke's account of Jesus' visit to the synagogue at Nazareth, an event in the structure of Luke's Gospel which is the inauguration of Jesus' ministry. The text from Isaiah 61 read by Jesus is clearly applied by Luke to Jesus himself.

> "He has anointed me to preach good news to the poor.
> He has sent me to proclaim release to the captives
> and recovering of sight to the blind,
> to set at liberty those who are oppressed,
> to proclaim the acceptable year of the Lord" (Luke 4:18-19).

The very deeds of Jesus demonstrated that the kingdom of God is an event which renews human life in all its dimensions. When the disciples of

John the Baptist are sent to Jesus to inquire whether Jesus is the "one who is to come, or shall we look for another," Jesus tells them to "go and tell John what you hear and see: the blind receive their sight and the lame walk, lepers are cleansed and the deaf hear, and the dead are raised up, and the poor have good news preached to them" (Matthew 11:3-5). The event of the kingdom brings healing to the body; it is also a message of good news to the poor.

In his excellent analysis of the biblical attitude toward poverty, Gustavo Gutierrez makes three points: (1) that poverty is a scandalous condition inimical to human dignity and contrary to the will of God; (2) that the people of God should live and operate their institutions in such a way as to prevent poverty from becoming established amongst themselves; (3) that God has special concern and compassion for the poor. It is in this latter sense that the beatitude "Blessed are the poor" is to be understood, says Gutierrez.

> "Blessed are you poor, for yours is the kingdom of God" does not mean, it seems to us: "Accept your poverty because later this injustice will be compensated for in the kingdom of God." If we believe that the kingdom of God is a gift which is received in history, and if we believe, as the eschatological promises—so charged with human and historical content—indicate to us, that the kingdom of God necessarily implies the reestablishment of justice in this world, then we must believe that Christ says that the poor are blessed *because* the kingdom of God has begun: "The time has come; the kingdom of God is upon you" (Mark 1:15). In other words, the elimination of the exploitation and poverty that prevent the poor from being fully human has begun; a kingdom of justice which goes even beyond what they could have hoped for has begun. They are blessed because the coming of the kingdom will put an end to their poverty by creating a world of brotherhood. They are blessed because the Messiah will open the eyes of the blind and will give bread to the hungry.[25]

The kingdom event also has implications for male-female relationships. Jesus is revolutionary in the way he relates to women, particularly when we compare him to the prevailing patterns of his time.[26] The kingdom event revolutionizes the realm of religion also where the Sabbath institution is renewed in line with ethical principles. "Man was not made for the Sabbath, the Sabbath was made for man." For every realm of life—the political, economic, male-female relationships, and religion—the kingdom event has significant implications. Human institutional life is judged and challenged to renew itself according to the new vision of the kingdom of God which is breaking into the world.

The New Testament concept of peace must also be understood in this context of the kingdom as an event which renews the totality of human life. The rabbinic writings and the New Testament continue the Old Testament tradition of using shalom ("eirene" in the New Testament) as a greeting which means a wish for well-being or salvation.[27] For example, after Jesus healed the woman who had suffered from hemorrhages for twelve years, he said to her: "My daughter, your faith has cured you. Go in peace, free for ever from this trouble" (Mark 5:34, NEB). After Jesus had forgiven the woman who had anointed his feet he said, "Your faith has saved you; go in peace" (Luke 7:50, NEB). Paul frequently uses the expression "grace and peace to you" in the salutation of his letters. Werner Foerster says that this positive meaning of the word "peace" as salvation in its deeper sense stands in contrast to the usual Greek meaning. Outside of the New Testament "peace" had a negative meaning, indicating absence of war, as an "interlude in the everlasting state of war."[28]

"Peace as the salvation of the whole man in an ultimate eschatological sense" is the fundamental meaning of the term, and "confirms the link with Old Testament and rabbinic usage."[29] This meaning is particularly evident in the song of Zechariah at the beginning of Luke's Gospel (Luke 1:76-79). Zechariah looks to Jesus to "give knowledge of salvation to his people . . . to guide our feet into the way of peace." Though the word "peace" is not used in the Magnificat of Mary, this poetry conveys also the sense that God is the bringer of salvation in its most holistic personal and sociopolitical nature. The same theme is evident in the angelic message of Luke 2:14: "Glory to God in the highest heaven, and on earth his peace for men on whom his favour rests" (NEB). This is no mere inner peace or spiritual peace, nor is this passage to be understood as a wish for peace. It is a "salvation which has come to the earth," says Forester.

The word "peace" has the same meaning of salvation in a holistic sense in the words of those who welcome Jesus at his triumphal entry to Jerusalem with the cry: "Blessings on him who comes as king in the name of the Lord! Peace in heaven, glory in highest heaven" (Luke 19:36, NEB). Peace has a similar meaning when Jesus weeps over Jerusalem and says, "If only you had known, on this great day, the way that leads to peace!" (Luke 19:42, NEB).

In much traditional Christian thought earthly peace and inner-spiritual peace with God are separated into two distinct spheres. The new covenant with Christ is viewed as an inner-spiritual peace that primarily restores the human relationship with God; it involves a kingdom which is not of this world. This duality imposes false categories on the New Testament.[30] How shall we interpret passages like John 14:27, where Jesus says, "Peace is my parting gift to you, my own peace, such as the world cannot give" (NEB)? Foerster cites Bernard Weiss and several other authors who argue that "if Jesus here borrows from the Jewish greeting, this is in itself a warning not to think in terms of peace of the soul."[31] Later in the Gospel, peace is not contrasted with inner anxiety, but with the affliction and trouble in the world (John 16:33). In Ephesians, the peace which Christ brings is directly linked to the social realm:

> For he is himself our peace. Gentiles and Jews, he has made the two one, and in his own body of flesh and blood has broken down the enmity which stood like a dividing wall between them; for he annulled the law with its rules and regulations, so as to create out of two a single new humanity in himself, thereby making peace (Ephesians 2:14-15, NEB).

In the conclusion to the book of Ephesians the author lists the Christian armor necessary to do battle with "cosmic powers, against the authorities and potentates of this dark world" (a reference, we shall piont out later, which refers to sociopolitical as well as superhuman forces). Christians are urged to "let the shoes on your feet be the gospel of peace, to give you firm footing" (Ephesians 6:15, NEB). In 1 Thessalonians 5:23, Paul views peace as salvation of the whole person. "May God himself, the God of peace, make you holy in every part, and keep you sound in spirit, soul, and body, without fault when our Lord Jesus Christ comes" (NEB).

As in the Old Testament, where the eschatological hope for peace embraces nature as well as the human world, so in the New Testament we have this same vision. It is most vividly expressed in Colossians 1:19 where the verb "to make peace" is used (along with the word, "reconciliation"). "Through him God chose to reconcile the whole universe to himself, making peace through the shedding of his blood upon the cross—to reconcile all things, whether on earth or heaven through him alone" (NEB).

Among the rabbis shalom was also a process of reconciliation between individuals and not merely nations. Thus, says Foerster, "we have frequent and emphatic reference to the making of peace (shalom) between men. . . . One might almost say that makes the role which peacemaking assumes among the rabbis nearest to the New Testament concept of love and takes the place in later Judaism which the requirement of love occupies in the New Testament."[32] The term "peacemaker" in the Sermon on the Mount ("Blessed are the peacemakers," Matthew 5:9) should be understood in terms of this rabbinic meaning of establishing peace and concord between human beings. "The reference is to those who disinterestedly come between two contending parties and try to make peace. These God calls his sons because they are like him."[33]

The third and fourth theses shall be elaborated in conjunction with each other. Jesus' inauguration of his kingdom of justice and righteousness led to a clash with institutions which preferred to maintain the status quo. Jesus' death on the cross was the price he paid for his social nonconformity. In his conflict with the powers, Jesus was constantly confronted by the temptation to use revolutionary violence. Jesus' response to this temptation was his nonviolent servanthood ethic, an ethic he also recommended to his followers.

The model of revolutionary violence for the sake of God's righteous cause is, of course, an important theme in the Old Testament. The principalities and powers often develop into very powerful forces resistant to change, sometimes becoming so demonic that it is difficult to see any goodness left in them. The Bible reflects a changing perception about how God is working to conquer the powers and bring them back in line with his creative purposes in history. One strand of the Old Testament views Yahweh as a warrior who destroys his enemies and who often calls upon his people to participate in that violence.[34] After the Exodus the people of Israel sing this song:

> I will sing to the Lord, for he has
> triumphed gloriously;
> the horse and his rider he has
> thrown into the sea. . . .
> The Lord is a man of war;
> the Lord is his name (Exodus 15:1, 3).

To understand Jesus' attitude toward violence we must understand the meaning of this holy war tradition in the Old Testament. Holy war, where Yahweh saves his people miraculously without their needing to act, is very different from the institution of war practiced by the kings of Israel with their armies and battle strategies. The Exodus, an event in the holy war tradition, is a miracle in which Yahweh defeats Israel's enemies without Israel participating in any violence at all to insure Yahweh's victory over the Egyptians.

> The Lord will fight for you;
> you need only to be still (Exodus 14:13, NIV).

This same tradition of Yahweh's miraculous intervention on Israel's behalf is reflected also in the battle of Jericho, the Gideon story, the Elisha stories (where a whole army is defeated just at the word of Elisha), and the stories about the conflict with the Assyrians who are routed without Israel doing anything. Isaiah, within this same holy war tradition, gives advice to King Hezekiah, as he faced Sennacherib, "that Yahweh had found Zion and was its sufficient defense (Isaiah 14:32) and that he would in his own good time give the signal for the overthrow of Assyria."[35] The people are to wait for Yahweh's miracle. The prophets again and again appeal to this tradition. They condemn the violence and cruelty of the nation and call on Israel to turn back to Yahweh and trust in him. We see this theme in 2 Chronicles which views wars as the result of Israel's unwillingness (especially its kings) to trust Yahweh (2 Chronicles 14:11; 16:7f.; 20:17).

Within this holy war tradition, the people were often called by Yahweh to participate in the violence. But this participation was done within the traditions of holy war. Holy war did not depend upon a standing army. A charismatic leader would rise up to lead the people, one upon whom "the Spirit of Yahweh rushed" (Judges 3:10; 14:6). The battles were conducted in strange ways, not as traditional military campaigns for instrumental political goals. The Jericho and Gideon legends illustrate this unorthodox form of warfare. The Jericho legend shows that the holy war concept should be interpreted in the context of sacrificial ritual. All its inhabitants and all its possessions are "devoted to Yahweh," and thus the city and all that goes with it are taboo. For this reason, Aachen, who violates this ritual act by keeping booty for himself, is killed.

Because Jesus stands within the prophetic tradition, he, like the Hebrew prophets, rejects the royal tradition of calculated warfare where kings no longer trust in God's deliverance but in their own standing armies. Jesus accepts the holy war concept of trust in God, but he gives the concept a completely nonviolent interpretation by extending the meaning of who are God's people universally to include even God's enemies. Love is to be shown to enemies, for they are objects of God's saving activity, potentially members of the covenant community. No longer are enemies objects of God's wrath to be destroyed because they are inevitably alien to God.

This universalization of the meaning of peoplehood had already taken place in the Hebrew prophets. As the concept of Yahweh's people was extended and gradually universalized to include those beyond Israel's own borders, the notion began to die away that Yahweh had enemies who were to be "devoted to him" and who must be destroyed as sacrificial objects. Yahweh's people are all the nations of the earth. In the Servant Songs of Isaiah, the notion of holy war seems to have disappeared altogether. The servant suffers "because he goes around to the nations preaching the kingdom of God, the Torah. . . . Instead of going like Sennacherib or Nebuchadnezzar with an army he goes around preaching."[36]

This tradition is picked up by Jesus and the New Testament. The New Testament is a selective reading of the Old Testament. In the reading of the Old Testament the tradition most distinctive to Israel among the nations is remembered. Within that tradition, Jesus extends the meaning of Yahweh's people to include one's enemies. This tradition expected miraculous deliverance from Yahweh. John H. Yoder says that

> when, therefore, Jesus used the language of liberation and revolution, announcing a restoration of "kingdom" community and a new pattern of life, without predicting or authorizing particular violent techniques for achieving his good ends, he need not have seemed to his listeners to be a dreamer; he could very easily have been understood as updating the faith of Jehoshaphat and Hezekiah, a faith whereby a believing people would be saved despite their weakness, on condition that they "be still and wait to see the salvation of Yahweh."[37]

In this context of his "trusting" attitude toward Yahweh we can understand Jesus' view of liberation and victory over the powers and principalities through his life and action as a servant. Instead of being persons who lord it over others, Jesus tells his disciples to serve their fellow human beings. Luke states this clearly after the disciples had been debating about their appropriate place in the kingdom. Evidently the disciples had understood Jesus to be inaugurating a traditional kingdom. Jesus says: "The kings of the earth lord it over their subjects; but it shall not be so among you. . . . For I am among you as one who serves" (Luke 22:24-27).

Jesus' clear rejection of revolutionary violence is especially evident when he makes his triumphal march into Jerusalem and cleanses the temple. The time was ripe for him to seize power. A number of his disciples were ready for it. Oscar Cullmann says that perhaps as many as half of Jesus' disciples came from the ranks of the Zealots, a religiopolitical party in the tradition of the Maccabean kings who wanted to restore the Davidic kingdom.[38] The enthusiasm of the crowd could have been translated into a violent revolution to overthrow Roman rule and set up a new kingdom. But, says Yoder, "it belongs to the nature of the new order that, though it condemns and displaces the old, it does not do so with the arms of the old. Jesus passes up his golden chance, and withdraws to Bethany." And Jesus withdraws not because his message is primarily spiritual, but because his social revolution is not a traditional violent revolution.[39]

The cross is both the negative consequence of Jesus' nonconformity to institutions threatened by his life and message, and also a positive demonstration of his radical love. The cross, above all, demonstrates his willingness to lay down his life for us. In demonstrating an alternative to revolutionary violence, Jesus introduces into the historical process the possibility of genuine reconciliation. Genuine reconciliation is possible because love overcomes all barriers, even the barrier between enemies. The ethic of the Sermon on the Mount to "love your enemies" (Matthew 5:44) should be understood in the context of Jesus' total life and ministry of teaching and healing. Everyone loves "those who love you." The ethic of the kingdom extends beyond the narrow loyalties of nation, class, and race to the whole of humankind, even to one's enemies.

The Zacchaeus story (Luke 19:1-10) is a remarkable example of Jesus' identification with, and concern for, those who the people regarded as their enemies. Zacchaeus was a rich tax collector. Given what we know about the oppressive tax burden of Palestinian peasants and how the tax collector was part of a system that enabled some to become rich at the expense of the poor, it is no wonder that the people murmured when Jesus asked to visit Zacchaeus. After all, had not Jesus declared himself again and again on the side of the poor? In the Zacchaeus story we observe Jesus' identification with both the oppressor and the oppressed. True liberation or salvation does not involve a class war, but the transformation of both sides. The outcome of Jesus' visit produces action by Zacchaeus that signals the kingdom. Zacchaeus promises to give half his goods to the poor and to restore fourfold to anyone he has cheated. To this Jesus responded: "Today salvation has come to this house, since he also is a son of Abraham. For the Son of man came to seek and save the lost" (Luke 19:9-10). Salvation here means shalom, an agenda that includes economic justice. In acting justly by righting wrongs Zacchaeus stands in solidarity with the tradition of Abraham.[40]

Our fifth thesis is that Jesus' servanthood ethic permeates every strand of the New Testament. *The New English Bible* translation of Matthew 5:48 summarizes this ethic: "There must be no limit to your goodness, as your heavenly Father's goodness knows no bounds."[41] Servanthood ethics goes beyond the mere "natural" level of returning love for love. As an ethic that knows no bounds, it is indeed "salt" and "light" (Matthew 5:13-14). In accepting this way of love with gladness and exultation, the disciple stands in the tradition of the prophets who were "persecuted before you" (Matthew 5:12). In other words, love of enemies is implied by the heart of the gospel itself, a gospel which reveals God as one who loves all, as one who seeks the salvation of both oppressor and oppressed. Indeed, all of humankind in its sinful rebellion is God's enemy, and yet God chooses to love us (John

3:16f.). The gospel is not to be understood primarily as salvation for eternal life beyond this life. Jesus' death means that salvation is made possible in history and is integrally related to Jesus' concrete historical figure. Jesus brings hope and liberation from oppression and various forms of human bondage. The cost of that liberation is his death. His death reveals his deep love for us. It is to this same ethic to which his followers are called.

The New Testament church is urged to practice the servanthood ethic of discipleship. In this respect no gap exists between the Jesus of the Gospels and the Christ of the Gentile churches of Greece and Asia Minor. Also no gap exists between the Jesus of history and the Christ of faith. In all the strata of the tradition and in all the types of literature in the New Testament the historical Jesus, who as servant ended up on the cross, is the Christ of faith.[42] Christ both serves as the model for the moral life and empowers Christians to live in the newness of life.

In these materials we are not asked to imitate Jesus in all particulars. We are not called to teach in parables, to engage in an itinerant ministry, or to be celibate like he was. At one point, however, we are called to imitate Jesus, in his role of servant and his death on the cross.[43] Both Matthew and Luke discuss the costly implications of Jesus' approach to renewal. This is reflected in Jesus' discussion of the need to "hate" father and mother for the sake of the kingdom. The disciple is called upon to transcend the more narrow natural loyalties of family in order to be committed voluntarily to the way of servanthood. If one restricts one's commitment to the preservation of the family, for example, one may never be willing to take the risks necessary for justice or peace. The peacemaker Martin L. King remained dedicated to civil rights even when his house was bombed. This servanthood will not always bring one into social harmony with one's fellow human beings but rather into conflict.

Many Christians have, of course, interpreted the texts about "taking up the cross" in quite different ways. The most common view is that our cross is the suffering which men and women of all ages have had to face because of illness, misery, defeat, and loneliness. As helpful as this pastoral use of these texts may be for enabling people to bear their suffering, this use of the New Testament is a misinterpretation of Scripture. The cross of human suffering laid upon people against their will is very different from the cross which Jesus chose voluntarily in pursuit of his servant calling.

The sixth thesis is that Jesus' way of life and death is the way of resurrection or victory over the "principalities and powers."[44] By principalities and powers the New Testament means the sociostructural forces and institutions that have been created by human beings. These institutional structures take on a power and momentum of their own once they have been created. They act back upon human beings to direct, shape, and order human behavior. As we said in our discussion of the doctrine of creation, these structures are not inherently bad: political and economic structures, family patterns, cultural forces, and technology are created by human beings who have been made in the image of God. At the same time these structures have been distorted and corrupted by human sin, such that they contribute to injustice, dehumanization, and bondage.[45]

The cross is not a defeat by these forces, but in the cross is resurrection. Christ has defeated the powers and is Lord over them. This means first of all that he enables persons to become free from the power of these forces. Christ empowers persons and the church as a body to be free from their enslavement and bondage to the powers. Persons no longer must behave according to the determining forces of these structures. For example, to be in Christ means to be set free from the dehumanizing sexual division of male and female, the unjust conditions of slave and free, and the hostility of Jew and Greek (Galatians 3:28). One is no longer compelled by virtue of one's sexual role, membership in a national or ethnic group, or identity with an economic class to live by the rules of that role, group, or class. One is set free to serve one's fellow human beings, regardless of who they are. God through Christ breaks the chain of evil forces and makes possible a new birth, a new creation.

This concept of being set free from the powers has revolutionary political and social meaning. The power of human institutions lies in their capacity to gain allegiance and obedience. As we pointed out in chapter two, no political system is able to function without compliance from the majority of the citizenry. Only because most people obey most of the time can governments remain in power. "The voluntary or habitual compliance of the mass of the population is the invisible but very real basis of the power of every government."[46] One view of power holds that the people are dependent on the good will of the governing authorities. An alternative view is that government power ultimately depends upon the good will and tacit support of the people. Gene Sharp points out that the latter view is the basis of nonviolent action or any kind of people movement employed to bring about political change.[47]

We can see the revolutionary significance of loyalty to Jesus Christ. Loyalty to Jesus Christ empowers people to live according to values that are contrary to the rules, roles, and expectations of the basic human institutions in their fallenness. In Christ, human beings are set free from the behavior patterns of sexism, racism, classism, and nationalism that have become ingrained in the family, the economic system, and the political order. A new movement of people loyal to Christ thus can create a powerful liberating force for change in the midst of the principalities and powers.

The seventh thesis is that what God through Christ creates in history is a new social reality, the church. The church by simply being itself, by being loyal to a new center of authority, Jesus Christ, represents a powerful political alternative in history which has potential revolutionary significance. As a body of people bound together by Jesus Christ, the church transcends national, racial, ethnic, ideological, and class lines.

This transcendence by a community of ideological separation is illustrated beautifully in Karl Barth's letter during the cold war to Christians living in East Germany under communism. Most Christians at this time tended to identify the church with the West and evil with communism. In other words, the church simply reinforced ideological division. Not so with Karl Barth. Barth knew persons in East Germany who were Christians, members of the one body, the church, under the lordship of Jesus Christ. Barth, therefore, wrote to them as one who was in solidarity with his fellow Christians in East Germany, not as one primarily in solidarity with Western anticommunism.

From this perspective Barth used the text from Jeremiah 29:4-7 to urge the Christians in East Germany not to long for political deliverance from the West but to make their witness in their setting under an alien ideology and to contribute to the welfare of East German society (Jeremiah 29:7). Barth did not fall into the trap of identifying the West with Christianity but rather spoke of the West critically, identifying its materialism and practical atheism.[48] This does not mean that Christians cannot or should not make judgments about the relative merits of different social systems. But making such judgments is "tricky" business, since such judgments are easily coopted by persons and groups engaged in ideological conflict. It is easy to criticize systems different than one's own, and much more difficult to see the shortcomings of one's own. In general, Christians should be suspicious of those who find all the faults with others and exaggerate the goodness of the system within which they live. "Judge not, that you be not judged" (Matthew 7:1) are appropriate words of caution to those who open their mouths too readily on the evils of communism, but close their eyes to injustice and militarism in capitalist societies.

Christ's victory over the powers creates a new social reality in history which can transform human institutions. Christianity is not primarily an ethic of heroic individualism. The new creation spoken of by Paul is a new social reality. In Romans 6, Paul begins the chapter by asking: "Shall we persist in sin, so that there may be all the more grace?" His answer is: "No! No! We died to sin: How can we live in it any longer?" In being crucified with Christ, Paul says we cease to be a slave to sin. And in being resurrected with Christ we are "alive to God, in union with Christ Jesus" (Rom. 6:11, NEB). This has significant moral implications for human social life. "You must now yield them [your bodies] to the service of righteousness, making for a holy life" (Romans 6:18, NEB).

The new creation in Christ is the basis for the moral exhortations in the four final chapters of Romans which begin with the injunction to "adapt yourselves no longer to the pattern of this present world, but let your minds be remade and your whole nature be transformed. Then you will be able to discern the will of God, and to know what is good, acceptable, and perfect" (Romans 12:2, NEB). The new creation involves obedience to a way of life which lives out a new kind of social reality no longer conformed "to the pattern of this present world." We find a similar emphasis in 2 Corinthians 5:17-18, where the new world brought about by Christ is linked to our ministry of the "service of reconciliation." According to Ephesians, the new creation has immediate social consequences. The wall of hostility between Jews and Gentiles is broken "so as to create out of the two a single new humanity in himself, thereby making peace" (Ephesians 2:16).

Christ's lordship over the principalities and powers not only frees persons from bondage to the powers, but the church, both corporately and through its individual members, is set free to contribute toward the restructuring of these powers. In the midst of the principalities and powers the church should make its witness, a witness which brings both critical judgment upon the failure of the powers to serve humane purposes and a creative contribution to the structure of social and cultural life. In other words, Christians become creators of culture after the image of God, but now on the basis of their new creation in Christ.

The Christian position is thus neither total acceptance nor total rejection of the social structures, but the Christian approaches these structures with a discriminating ethic. Sometimes Christians may find that they can cooperate with institutions. Other times they can expect to face difficulty and conflict which may require that they bear the cross of suffering and perhaps even death. We must, however, keep the cross in perspective. The cross arises out of conflict with the powers in the midst of the goal to seek the welfare of the polis. The cross itself arises out of the prior motivation of compassion, a compassion which leads Christians to seek liberation, justice, and wholeness for fellow human beings. Though Christians must be prepared for the cross (the cost of discipleship must be counted), the goal of their action is the reestablishment of friendship among fellow human beings, a friendship which is righteous and just.

Serious distortions of the gospel can result if the cross is not viewed as a consequence of compassion for the welfare of the polis. The one distortion is pacifistic withdrawal and the other is the violence of fanatical confrontation. For example, the position of some Mennonites of withdrawal from the world results from an ethic of suffering without a corresponding compassion for the world.[49] Christians also often commit the error of relating to the powers with the violence of fanatical confrontation. It is easy to slip into messianic delusions without the servanthood spirit of Christ, because it is extremely difficult to remain compassionate as one confronts the injustice, self-interest, and status quo defensiveness of the powers that be. The temptation to strike out with hate, to expose and humiliate the opponent is great. When that happens, the opposition can only respond defensively, with stronger opposition. This produces an even greater self-righteous contempt for one's opponent.

The Christian who is genuinely interested in liberation, for both oppressor and oppressed, seeks to create space for the opponent to respond creatively. The ultimate purpose for confronting the powers is to create space for change, so that the enmity can be broken down and friendship based on justice can be established. Jesus' encounter with Zacchaeus must have done that. Both Gandhi and Martin L. King, who ultimately sought for reconciliation and friendship with the opponent, demonstrated a remarkable capacity for patience and flexibility so that the opponent could respond creatively. This should not delude us into thinking that compassion guarantees success. Though Gandhi and King were at times successful, they were both assassinated. But we must be able to distinguish between our own violence of fanatical confrontation which produces a cross that is the result of our own foolishness, and the foolishness of the cross which is based upon a courage grounded in compassion and justice.

B. ESCHATOLOGICAL HOPE:
THE PERFECTION
OF HUMAN INSTITUTIONAL LIFE

The relationship of the Christian to the principalities and powers is affected in two ways by the vision of an eschatological future or final age to come. In the first place, the eschatological vision is a motivating and driving force behind vigorous involvement in social structures. Too often the expectation of a new age beyond history has cut the nerve of vigorous political and social activism. The eschatological vision of a new age to come should function in just the opposite way. As a vision of the future, it calls human beings to seek new possibilities within the present. As a hope, it is a driving and motivating force that protects Christians from despair. The only way the dangers of escapism can be avoided is if the vision of the future is firmly linked with the experience and reality of redemption in the present, a redemption which is a partial realization or anticipation of the future.

A closer look at the New Testament eschatological vision reveals that human cultural activity and institutional reality is not completely destroyed, but is taken up, transformed, and given a role in the eschatological future. The vision of the book of Revelation consists of a new heaven and a new earth in which a new city, Jerusalem, is established on the earth (Revelation 21:1f.). The vision goes on:

> I saw no temple in the city; for its temple was the sovereign Lord God and the Lamb. And the city had no need of sun or moon to shine upon it; for the glory of God gave it light, and its lamp was the Lamb. By its light *shall the nations walk, and the kings of the earth shall bring into it all their splendor.* The gates of the city shall never be shut by day—and there will be no night. *The wealth and splendor of the nations shall be brought into it;* but nothing unclean shall enter, not anyone whose ways are false or foul, but only those who are inscribed in the Lamb's roll of the living (Revelation 21:22-27, NEB, emphasis added).

The highlighted passages suggest that political life, including even the wealth and splendor of it, is not destroyed but taken up into the new age which is to come. This vision is consistent with a theme in the Old Testament prophets in which the mountain of the house of the Lord is the center to which "all the nations shall flow" (Isaiah 2:2-4; Micah 4:1-3). It is also consistent with ideas of other parts of the New Testament in which the purpose of God is that "the universe, all in heaven and on earth, might be brought into a unity in Christ" (Ephesians 1:10, NEB; see also Colossians 1:20). This vision is consistent with what we said about creation. Human cultural activity, since it is an expression of the "image of God," is not to be destroyed, but taken up into God's purposes, and transformed to be an expression of God's glory.[50]

This suggests that utopian thinking and futuristic projections of alternative ways to live and structure political life have an important role to play in a political ethic. Too easily and quickly futuristic visions are dismissed as unrealistic and unworkable. However, the creative imaging of alternative futures is one way in which social transformation comes about. These alternative futures must be given their full expression and full weight so that they might serve as a stimulus to the way we structure political institutions in the present.

Secondly, however, we need to say that in another sense the age to come is "beyond" history. The new age is always future, still to come. "Beyond" does not mean that the future is outside of time or history, that history cannot or will not be transformed into God's kingdom, or that it is asocial or apolitical. This interpretation of "beyond" would cut the impact the future hope has on the present. It is "beyond" in the sense that it is always ahead of the present. The present is never a full expression of the perfect age which can be. The future is always transcendent of us and our political institutions. We can never claim to have made it. We can never justify our actions according to the view that if we do just this one more thing, then the kingdom will arrive. The "beyondness" of the future guards us against the false optimism of the notion of progress—that things are getting better and better all the time. The transcendence of the eschatological future may well lead us to conclude just the opposite. Human institutions are not getting better. Judged by the eschatological vision, things may be getting worse. But this judgment upon us should not produce a note of despair. Rather, it should compel us to move forward, driven by the hope that is in us.

A tension always exists in the Christian faith between the experience of radical rebirth and renewal and the "not yet," the continual battle with sin in one's own self, in the church, as well as the pervasive presence of evil in the world and culture around one.

How should we view the relationship between God's redemptive activity in history which results in transformed lives and in transformed social realities, and the continued fallenness of not only the world but also the lives of Christians and the church, an imperfection which leads Christians to speak of a final perfection only in the age to come?

The temptation of Christians over the centuries has been to attempt to resolve this tension. One resolution of the tension is to assert in one way or another that the new age has been realized or is about to be fully realized within history. One version of this position puts its faith in a remnant, a specially called-out prophetic group which is regarded as the transformed community to be the witness of the way, the truth, and the life. This community believes that it possesses the light in a way that is distinct from the mass of humankind.

This group may be content simply to witness to the truth of its position, suffer, and see its cause vindicated in the age to come. Or it may see itself as a vanguard to help usher in the kingdom for all of humankind because it hopes for the full realization of the kingdom within history. Those who expect a full realization of the kingdom within history may either expect that kingdom to come about by a gradual growth in human insight and reason or they may take a more conflictual view, holding that transformation can only occur when the oppressed rise up and overthrow the oppressor. Still another version of this position is where a group or institution which already holds the dominant position in society regards itself as God's special agent for the realization of the kingdom.

When the eschatological tension between the kingdom as "already realized" but "not yet fulfilled" is resolved in the direction of the "realized" pole, four kinds of distortions of Christian faith may result: self-righteousness, violent fanaticism, self-deception, and sentimentalism. Self-righteousness results when the remnant regards itself as the sole possessor of the truth. In the very act of regarding itself as right and everyone else as wrong, it commits the sin of pride. It forgets that Jesus' most severe judgment was upon the religious elite who regarded themselves as better than others.[51]

Violent fanaticism results when the vanguard comes to see itself as the agent for the initiation of the kingdom for all of humankind. It loses patience in the struggle against evil and takes upon itself the messianic mission of seeking to destroy evil by violence. Self-deception is at the root of this fanaticism, for in the very process of using violence, by acting in such a way as to destroy those who do not see the light, it both corrupts itself and builds into the very ends it uses, the evil it set out to destroy. It forgets that evil cannot be overcome by evil, but evil can be overcome only by good, as revealed in the Christ as the suffering servant.

poverty also corrupts

Another form of self-deception is involved when a dominant institution, which regards itself as the visible expression of God's kingdom on earth, nevertheless engages in all kinds of compromises with the sinful human condition by aligning itself with power and privilege to protect its own position. It forgets that Christ exercized his lordship as the servant, not as one who lords it over others.

Sentimentalism results from the naive optimism which expects the kingdom to come in gradually if only human reason and the underlying goodness of people prevail. Such sentimentality is continually shocked by the depth of evil in the human condition, for it fails to consider the cost of human liberation as revealed in the cross.

doctrines which confuse our lives

The other improper resolution of the eschatological tension is to stress in one way or another the "not yet realized" nature of the kingdom of God at the expense of the experience of its realization. One form of this kind of resolution separates justification and sanctification, and emphasizes salvation as primarily a change of a person's status before God. Under this view, the cross is seen primarily as the way in which, through Christ's sacrifice, God's justice is satisfied. Thus, to those who have faith in Christ, their sin is no longer accounted to them, since Christ "paid it all."

Forgiveness of sin is emphasized at the expense of repentance, which involves not only the acknowledgment of sin and the cry for mercy, but also the turning away from sin to a new way of life. Very little emphasis, if any, is placed on the fact that the fruit of the Spirit should be expressed in daily living. Sunday after Sunday Christians come to church to confess their sins, to ask for forgiveness, to receive God's grace through the sacraments, only to return to the world basically the same as their fellow human beings, giving no real evidence of the new life in Christ, having no light to let shine in the world. Such a resolution of the eschatological tension can be described with the famous phrase "cheap grace," forgiveness without repentance, salvation without the newness of life.

In another form, this resolution of the tension results in escapism. One type of escape is to regard faith in Christ as primarily insurance against judgment and hell. Another type of escape is reflected in those who experience the world only as radically evil. These Christians believe that the signs of the times point to the imminent return of Christ to establish his kingdom. Since salvation is entirely oriented toward the future, nothing can be done in this age except to have faith and wait for Christ's return. This resolution of the tension results in an inner psychic escape from the hard realities of the present—all of which functions as a drug—in order to live in a world of dreams.

Still another form of resolution of this tension is shaped primarily by an analysis of the human condition. We see this reflected particularly in the theology of Reinhold Niebuhr. Niebuhr stresses the pervasiveness of human sin, especially as it expresses itself in the power and self-interest of various collectivities like nation-states and economic interest groups.[52] Since his position begins primarily from an analysis of the sinful human condition (rather than the other basic type of resolution of the eschatological tension which starts from the experience of the new birth), the redemptive possibilities of history are underemphasized. History reveals only human sinfulness and inadequacy. Though the Christian faith gives hope, this hope is only for an ultimate fulfillment beyond the tragic necessities of the historical process itself.

In this view the meaning of the Christ event is twofold: ideal love revealed in the cross judges all human action as corrupted by human sin, and at the same time the cross points toward the future hope which can result in human fulfillment beyond history. Since in Niebuhr's view sin is inevitable in history, Christians must adapt themselves to the sinful human condition and make the necessary compromises with selfishness and power. The ideal of the cross always stands as a norm of judgment over these compromises as well as guide toward seeking some relative degree of justice in the social order. This justice is possible because it takes sin into account while at the same it is relatively good because the norm of love stands as a judge upon relative justice.

Niebuhr's position is a serious distortion of the Christian faith because it does not sufficiently emphasize the basic thrust of the whole biblical story: God's redemptive activity in history to make his people into a new people who, because of their trust in God, are given new possibilities of obedience to God's will. Niebuhr is so preoccupied by the question of what human possibilities are that he underemphasizes the possibilities of God's redemption. In contrast to liberalism which was too optimistic about human possibilities (and which Niebuhr battled against), Niebuhr was too pessimistic about human possibilities. Both liberalism and Niebuhrianism are rooted, however, in the common presupposition that the basic starting point for theology is the question of human possibilitiy. In this respect both are distorted by a common failure: lack of trust and faith in God as the energizer, the redeemer, the one who acts creatively through human culture, who frees persons from sin (that means the principalities and powers) and gives to human beings new possibilities of obedience.[53]

Niebuhr's position also builds into its thought structure the justification for a series of compromises with sin that makes the Christian faith an innocuous and weak movement in human history; for what is the consolation of a hope beyond history? How is this hope anything other than an "opiate" which allows people to tolerate human sin and oppression (because they are inevitable)?

Those who assert the inevitability of sin thereby engage in a subtle justification of it. For if it is not possible to have done otherwise than to have sinned, then we cannot be held accountable for what we do. Or, if indeed we are accountable and all we can do is ask for forgiveness, then are we not again in danger of "cheap grace"? Forgiveness which cuts the link to repentance and the possibility of the new life is not a forgiveness which frees and liberates. It is simply a security blanket. Furthermore, such a position is tempted to compromise much too quickly. Despite the fact that love always stands as a norm over the relative degree of justice possible in history, since compromise is inevitable, the temptation is to settle for the compromise all too readily.[54]

In Christ it is possible not to sin, though we ourselves can never claim to be totally pure and free of all sin. We never know for sure whether our actions or the motives out of which we have acted are pure. To claim perfection for ourselves is to commit the sin of self-righteousness.

On the other hand, it is just as grave an error to say that sin is inevitable, that every time we act we must sin. To assert such is to deny the possibility of God's redemptive action in history. It is to deny the possibility that God through us is capable of liberating or freeing us to engage in a deed worthy of his praise.

Nevertheless, the eschatological perspective should make us aware that all human visions, institutional structures, and human acts are limited and imperfect expressions of the kingdom of God. This applies to all realms of human institutional life. Yet we are driven by our experience of God's compassion for us to act compassionately toward our fellow human beings in the midst of a sinful and corrupt world. We are called in that world to radical discipleship. "There must be no limit to your goodness, as your heavenly Father's goodness knows no bounds" (Matthew 5:48, NEB). We should not give any grounds, either theological, ethical, or practical, to water down or compromise that moral claim upon us. But neither should that moral claim lead us into such an inordinate preoccupation with being right or pure that we are incapable of action, or that we are no longer capable of taking the risks of action in a world of sin and imperfection.

In this context Martin Luther's doctrine of justification by faith can play an important role. Through Christ's death and resurrection, God has forgiven our sin, if we will but trust in his promise to us. An enormous freedom is given to Christians in this idea. God sets us free to risk all for the sake of the kingdom of God. If we take this perspective, then our basic question will not be, How can I act in the world without sinning? but, How can I through God's power and forgiveness live freely for the sake of the kingdom of God? This does not mean that because I am justified before God I can sin boldly that grace may abound. Justification by faith must not lead to cheap grace. Justification by faith means that I am set free to be a disciple in the world, confident of God's forgiveness when I fail.

We have emphasized the political-ethical meaning of the cross. The cross is the voluntary suffering Jesus takes upon himself as the cost of his radical response to God's love for human beings. To this same cross Christians are called to obedience. But the cross is also a symbol of God's forgiveness of human sin. In the cross Jesus paid it all, and those who trust in him are set free by his grace. Both of these perspectives must be held together. Neither can cancel out discipleship. The cross of discipleship must be held in relationship to the cross which paid it all.

Both perspectives must be held together in the celebration of the high point of the liturgy, in the Lord's Supper. The Lord's Supper is, on the one hand, a celebration and remembrance of Christ's sacrifice for us through which we have the forgiveness of sins. On the other hand, the meal is a symbol of a new fellowship (koinonia) of persons bound together by love who in the present eating together have a foretaste of the messianic banquet. Thus to eat the Supper with a spirit of disunity and hate is to violate the very meaning of the Supper and to bring judgment upon oneself. Liturgy without repentance and ethical renewal is a sham. That is why if one has a grievance with a brother or sister, one is, according to Jesus, to leave one's gift at the altar and first go and make the matter right. On the other hand, the Supper is for sinners, for those who need God's grace and forgiveness. If ethical perfection were to be made an absolute condition for eating the Supper, then none of us would ever partake. Nevertheless, the fullness of the Supper is expressed when we can offer to each other both a reconciling spirit of love and at the same time come to the Supper expecting God's grace of forgiveness where we lack that love. ○

PART III
NORMATIVE PRINCIPLES FOR ACTION IN THE WORLD

5 JUSTICE: THE GOAL OF SOCIAL INSTITUTIONS

We said earlier that the Christian ethical responsibility of peacemaking is not limited simply to the prevention of, or peaceful resolution of, overt violent conflict. Peacemaking must be extended to work for those overall conditions of society and the physical environment which can lead to a full and holistic human development for all persons. In the past, unfortunately, Christianity has usually been identified with the status quo forms of social organization in which there have often been gross violations of justice. Full human justice within social institutions, of course, is a utopian ideal that always stands in tension with the sinful human order. Nevertheless, we need to define the goal toward which Christian responsibility is to be directed, so that at least we can determine how relative approximations to this goal can be reached.

A. FROM THE COMMUNITY OF FAITH TO POLITICS

In order for Christians to relate their theological perspectives effectively to the human situation, they must be able to translate the theological-ethical norms that are meaningful within the community of faith into principles that are applicable to the political order. This translation process is necessary in order to bridge two gaps: the gap between the more particular community of faith and the larger political community, and the gap between the church and political institutions.[1] Some would also argue that there is a *necessary* conflict between political institutions and the church, because the essence of politics is the "sword," i.e., the ultimate sanction is violent force. Though violent force is present in political institutions, political institutions cannot be reduced to this definition, as if violent force were necessary for political institutions to remain political. The essential purpose of political institutions is cooperation for the sake of the common good. Coercive violence is often not operative. We tend to exaggerate its importance because so often the question of the use of force is what generates our debate and attention.

A tension does exist between the faith community of Christian people, who supposedly share a common language about their basic commitments and values, and the political community which represents a plurality of faith communities and thus does not share the same language as those within a particular community of faith. If we are to relate our Christian values to the larger political order, we, therefore, must find a way to "deconfessionalize" our ethical language so that it can relate to the broad concerns for the common good of the political order.

One way in which most Christians have sought to deconfessionalize faith so as to relate faith to politics is through natural law. Natural law can be generally defined as those universal moral principles knowable by all persons through the use of reason that can serve as a guide for policy in the administration of political and economic institutions. The assumption underlying natural law theory is that a universal moral reason exists which can be known independently of the particular faith stance of community in which one is a member. No particular content can be ascribed to "Christian" ethics relevant to social institutions that is distinctive from what can be known by all rational human beings.

I agree with Stanley Hauerwas' critique of this approach to Christian social ethics. He argues that such a stance destroys the distinctive content of Christian ethics by attempting to abstract ethical principles from their narrative framework, from the biblical story of creation, Fall, redemption, and hope, within which Christian identity is given shape and meaning. Natural law ethics reduces ethics to minimalist principles, i.e., what all persons everywhere using their common reason can agree to. Such a view, says Hauerwas, undermines the distinctive contribution of Christian ethics where our character and the acts that express our character are shaped by the story of God's gracious activity through history culminating in Jesus Christ. Hauerwas argues that we should not flee from the particularlity of this concrete history, but rather embrace the biblical story so that it can shape our lives more profoundly and empower the church to be truly the church in all its distinctiveness. Hauerwas believes this approach is especially crucial for the Christian stance of nonviolence, for an ethic of nonviolence is ultimately rooted in our trust in God, not in our efforts to try to control history. By contrast, natural law theory leads to the justification of violence because it believes that human beings should be in control of political and economic institutions. Hauerwas says the church must above all be the church, living out in its communal life the ethic of the peaceable kingdom.[2]

Though I agree with Hauerwas' orientation (I believe I have started where he has by defining Christian identity within the framework of the biblical drama), he has not gone far enough in illuminating how Christian ethics operates as Christians live and work in the world in institutions other than the church. It is necessary, therefore to translate the gospel out of its narrative framework in order to define and then apply those mediating principles to institutions other than the church. Though these mediating principles are firmly rooted in the Christian faith in that they are not necessarily principles all human beings would adhere to as a result of the exercise of reason, they are also translated in such a way that they can be applied to institutions which do not share the Christian narrative framework. This entire book is an exercise in that translation process—showing how Christian nonviolence can apply to the world of international politics. How do Christians help shape institutions and policies in such a way as still to remain faithful to the narrative biblical framework of the church? Furthermore, no direct application of theological-ethical norms to political reality can be made, since political institutions exist for quite different purposes than the church.

I start from the assumption that the church is made up of a particular group of people who have chosen membership in that community as a response to God's call to them to serve a special God-given task in the world. By contrast, we are all born into the political order where we are thrown together out of necessity to order our common lives with respect to physical survival and welfare. Christians make a serious mistake when they fail to keep this distinction clearly in mind. They then either seek to make political institutions operate as if they were a church by seeking to impose upon the political order a particular Christian standard of morality (the tendency of the evangelical right), or they seriously compromise the standards of the church so as to conform to the general mores of the political order (the tendency of the mainline denominations). This later tendency is evident in the church's almost universal support of the state when it has engaged in war.

The key issue for the church is how to remain faithful to its own norms as a community of faith and at the same time be relevant to the larger political community. In this section of the book I seek to elaborate two mediating ethical concepts, justice and nonviolence—concepts which are both relevant to political reality and at the same time reflect basic values of Christian faith. In the previous section of the book I drew heavily upon the language of faith and the Bible. In this section I will seek to speak of justice and nonviolence in terms which relate to the more strictly humanistic language of the larger political community. In this section my goal is to search for common ground, to find points of contact where Christians can cooperate with others for the sake of larger political objectives.

The relationship between the community of faith and the political community can be illustrated with two overlapping circles. The area in the middle where the two circles overlap reflect the arena where the church can involve itself creatively in cooperating with the larger political community

for common ends. Even where the two circles do not overlap, the church plays an important role in initiating critical action and words of judgment within the political community that, if heeded, will make politics more humane and more likely to endure.

To be a Christian means that loyalty to the "Christ" paradigm is the final standard by which to evaluate Christian action. To declare oneself a Christian means to confess that ultimate reality is fundamentally revealed in the biblical paradigm of redemptive history, a norm that reaches its culmination in the Christ event. It is neither possible nor proper, then, for Christians to attempt to develop the norms for politics on independent rational or philosophical grounds apart from revelation. That would, in effect, mean that revelation is not really the absolute presupposition from which Christians operate, that something alongside faith is of equal value.

On the other hand, Christian solidarity with all human beings is the context for social and political action in the polis, in the social order where all humans must seek to cooperate together for the sake of the general good. In this task of shaping the common good, Christians bring their own norms of faith to bear upon political action. The concepts of justice and nonviolence can provide such a normative framework. These principles help the Christian make discriminating judgments about the ends or goals toward which the polis is being shaped, as well as the means by which persons and groups are to bring about these ends. At the same time they are concepts which connect with the concerns of non-Christians who are also interested in the shape of the polis.

B. CONCERN FOR STRUCTURES, NOT JUST INDIVIDUALS

It is probably fair to say that most Christians, where they see individual persons who are suffering and in personal need, consider it their moral responsibility to give help. The model for this aid is provided in the New Testament by the Good Samaritan story. Where there is famine and hunger, most Christians consider it their obligation to give of their abundance to those in need. When disasters strike, such as tornadoes, earthquakes, or disease, Christians consider it their moral duty to help the victims. This kind of moral sensitivity is to be praised, and it often does a great deal of good in the world. But it is not enough, and sometimes it may even do more harm than good.

Compassion must express itself in seeking justice. Those concerned about justice seek not only to treat the victims of famine, disease, or war, but seek to find out what are the underlying conditions which produced the victims. Often the fault lies not in particular individuals who are especially demonic, but in the institutions or structural arrangement of a society. As we said in the previous chapter, Christians must seek to liberate persons from, or seek to transform, the principalities and powers so that these structures serve their God-intended functions. To try to convert individuals or to treat the victims of disaster without struggling to change the structural conditions which cause the disaster is to fail to fulfill Christian social responsibility.

The basic problem is how decision-making power and economic resources are distributed in social systems. The problem of hunger, for example, can be multifaceted—involving economic systems which are producing gross inequalities in the distribution of wealth, trade relationships between more wealthy and poorer states, the availability of world markets, technological developments such as mechanization of agriculture, or even food aid which depresses prices within a country so that it is no longer profitable to produce one's own food. It is possible for direct aid actually to produce more victims than it helps. Thus it is important for Christians to think much more carefully about the structural conditions or institutional arrangements both internal to a society and in the international system as a whole. Christians must apply the principle of compassion in a way that at the deepest level frees victims from exploitation, oppression, and human misery on a long-term basis, and creates conditions that lead to human health and wholeness. We need to understand the *causes* of human misery, not look primarily at the effects; we need to understand the importance of *structures*, not look primarily at individuals as the problem and solution.[3]

C. JUSTICE AS A NORM
1. Approach to Justice

Justice is an ethical term particularly applicable to institutions. The basic root meaning of justice is what is due to a particular person or group.

In this context we are especially concerned about how decision-making power and goods and resources ought to be distributed within political and economic systems.

Many views of justice and various methods by which to arrive at a definition exist. Some have attempted to develop a purely rational method for determining a definition of justice. One of the most significant and influential for Christian ethics is John Rawls' *A Theory of Justice*. Rawls proposes that we arrive at a definition of justice by putting ourselves in an "original position" behind a "veil of ignorance." By this Rawls means that we are to imagine ourselves in a situation where we do not know what position we will have in society. We do not know whether we will be rich or poor, or whether we will be in a decision-making role. What view of justice would we advocate assuming we were to operate in our rational self-interest? Because we do not know our position in society, Rawls believes that we will develop a more universal, and thus objective, view of justice than we would if we were to define justice from the standpoint of a particular group in society.[4]

The outcome of Rawls' method is a definition of justice consisting of two principles. The first principle of justice is "each person is to have an equal right to the most extensive basic liberty compatible with a similar liberty for others."[5] This principle, says Rawls, is prior to the second principle of justice which he states as follows: "social and economic inequalities are to be arranged so that they are both (a) to the greatest benefit of the least advantaged and (b) attached to offices an positions open to all under conditions of fair equality of opportunity."[6]

Rawls' position turns out to be essentially a rational defense of the American liberal creed. Derived from the first principle would be the various rights defined in the Bill of Rights of the U.S. Constitution which protects the liberty of citizens with such rights as freedom of speech and assembly and the free exercise of religion. These rights are protected against the tyranny of the majority who cannot vote away these rights for the sake of a greater good for the greater number.[7] Rawls argues that we would not choose utilitarianism as our first principle of justice in an "original position" because considering we might be in the minority we would be unwilling to give away our basic liberty to the majority if that were in the interest of the overall greatest good. Individual liberty is more basic than the general good of society.

Rawls' second principle basically boils down to equality of opportunity. Inequality in a society is permissible, provided that everyone has a fair shake. People should not be discriminated against because of race or creed. Educational resources should be available to all so that persons can compete fairly in the system. The laws of a society should operate by procedures that are fair to all persons. In sum, the process should be fair, though the outcome may lead to inequality.

Rawls, furthermore, qualifies inequality by saying that inequalities can only be considered just "if they result in compensating benefits for everyone and in particular for the least advantaged members of society."[8] This principle, however, gives little guidance to social policy. It is quite difficult to verify whether a particular policy has benefited the least advantaged. Rawls' position, in effect, allows for considerable inequality. It can support those who believe that the accumulation of capital in the hands of the few will eventually "trickle down" and benefit the least advantaged. Thus Rawls' theory of justice not only is a rational defense of liberalism but also supports the underlying theory of justice of industrial capitalism. It is revealing that from the "veil of ignorance" Rawls should defend the underlying theory of justice of the society in which he is a member.

Both the method by which Rawls arrives at a theory of justice and the principles that result from the application of his method are open to question. Stanley Hauerwas rightly finds his approach problematic because it fails to take into account adequately the narrative or contextual element of ethical reasoning.[9] As Rawls' own position corresponds strikingly to the context in which the position was developed—American liberalism and industrial capitalism—we cannot claim an objective moral standpoint divorced from our particular stance in society. From a Christian perspective, we should wholeheartedly affirm that being Christian means to have our views of justice shaped by a particular community, the church.

The church's definition of justice grows out of the special context of the biblical drama of God's redemptive activity culminating in Jesus Christ. This narrative context in some respects will result in agreement with Rawls' principles of justice, but in other important respects goes beyond Rawls. It is the task of the Christian from a Christian narrative context to give an account of an alternative definition of justice and in the context of the public arena of debate rationally explain why a Christian definition of justice is more adequate, just as Rawls has sought to give his rational account. In this sense, ethical debate is a rational enterprise and does not simply involve the assertion of one view against another. The next section defines justice from a Christian perspective and explains why that position is a more adequate account of justice than Rawls' and other positions.

2. Biblical Justice: Seeking What Is Due for the Disadvantaged

The starting point for a biblical view of justice is the expectation that all human beings should live a holistic life of material, social, and spiritual well-being. God's justice, which we are to pattern our lives after, is distributed particularly to the disadvantaged or the most undeserving (the poor, weak, slaves, sinners, outcasts) in order to bring about their salvation or wholeness. Poverty, oppression, slavery, and other forms of human deprivation are fundamentally alien to God's compassion for all human beings. "There shall be no poor among you" (Deuteronomy 15:4). In the words of Jesus' sermon in Nazareth:

> "The Spirit of the Lord is upon me,
> because he has anointed me to
>   preach good news to the poor.
> He has sent me to proclaim release
>   to the captives
> and recovering of sight to the blind,
> to set at liberty those who are oppressed,
> to proclaim the acceptable year of the Lord."
>   (Luke 4:18-19)

Thus Stephen Mott argues that a fundamental aspect of biblical justice is the principle of redress. "Biblical justice is dominated by the principle of redress which postulates that inequalities in the conditions necessary to achieve the standard of well-being be corrected to approximate equality."[10] In a situation of loss of freedom or loss of economic independence as a result of severe poverty or political oppression, the social conditions must be put back in order so that people can begin again with a situation of equality. It is this view of justice which underlies the concept of the year of Jubilee. When people are ground into poverty and overcome with debts to the point that they may even become slaves to others, the situation must be redressed. The original lands must be restored to the family and debts erased so that persons can begin anew.

The theological presupposition underlying this view of justice is that the resources of the earth belong to God for the sake of the well-being of all persons. When power and wealth are distributed so unevenly that poverty and oppression result, then they must be redistributed from the haves to the have-nots in order to meet basic human needs.

Mott summarizes well the implications of this view:

> When God's justice motivates us, our basic loyalties and sympathies will be profoundly affected. We can then identify with the welfare mother whose real income decreases because the legislature avoids raising taxes by eliminating cost of living increases for welfare

recipients. We shall appreciate the viewpoint of the black worker who fights prejudice to get a job only to lose it because the economics of treating inflation through increased unemployment often result in the last hired being the first fired. We shall feel the discouragement of the laborer who works full time yet remains in poverty. We shall share the frustration of the Third World laborer who has seen the government that he worked to elect overturned in a coup by elitest forces who receive support from a foreign government. We can feel the despair of a father in another land who sees the marks of torture on the body of his son who died in prison and wonders why money from a foreign country goes to finance a dictatorship infamous for its violation of human rights. Our perspective will include the woman whose husband is dying of liver cancer as a result of working with vinyl chloride, which is produced in his country because its production is too strictly regulated in the manufacturer's own country.[11]

3. Critical Analysis of Various Views of Justice

a. *Another Look at Rawls*

John Rawls' view of justice is fundamentally individualistic, failing to take into account the way our group solidarities define human identity and thus determine what share of the pie persons will receive in an economic and political system. From his individualistic starting point, Rawls defines justice as securing liberty and equal opportunity for individuals. Rawls assumes that individualistic starting points will satisfy the requirements of justice.

David Wills illuminates the inadequacies of Rawls' theory of justice as it applies to racial justice in the United States. He points out that the liberal ideals of justice centering on "freeing the individual from all forms of arbitrary treatment"[12] does not adequately take into account the way blacks as a group are locked in disproportionately to conditions of unemployment, underemployment, and poverty because of the fact that they belong, for the most part, to an economic underclass. The standard liberal specification of the meaning of equal justice in the economic sphere—equality of opportunity—assumes that the requirement of justice can be met by providing individuals

> with equal opportunities to achieve success by their own efforts. If, given such equal chances, different individuals achieve by virtue of their personal skill and diligence widely varied incomes and possessions, that is not to be regarded as unjust. That there are winners and losers is no injustice as long as the race is fairly run. This principle

(equality of opportunity) is also a characteristic element in the liberal definition of racial justice as the non-discriminatory treatment of individuals. Racial discrimination is unjust precisely because it interferes with the free running of the economic race.[13]

Wills says that by focusing on "whether the race has been fairly run" precludes the possibility of making a judgment about the justice of the outcome, an outcome which still results in vast inequalities between blacks and whites in the economic sphere. Liberalism focuses upon justice defined as nondiscriminatory treatment of *individuals* and fails to take into account the disadvantages resulting from *group identity*—the *structural* factors that forever operate in a society to prevent black people as a group from receiving their due proportion of the economic pie. These conditions are built into economic and political structures as a result of long periods of slavery and racial discrimination which continue to have a detrimental effect on blacks as a group. (See my earlier discussion of principalities and powers on pp. 61ff. and 90ff.

Wills argues that the notion of compensatory justice (which I believe is identical to Mott's principle of redress)

> challenges the whole individualistic framework upon which liberalism customarily relies. To speak of the obligations laid upon the contemporary white population by the injustice done by prior whites to now deceased blacks is, after all, to acknowledge in racial group identity and its continuity over time a moral significance which conventional liberalism has persistently sought to deny. It is to admit that the differential between white and black median family income reflects an injustice that must be understood in terms of the groups involved—and not instantly translated into a pattern of discriminatory action against discrete individuals. It is also to admit that American economic life is less a race among individuals freshly run with each generation than it is an uninterrupted contest in which kinship groups struggle to preserve or improve the positions gained by previous generations. It is to admit, finally, that the idea of equality of opportunity, conventionally understood, is of limited use in defining the meaning of racial justice—particularly economic justice between the races.[14]

Taken seriously, the principle of redress or compensatory justice would require the equalization of blacks and whites in the economic sphere, and would thus require Americans to come to terms with economic inequality and economic class. Wills believes that such an imperative drives one back again to the socialist tradition. The language of "capitalistic exploitation," whatever its inadequacies as an economic account of the nature of class injustice, at least enables us to acknowledge and condemn the unjust human relationships which industrial capitalism has so evidently created and maintained.[15]

b. *Marxist-Socialist Views of Justice*

I do not mean to equate Marxism and socialism, nor smooth over the various shades of Marxism and socialism. For our purposes here, however, it is fair to say that most Marxists and socialists share a similar understanding of distributive justice, though they may disagree radically in their social analyses of the causes of injustice and in the manner in which they believe social change comes about. Both Marxists and socialists are committed to the view that economic resources should be distributed as equally as possible in order to meet basic human needs. They are committed to the fundamental unity of the human family and thus oppose economic systems which divide persons and groups from each other because of competitive economic interests.

It is thus understandable why some Christians are attracted to socialist and Marxist views of social justice, given the biblical view of justice as meeting basic human needs by distributing resources as equally as possible to secure the well-being of the entire human family. Christian support for socialism, which goes back to mid-nineteenth-century England, was a powerful force in the social gospel movement in the early part of this century, and continues to be persuasive, particularly for Christians in the third world. Paul Tillich is purported to have told a group of students in 1957 when asked whether he supported socialism: "That is the only possible economic system from the Christian point of view."[16]

I find myself in fundamental sympathy with the view that resources should be distributed in a society to meet people's fundamental needs. This view is based on the underlying premise that each person is of such worth that a society has the responsibility to insure that people have the most basic minimal resources that are necessary for human survival. No matter what a person's merit or worth, and no matter how the market functions in a society, everyone has a right to have his or her basic needs met by society.

I have referred so far to this position in terms of "basic" or "primary" needs. Even though it is difficult to determine precisely what a basic minimum is or what the basic needs are, I shall assume that it is sufficiently clear to a society so that a basic social minimum can be determined. It is, of course, much more difficult to determine what "needs" means on a global level. By a basic social minimum I mean at the least the necessities of food, clothing, shelter, education, and the right to a livelihood so that one can support oneself.

Basic human rights defined by the liberal creed (freedom of speech and the free exercise of religion) are also human needs; these aspects of justice are addressed at another point of the chapter. It is, however, important to indicate here that most Marxist views do not have a broad enough view of needs. Democratic socialism is really the only view which adequately combines a concept of economic equality with liberal democratic views of human rights. Beyond these primary needs or goods which everyone ought to be entitled to, the needs of persons vary greatly. Some persons need very little in the way of material comfort, whereas others *need* a great deal. Some persons need a great deal of culture such as books, music, and art, whereas others have a greater need for things such as homes, cars, and other comforts. It seems, therefore, highly inappropriate to determine needs beyond a basic social minimum.

The big question with a *needs* view of justice is whether distribution based on individual competition should be completely ignored. Once a basic social minimum is achieved, should then a society not recognize various individual contributions based on merit? Some argue that to guarantee even a basic social minimum would abolish all incentive to work. On the other hand those societies which have developed a more radical egalitarian notion of justice seem also to have evolved a less individualistic and more communal motivation. The most notable example is in contemporary China where the motivation to work is governed not primarily by individual reward but by the contribution one makes to the common good (though, I understand, this may be changing). This communal motivation is achieved through the pressure of the collectivity as a whole upon the individual. It is difficult to determine to what extent this more communal orientation is consented to voluntarily by most Chinese, and to what extent this consent is gained through coercive force. Probably the best system lies somewhere between a society based on individual initiative and one with a more communal orientation.

A notion of justice that insures a basic social minimum so that persons have some measure of equal opportunity to wealth and power can be combined with the value of individual freedom which allows for some inequality that reflects diverse motivations, interests, and definitions of need. However, insuring that people have a basic social minimum must be a first priority, and only after that condition has been met can inequality be justified. Some would agree that this notion of justice is not nearly egalitarian enough. But just by adopting the notion that justice requires a basic social minimum, major change would be called for in many societies.

Some would argue that to guarantee that someone's basic needs are met undermines the incentive and responsibility of the individual for his own welfare. They believe that some people would just become freeloaders on the system. It has to be acknowledged that some persons might be content to accept the social minimum and simply live off social handouts. Most people, however, want much more than a basic social minimum for themselves. Most people are motivated to live for values that go far beyond basic survival, including the benefits that arise from those goods which are produced by society as a whole (e.g., public education, public transportation, and public recreation). People most in need of a guarantee of a basic social minimum are usually the old, the very young, the sick and handicapped, single parents with dependent children, and others. It is unfair to place such an immense burden on one or several people who struggle to survive in the face of immense hardship—hardships which are often beyond the control of persons to ameliorate. It is clearly contrary to Christian compassion to fail to have concern for and care for the fatherless or motherless, the widow, the poor, and the stranger within the community.

c. Human Rights

Another way to focus the issue of justice is to reflect upon the meaning of human rights. There are at least three levels to the human rights discussion: (a) political and cultural rights, (b) the right to social and economic well-being, (c) the right to live without serious threat to the environment which sustains life.[17] According to Stephen Mott, though the Bible does not talk of human rights, the

> desire for the well-being of each person leads to the idea of basic rights for each person.... Human rights are a crystallization of the claims that a person has when valued as an end.... Since human dignity is bestowed, based in God's love, the rights necessary concretely to protect and express that dignity are also bestowed.... Every right implies a duty. Rights free us from indignity and oppression and at the same time mandate respect for others.[18]

By political and cultural rights are meant those rights stressed by liberal democracies, the rights guaranteed, for example, by the American Constitution. These rights include among others the right of speech and freedom of assembly, the right to organize and advocate a point of view in the body politic, the right to vote and determine one's own political system, the right to the free exercise of religion and to a lifestyle that is sufficiently compatible with others that it does not destroy their liberty, the right to a fair trial, and freedom from torture and unjust detainment and incarceration. These rights are by no means universally upheld in the world community. In fact, they are grossly violated in perhaps well over half the population of the world by both rightist and leftist states. Christians should support such rights. Christians concerned about the preservation and protection of these rights should understand what those structures are like where such rights exist, and what the possibilities are for modifying existing structures or creating new structures where these rights are not yet recognized and protected.

At a second level are the rights connected to social and economic well-being. Among these rights are the rights to adequate food, decent housing, adequate health care, a job or a meaningful way to earn a livelihood, and an adequate education. Socialist economies tend to emphasize these goals. Scandanavian countries like Norway and Sweden are noted for their accomplishments in meeting basic social needs. China has made tremendous strides from the pre-revolutionary days of Chiang Kai-shek. The Soviet Union and most East European Marxist states have, at least to a considerable degree, been able to meet the most basic social and economic needs of their citizens, though they still have inequality and have not been able to fulfill adequately the first category of rights.

Capitalist societies have brought about immense material well-being, but inequality is often great. In many of these societies are pockets of poverty in the midst of extreme wealth for some. Unemployment is unknown in China. It is a permanent feature of industrial capitalism. So the human rights discussion is more complex than it is often made out to be. Whereas under one system certain rights in the political and cultural realm are well protected (the United States), under another system social and economic well-being for all seems to be better protected (China). We need to ask ourselves whether some structures can preserve and protect both kinds of rights. Democratic socialism claims to be a system which protects both political rights and aims at greater economic equality.

At a third level is the right to live without serious threat to the environment which sustains life. Normally these considerations do not enter into the human rights discussion at all. Here we refer to the threat of nuclear devastation and the increasing threats to the environment by pollution. None of these human rights arenas can easily be confined within the borders of a nation-state, but this area in particular must be dealt with on a global scale. What one state does to the atmosphere or the ozone layer or to the ocean depths has a direct affect on all the inhabitants of the globe. Christians must be, therefore, concerned about the global structures which seek to preserve a physical environment that is inhabitable. The concern about the control of nuclear weapons is not *another* issue, but is itself a human rights issue. Former President Jimmy Carter, for example, failed to link nuclear disarmament with the human rights discussion when he emphasized human rights as an important component of U.S. foreign policy.

Our obligation to future generations must also be noted. Is it legitimate for us to consume all our natural resources now in order to achieve social justice in our own generation? The resources of the environment do not belong to one generation, but belong to all of God's people, including future generations as well. We should act then in our generation so as to insure for future generations that they live in an environment which can sustain life. This requires that we develop institutions that serve the common good and that protect the environment for future generations so that they might have equal opportunity. A just society, then, is one that also saves for future generations.

d. *Merit View of Justice*

One view of justice is that persons or groups merit what they are due. Persons or groups should be rewarded appropriately for what they accomplish. Similar merits should be awarded similarly. Thus, if persons work hard and contribute to society, society owes them an appropriate reward for their contributions. Today "merit" is usually defined as work contributed, a contribution that is valued by society. Merit has sometimes been defined more aristocratically as reward for a person's predefined worth, status, or position in society.

Justice defined in terms of merit is problematic for several reasons. In the first place, a Christian should start out from the theological principle that all persons have intrinsic worth no matter who they are, regardless of what natural endowments they are born with, within what social environment they are born into, or what they are able to achieve. People should be valued from this perspective not primarily in terms of what they achieve, but because of who they are, as created and valued equally by God.

Second, from both a theological perspective and by reflecting upon the human situation, we know that what we are and what we receive from society in the form of wealth and power is often a gift or accident, not simply a result of our own effort and accomplishment. We do not choose our family or social environment. Factors concerning birth may determine more than anything how much we eat, what our intelligence will be (since lack of protein in early life damages brain development), how long we will live, and what kind of education we will have. Gifts we receive from other persons can fundamentally alter our chances in life. The opportunities provided by home and school, the encouraging word of a friend, a chance meeting or occasion may have more to do with our achievement than our own efforts. From a Christian viewpoint the human experience of gift and grace should inspire an attitude of thanksgiving. From this perspective our life itself is a gift. The environment which nourishes and sustains us is a gift. From the standpoint of Christian faith, who we are is a function of the grace of God and at the deepest level we do not really earn anything.

Third, it is impossible to run a society on the basis of a notion of justice based on merit or worth. Who is to determine who merits or is worthy of receiving goods when they are scarce? By whose standard of worth would we make such judgments? Suppose we have a scarce supply of kidney machines and we cannot meet the demand for them. Should one try to give the scarce resources to the persons who most deserve or merit a machine? How would one make that decision? Who would make the decision? It would be more just, from a practical standpoint, simply to make a random selection by drawing names out of a hat, giving everyone an equal opportunity to be selected rather than to try to determine who gets scarce resources on the basis of merit or worth.[19]

e. Justice as Determined by the Market

Another view of justice is that the fair wage for a person's contribution of labor in a free competitive market is what is due. This position assumes that, if the market is allowed to function competitively, fair prices and wages will automatically work themselves out. If the economy has an oversupply of labor in one area, wages will be forced down and persons will be forced to work in areas where the demand for labor is greater and wages are higher. This position assumes that a free competitive market will automatically balance things out. Persons holding this position favor a social system that enhances everyone's freedom to work within a free competitive market without undue external interference by government.

The underlying assumption of a free competitive market view of justice is that justice will result when each person pursues his own individual self-interest. This assumption does not seem to be true in actual practice. The theory of capitalism assumes a relatively large number of entrepreneurs competing with each other with a relatively equal amount of power and wealth. However, the actual practice is that certain people and groups gain an advantage in wealth and power. Once this advantage is gained, their power and wealth accumulate in an almost exponential way. It then becomes possible for these persons to develop a monopoly or extraordinary power so that the market no longer functions competitively. Once a person or corporation is able to save and use capital for more technological development, they can gain further advantage and contribute to an increasing gap in power and resources. As the gap increases and wealth and capital become concentrated in fewer hands, the market works less freely and competitively.

Second, this theory of justice assumes that persons start out in a relatively equal condition, and does not take into account the aspect of accident of birth that we already mentioned.

Third, this view is not able to take into account the "tragedy of the commons," as Garrett Harden has put it.[20] Harden imagines the situation of a common pasture land that is available for cattle. Each farmer, operating out of his own interest, grazes as many cattle on the common lands as is possible so that he can maximize his own profit. The consequence is a disaster for the commons since the commons is overgrazed and the grass is killed so that no one can profit until the commons recovers. Harden views the "tragedy of the commons" as symbolic of the modern problem of the environment. No one person acting alone is destructive of the environment, but a number of people, each acting the same way, destroys the very conditions for survival. The competitive market position holds to the assumption that the supply of natural resources is unlimited. It assumes that harmony can result even when many persons pursue their self-interest. It fails to face the issue of scarcity and limit that results when all pursue their own self-interest simultaneously.

Fourth, the free competitive market view of justice does not deal with the hardship resulting from the short-term fluctuations of the market. It holds that supply and demand will balance out in the long run. This view lacks compassion for persons and groups who cannot easily adjust by finding new work, moving to a new location, and retraining if they suddenly find themselves out of work. It is often out of these short-term fluctuations that more chronic conditions or lack of opportunity may develop. This position tends not to have compassion for those who, by virtue of birth in societies where opportunity is not equal, remain in a permanently disadvantaged position. Furthermore, because capital is increasingly mobile among cities, states, and countries, corporations can play one region against the other. Capital can go where the tax breaks are best and labor is cheapest. For many multinationals that means going to other countries. Such moves can create long term detrimental consequences for workers.[21]

f. Utilitarianism

Some believe that justice is achieved when the sum of goods or satisfactions of a society are maximized as much as possible. This sum total of satisfaction can be distributed in various ways. Sometimes satisfaction or the good is defined simply as the highest average of satisfaction. Another view is that the sum total of satisfaction or good should be maximized for the greatest number of persons.

The utilitarian position defines right action according to the quantity of good brought about.[22] A pure utilitarian theory, to achieve the greatest sum of satisfaction for the greatest number in society, allows in theory for the sacrifice of the liberty and life of the few for the sake of the greater good. This view is fundamentally contrary to the value placed on the individual by the Christian faith. It also threatens the fundamental emphasis of biblical justice: that we are to seek justice for the least advantaged members of society. It is especially the poor, the weak, and the outcasts of a society that would be so easy to cast aside in the name of a utilitarian calculus of the greatest sum of good for the society as a whole.

Here John Rawls' critique of utilitarianism corresponds with the Christian view. Rawls argues that if we were to put ourselves in a position in which we did not know what position we would have in society (i.e., if we did not know whether we would be rich or poor, a leader in the society or a dissenter), we would not agree to a notion of justice that would sacrifice the liberty of the few for the sake of the benefit of the majority.

In summary, from a Christian narrative context, the goal of justice is to meet basic human needs. Since all persons are valued by God, all persons and groups have basic rights that are "due" them. These rights are political, cultural, economic, and social. They include environmental conditions capable of sustaining life. From this perspective, justice must go beyond equal opportunity for individuals (Rawls). Authentic justice seeks to redress wrongs and to compensate groups or classes of people for past injustice (the notion implicit in the biblical concept of Jubilee) so thta basic human needs which undergird a life of wholeness (shalom) can be met. In particular, merit, market and utilitarian views of justice are inadequate from this perspective.

D. JUSTICE AND THE INTERNATIONAL ORDER

In the preceding section we discussed a general theory of justice without specifying how justice applies to international institutions. Here we can only suggest some general guidelines about how justice applies to the international order, as the topic of this part of the chapter could be the subject of an entire book.

I. Recognition of Complexity

Can principles of justice be translated into guidelines for the international order? The difficulty at the international level is not so much the definition of ethical guidelines as such, but the lack of international institutions to implement these principles. For example, John Rawls applies the principle of equal liberty to the relationship between states in the international system:

> The basic principle of the law of nature is the principle of equality. Independent peoples organized as states have certain fundamental equal rights. The principle is analogous to the equal rights of citizens in a constitutional regime.[23]

This principle has been established in international law as the right of peoples to self-determination without intervention of foreign powers, and the right of self-defense against attack. The analogy goes this far, but then it begins to break down. For within a society, institutional structures can enforce compliance with the principles of equal liberty, and in cases where individuals have acted in self-defense, institutional structures are available to assess whether that act of self-defense was justified. If not, the person is subject to punishment under law. Of course, with nations these institutions are presently very weak, and the tendency of nations is to act in their own behalf without the institutional safeguards which insure that acts of war are genuine acts of self-defense. Institutions are lacking to make sure that armed force is not used unnecessarily, and also that war is conducted in such a way as to restore and insure future peace.

Can the principle of distributive justice be applied to the international arena?[24] The world community is increasingly interdependent economically. This interdependence basically serves as a benefit to people, for they basically cannot survive without dependence upon each other for the exchange of resources, technology, and goods. But the people of the world are not indifferent about the way in which the mutual advantages of cooperation are distributed. Thus the question of distributive justice arises at the international level just as it does at the societal level. Not only is it very difficult to determine what distributive justice means at the international level, but these questions are much more difficult to handle at the international level because of severe weakness and practical nonexistence of international institutions to bring about a just distribution, even if we could agree what a just distribution means.

The most critical issue is what institutions and procedures best suit these principles of justice we have outlined. Considerable room for variety and different judgments exist, depending a great deal upon the history and traditions of the people concerned. Under the right conditions, the types of social systems compatible with justice could range all the way from a quite competitive free market system to a socialist system where the means of production are collectively owned. Which particular institutional structures really serve justice will always be somewhat uncertain. Such a debate is now raging, for example, about the role of multinational corporations. Do they serve the requirement of justice, or do they operate so as to work against the least advantaged persons of society?[25]

Such questions can be settled only by careful empirical inquiry, and here each situation must be studied case by case. In settling these kinds of questions, ethical reflection needs to be integrated with other social scientific research and policy considerations to determine what institutions and policies are more likely to be just. As a theologian and ethicist, I am not competent to make judgments about development strategies or trade policy because these judgments require careful empirical analysis demanding the expertise of social scientists and policymakers. On the other hand, policy judgments cannot be left to the experts, because policy discussions also inevitably involve value commitments. Empirical analysis itself is not neutral but is shaped by larger overarching worldviews that often contain an implicit theological or metaphysical position. We must be aware that people tend to derive their values and perceptions of the world from groups with which they identify themselves, and this includes the so-called objective analysis of scholars. As Christians we cannot leave policy judgments to the "experts" when they are pursuing ends or advocating means that are not commensurate with the Christian faith. On the other hand, Christians must also have a certain degree of modesty about the policies they recommend lest they confuse their own judgments, involving empirical analysis on which honest persons can disagree, with the gospel itself.[26]

The requirements of international justice demand such significant changes that the problems we confront seem overwhelming and unmanageable. Justice at the global level would require massive changes in many societies where basic human rights are being violated regularly. Economically, global justice requires that all persons in the world have the right at least to the same primary goods or social minimum necessary for survival. The fact is that gross inequality exists on the globe and the gap is growing. The disparity between the rich nations and poor nations is as great as the disparity between the rich and poor in the most unequal countries on the globe. To call for a "basic social minimum" requires some adjustment to what that language means within very diverse cultural traditions and social systems. Nevertheless, this very minimal notion of social justice would entail some rather significant readjustment of the behavior of the richer nations of the world. Yet one cannot mandate change without considering what is realistically feasible given the fact that global injustice is a function of many decision-makers acting often quite independently of each other.

To understand the roots of human misery in any society, let alone at the international level, is difficult because of the complex interaction of many factors that produce that condition. Nevertheless, certain common factors need to be taken into account in every analysis, if we are to intervene appropriately so as to help alleviate rather than increase human suffering. We need to understand the way in which these factors interact to produce a particular set of environmental, historical, social, political, and economic conditions that shape it in definite ways.

Every society has a complex interaction between six variables: the natural resources and physical environment of that society; the type of technology and available capital for the development of technology by means of which human beings control their environment; the system of exchange within a society through which goods and services are distributed to people; the complex social arrangements of communities as these reflect fundamental cultural, religious, and social values; the political structures which determine the degree to which persons participate in and have control over decisions which affect their lives; and the cultural or religious values themselves which impact upon how people cope with their social condition. Human misery can arise because of failures in any one of these arenas. Usually it arises out of the complex interaction of most or all of these variables.

The conflict in El Salvador, for example, which has caused immense suffering for many poor and powerless people is the result of a combination of an inadequate supply of land for peasants to adequately support their families and an entrenched oligarchy that controls that land for the sake of certain economic interests. The system is sustained by a government which either encourages or fails to restrain military or terrorist groups who use torture and violence to repress any dissent or organized attempts to change that society.

The problems of El Salvador are integrally connected with both global ideological conflicts and corporate economic interests. The United States gives military support to the government in order to keep "stability" in the country over against what it perceives as the communist threat and Soviet expansionism. And while the peasants suffer for lack of food and land, corporations who control the best land export crops to meet the needs of affluent consumers in the United States and elsewhere.

Human misery in any society can arise because of failures in any one or combination of six areas: (1) a failure in the proper relationship of people to the natural environment as a result of lack of food, fertile land, clean water and air, or energy to perform vital functions; (2) inadequate or inappropriate technology that does not integrate well with the other social and cultural values of a community; (3) exploitation that results from the exchange of goods and services that are not of equivalent value or where one party to the exchange uses excessive coercion; (4) a breakdown in fundamental social institutions such as the family or religious order without replacement of these institutions by ones which can give meaning or dignity to human life; (5) a political system in which those in authority exercise power in ways that are not for the common good but for their own self-interest, a political system which adversely affects those not in power, but who nevertheless do not have access to or control over these decisions; and (6) cultural values which do not motivate persons to work for social change.

What we have learned in the past several decades, often at great costs and with painful results to human beings and the physical environment, is that changes in one area inevitably have an impact in other areas. This is especially the case with technology, which many still naively assume is neutral. The building of a dam on a river not only affects natural environments which have developed over thousands of years, but it can disrupt human communities, their values, and their economies. The introduction of running water in a village not only changes physical comforts of people, but can affect an entire pattern of social relationships in a village where people are accustomed to coming to a common well to draw water. Decisions which are seemingly neutral with respect to certain areas of human life turn out to have an enormous impact.

The decision, for example, of the U.S. Congress to appropriate vast sums of money for an interstate highway system rather than a superior system of public transportation has had enormous consequences for vast areas of American life. Above all, it was a decision to favor the automobile. That in turn favored a certain set of businesses and industries, rather than others, ones that are tied to the automobile—gas stations, motels, fast food restaurants, tire manufacturers, the trucking industry, and road construction. The system has changed cities by creating a sprawl of suburban dwellings, businesses, and shopping centers around inner cities which have been left to decay. The interstate system expropriated vast acres of fertile agricultural land, cut communities in half, and almost instantly created undesirable living areas and new slums along the routes within cities.

Small towns along old roads died without the automobile traffic, as new centers of motels, restaurants, and gas stations sprang up at the interchanges along the interstates. Carbon monoxide from the automobile forced cities to face problems of air pollution. The United States became more and more dependent upon foreign oil to run this system. United States foreign policy is increasingly shaped by the politics of Middle East oil. In the meantime the rail passenger system was left to decay as railroad stations were closed. Miles of tracks fell into disrepair, railroad cars became obsolete, and railroads went bankrupt.

This issue of the interdependence of technology and other social systems is put well by Richard Barnet:

> When a society buys an energy system, it is also buying a particular path of development. By choosing to burn up imported fossil fuels, to develop new coal technologies, to take the nuclear option, or to develop new alternatives—solar energy, fusion, harnessing of the ocean winds—leaders are also making decisions about how dependent society will be on scarce minerals, how much water it will use, how many jobs will be created, which cities and regions will rise and fall, and who will hold political power.[27]

Above all, many have failed to take into account the impact of Western technology and industrialization upon third world countries. The assumption that a Western capitalist model of modernization and industrial development would be the solution to human poverty in these countries has proven for the most part to be an illusion. A typical third world city illustrates the problem dramatically. The center of the city is not unlike New York, London, Berlin, or Zurich, a symbol of dynamic modernization consisting of modern skyscrapers, modern streets, and traffic with busy pedestrian traffic of well dressed people. This city is composed of a world of quiet streets where these people live, homes that exhibit luxuries often rare in Western industrial cities, a plentiful supply of domestic servants. Surrounding both of these zones are endless miles of slums. According to Peter Berger, who describes these three zones in his book, *Pyramids of Sacrifice*, a critique of the capitalist ideology of development must ask two questions: "Who benefits? and Who decides? The question can also be put as: Whose growth? and Whose market? . . . The question of who benefits from development can be translated into spatial terms, into the question of how these three urban zones relate to each other."[28]

The key to understanding the relationship of these three urban zones to each other is dependent upon seeing the interdependence of three entities: the multinational corporation with its investments in third world countries, the local governing elite of the third world country which can support an environment favorable to the corporation, and the military and political support of that elite by Western industrialized countries, chiefly the United States, that can secure so called stability in a host country that is favorable to corporate interests.

According to Richard Barnet, military power is able to facilitate dynamic growth and capital accumulation so that certain key third world countries—notably countries like Brazil, South Korea, Philippines, Indonesia, and others—are thoroughly integrated into the international economy. Barnet says that all these countries follow in varying degrees the Brazilian model:

> Attractive terms for foreign private investment, heavy commitment to high-technology industry and to the "infrastructure" of industrialization (roads, highways, dams, etc.), and, most important, tight control of wages and brutal discipline for the labor force. The model produces high growth rates, highly unequal distribution, and, inevitably, repression. It is not possible to bias the economic system so decisively against workers and those without any economic role at all without substituting systems of terror to perform the function assigned in democratic societies to the economic lottery—the chance to be rich through hard work and ingenuity. Where there are no incentives for a majority of the population, the Knout, the tracheon, the electric shocker, and the death squad are the means of assuring social peace.[29]

This system of industrialization has had particularly devastating effects on traditional agriculture. The combination of the mechanization of third world agriculture and industrial growth around big cities has led to a mass migration of peasant farmers to third world cities, a phenomenon which is responsible for creating vast slums in almost all major third world cities. Large corporate farms on the most fertile land in countries like Guatemala (owned by United Fruit) or in the Philippines (owned by Dole Pineapple) have displaced the small plots of peasants who were once able to eke out at least a subsistence living, and have driven them to the cities where they seek work in the modern factories, the product of Western industrialization. These factories, however, are unable to provide sufficient number of jobs for the millions who are moving to the cities, because for the most part these factories, following the Western development model, are technological-intensive rather than labor-intensive.

Even where multinational corporations have moved to third world countries because of the cheap labor and have employed unskilled laborers, the net impact of Western industrialization has been to produce higher unemployment. The industrialization of the third world has not created factory jobs in the cities comparable to the loss of employment. According to Barnet, "A smaller percentage of the Latin American work force was employed in the manufacturing section in 1970 than in 1925 despite the burst of industrialization that had occurred in intervening years."[30]

Another dimension to this problem is high population growth rates. The problem is that these growth rates will likely not be reduced substantially until economic conditions for the poor improve substantially. Thus many third world countries find themselves in a "Catch-22" situation.

The peasant who remained in the country at least had a chance at survival since he lived on the land and could produce his own food. If he moves to the city and fails to find employment, his chances of survival are very slim. Thus in Salvador, the capital of the state of Bahia in the northeastern part of Brazil, one of the main squatters' settlements (100,000 people) is on a landfill where garbage is dumped into the bay. As garbage trucks dump their loads they are met by crowds of people ready to pounce upon the contents.[31] Paradoxically, in many countries where persons are starving or malnourished from lack of food, agricultural products are simultaneously exported from the country. Fertile land in Latin America is used to grow bananas, coffee, strawberries, and other products which are exported by companies to markets in affluent countries without being distributed in the exporting company to benefit the poor. Profits from these exports increase the wealth of corporations like United Fruit or Dole Pineapple and they help the balance of payments of a third world country and enable it to pay its debts to industrialized countries for military hardware or for loans for developing technological-intensive industry or the infrastructure of a country. The overall growth rate of a country may look good, but only the few benefit from this economic growth—the corporate structure and the government bureaucracy—the few who live in the luxurious dwellings near the inner city. The vast majority not only do not find their situation improving relative to the overall growth of the country. For many, the situation has worsened, resulting in deep human misery.

2. Areas of Concern

We shall now identify four arenas in which Christians must become involved in order to help bring about more justice at the international level. This is by no means an exhaustive list. Nor do I presume to do a thorough analysis of each arena or prescribe a precise course of action. The four arenas I will briefly focus on are: (1) human rights advocacy, (b) helping shape the role of the multinational corporation toward distributive justice, (c) helping shape the priority of governments away from military spending toward more commitment to social programs, and (d) helping shape a third world development strategy that genuinely helps the poor. In each of these arenas, the church can contribute to justice at two levels: by its own lifestyle and actions as a corporate body and at the individual level as members work in various institutions and for social causes, and by the way in which the churches seek to influence public policy. In chapter eight we will outline more specifically these forms of action.

a. *Human Rights Advocacy*

We are at a time in world history when fundamental violations of human rights are occurring in most countries of the world, and in some countries on a massive scale. All one needs to see this fact documented is examine the yearly report of Amnesty International. Western democracies generally support within their own societies political and cultural rights like freedom of religion, freedom of speech and assembly, the right to remain free of unjust imprisonment and torture, and the right of a fair trial. It is often too easy for persons in these democracies to become hypocritical in their criticism about the violation of these rights in nondemocratic socialist or Islamic countries. These same persons often support military aid to totalitarian and repressive regimes who use military force to violate human rights. It is quite common for U.S. leaders and the religious right in America to condemn socialist regimes like Cuba or the Soviet Union but look the other way when rights are violated in countries to which the U.S. gives or has given military aid—the Philippines, El Salvador, Guatemala, Chile, or Vietnam.

Amnesty International has provided a model of concern for human rights that transcends ideological interests. It seeks to transcend ideology by being impartial in its research into and publication of the violation of human rights by examining these problems country by country on a global scale. Its members also become advocates of political prisoners without regard for ideological, economic, religious, or racial orientation. "Adoption Groups" work for prisoners of conscience in countries other than their own. These countries are balanced geographically and politically to ensure impartiality. Consequently Amnesty International has gained credibility throughout the world. Though countries may become quite defensive in the face of the publication of rights violations by Amnesty International and may not act accordingly to correct these violations, governments are often sensitive to citations of violations by the organization because of Amnesty International's credibility. The organization has actually achieved a remarkable degree of success in getting prisoners of conscience released.

Together with the one-by-one approach of Amnesty International, the church must also seek to shape public policy. Here it has a special role in Western democratic societies in monitoring foreign policy which sometimes supports repressive regimes in the name of national security or anticommunism. Christians must guard against a double standard of either overlooking violations of rights contributed to by the foreign policy of their own country, or of overlooking or downplaying rights violations in countries more akin to their own ideological bent.

b. *The Multinational Corporation and Global Justice*

The multinational corporation plays a very mixed role in the international system in providing an environment of peace. For the most part it probably contributes to the prevention of war between countries (a form of negative peace as defined in chapter one). As pointed out in chapter two where the transnational network model of the international system was treated, the multinational corporation contributes immensely to an integrated network transcending national boundaries of trade, communications, transportation, technological interdependence, resource interdependence, and reliance upon transnational institutions for monetary stability. The modern technology of communications, transportation, and accounting and business techniques has made the multinational corporation possible. A company may have its corporate offices in one country, obtain raw materials in another, manufacture components in a third country, use cheap labor in a fourth to assemble the components, seek a tax haven in a fifth country, and market the materials in still another country. Thus the multinational corporation has a vested interest in stability. Not only would war disrupt this network, but strong national identities which inhibit trade flows might do so as well. National boundaries essentially do not exist for the multinational corporation.[32]

This economic network works fairly well when it involves equals in terms of technological advancement and economic well-being. It serves well to integrate the European community, the United States, Canada, Japan, Australia, and New Zealand. It even enhances the integration of communist and noncommunist countries. Despite ideological differences, it is in the economic interest of many to maintain strong economic ties between Eastern and Western bloc nations. The U.S. grain embargo against the Soviet Union, as a result of the Soviet invasion of Afghanistan, probably hurt the U.S. farmer more than it hurt the Soviet Union. Economic interests thus tend to transcend ideological conflict.

This system works, however, much less well when it involves the interaction of the highly industrialized world of the North with the third world nations of the South. In this situation the multinational corporation tends not to contribute to positive peace, a situation defined in chapter one as the just relationship between peoples and groups. The relationship between the multinational corporations, who have the support of the elites in third world countries, to the poor or those in the slums around the central cities of third world countries is often one of exploitation—a relationship where the goods and services exchanged are not of equivalent value and one party to the exchange uses a substantial degree of coercion.[33]

We will simply cite three examples of how this system works in the extractive mining industries. Our list could be substantially expanded in other areas as well. Since 1964 covert operations and military aid have kept a corrupt Mobutu regime in power in Zaire, a country which exports 90 percent of the world's cobalt and 6 percent of its copper. Though Mobutu nationalized the copper mines, he is almost totally dependent upon the operation and management of the copper economy by Western interests. Eighty-five percent of the copper is shipped to Antwerp for processing and 25,000 Belgian jobs depend on the present copper arrangements.

Because of a collapsing economy, corruption, and poor administration, the International Monetary Fund, the World Bank, and the Common Market Commission essentially run the Finance Ministry and the National Bank in return for another one billion in loans. The Mobutu family stays in power through military aid and the copper mining interests are protected. Yet many of the people of Zaire suffer from protein deficiency. Three fourths of the Zairians are subsistence farmers earning a per-capita income of $25-$50 per year. Though the country was once an exporter of food, it now spends $300 million a year to import food.[34] Economic forces led to a distribution of resources that increased poverty rather than overcame it.

In 1910 Daniel Guggenheim bought Chile's Chuquicamata copper mine for $25 million. By 1920 all the important copper reserves of Chile and Mexico were in the hands of American companies. Between 1922 and 1968 the companies invested $30 million in Chile's copper mines and made a profit of $2 billion, almost two thirds of which was taken out of the country. For many years Chile welcomed foreign investors. While these companies, the United States, and other governments benefited greatly from these favorable circumstances, the Chilean people benefited very little. Thus by the 1960s, when Chile had become almost bankrupt, many in Chile began to demand that something be done about the copper companies. In 1964 and 1970 Christian Democrat Eduardo Frei and socialist Allende "differed only on whether the Chilean government should nationalize a controlling interest in the mines or take them over altogether." Allende won and took over the Kennecott and Anaconda mines.

The story has been told in detail about what happened in Chile. Through the work of the CIA, the U.S. government followed a "destabilization policy" that within three years brought down the democratically elected Allende regime in a bloody coup. Within a short time a new ruling junta settled with the copper companies on favorable terms and announced that Chile's copper was once again available for foreign investors. Though the nationalization of the copper mines was not the only or even the primary cause of the U.S. policy toward Chile, "the expropriations were seen as a dominoes problem, much like the insurgency in Vietnam. If one small country could get away with taking back its mineral wealth, where would it end."[35]

By the mid-1960s the aluminum companies of Alcoa, Kaiser, Reynolds, Anaconda, Revere, and Alcan had acquired about 13 percent of the island of Jamaica—225,000 acres of bauxite-rich land. The Jamaican economist, Norman Givan, noting the high unemployment in his country and the low earnings of the people, explains the relationship of these companies to Jamaica:

> . . . the Caribbean bauxite industry is a classic case of economic imperialism. It is entirely owned and operated by a small number of vertically integrated North American transnational aluminum companies (except in Guyana, and then only since 1971). These companies also control the bulk of world production and reserves of bauxite and they dominate the world aluminum market. Capital and technology for the Caribbean bauxite industry come from the transnational aluminum companies. There is no "market" for its output other than the plants of the companies. Prices are fixed by the companies according to their convenience. Levels of production and the rates of investment and expansion are matters of company policy, determined by the global economics of the transnational firm. Only a part of the value of the industry's "sales" actually accrue to the Caribbean economies; and only an infinitesimal fraction of the value of the end products flows back to Caribbean people. . . . Bauxite valued at $50, say, yields aluminum products that can be sold for anything up to $2,000. Evidently, the crucial activities in the generation of value and of industrial external economies are the processes of reducing aluminum from alumina and transforming the primary metal into semifabricated products used by manufacturers. But the Caribbean countries, in spite of their possession of some of the world's largest bauxite deposits, have been confined to the simple low-value activities, and particularly to the extraction of the bauxite ore and to that alone. . . . Thus, the Caribbean bauxite industry is entirely subject to the needs, policies, and authority of corporate monopoly capital based in North America.[36]

Several of these bauxite-rich countries organized themselves in 1974 into the International Bauxite Association in order to try to enhance the benefits for their countries. Unlike OPEC, they did not become an effective cartel largely because Australia and Brazil, countries with larger reserves than the Caribbean producers and with close ties to the U.S., did not cooperate in confronting aluminum oligopolies.

The Jamaican and Chilean experience illustrates the problem that third world countries have in gaining what they regard as appropriate compensation in the face of the overwhelming military and economic power of first world nations. In these cases we see examples of the absence of positive peace. They are classic cases of exploitation: appropriate compensation is not made for goods and services provided; and the multinational corporations have the coercive power, either through economic manipulation, indirect military support, or covert operations like the CIA, to maintain control over third world countries.

John Bennett and Harvey Seifert identify four general possibilities for improving the way multinational corporations function in the world.[37] One area is to increase sensitivity among managers and stockholders in companies. Here Christians have a special contribution to make.[38] Another area of action is regulation by legislation, though that is often very difficult to do by one country alone. This suggests also that international authority through agencies like the United Nations need to be made more effective. Bennett and Seifert say:

> As an immediate remedial step, fact-finding and publicity by international agencies could have significant influence. Effective control, however, requires a body of international law to apply to such intricate and huge international business operations. A similar need exists in postal delivery, airplane hijacking, and pollution of international waterways. This requires a revitalization and reorganization to keep pace with recent revolutionary changes in the world economy.[39]

Finally, they suggest that nationalization or socialization may need to occur in some cases if regulation fails, or in cases like the mining of the seabed, internationalization may be more appropriate.

c. Military Spending and Its Effect on the World Economy

The quality of global life is being seriously threatened by massive military expenditures. In 1982 world military expenditures were over $550 billion. Ruth Sivard estimates that in the mid-1930s when national governments began to respond to the Hitler threat the total outlay of all governments for military spending was $4.5 billion or about $40-50 billion at today's prices. That means today we are spending over thirteen times more. By contrast with economic and demographic change this is striking. "The rise in military power vastly exceeds the increase in the population to be protected and in the economic base to support it."[40] Between 1960 and 1976 the U.S. spent $1,179 billion for military expenditures; the Soviet Union spent $966 billion. The 1980s continues to be a time of renewed competition between these powers for military superiority. The superpower role does not come cheaply for either country.

"At $855 per capita in 1982, military expenditures in the U.S. compared with $75 in comparable prices just before World War II. Although there has been a substantial increase in the country's economic product, the military effort has risen faster than GNP and the burden on the economy as a whole now stands at 6.5% as compared with 1% pre-war. . . . In 1980 the annual product of the USSR was still less than half as big as the U.S., and its military outlays took 10-12% of it."[41]

Military spending is an even greater problem for third world countries. Many of these countries have rapidly growing populations and it is all they can do to maintain present standards of living. They do not have extra capital that would enable them to develop their resources more fully, to expand their transportation and communication systems, or to build more schools for the education of their children. Thus to put their own money into military equipment has an even more adverse effect than in a technologically developed country like the U.S. or the Soviet Union. We can see this impact if we look at two charts comparing military and economic growth of developed nations and developing nations between 1960 and 1976.[42]

COMPARATIVE MILITARY AND ECONOMIC GROWTH
1960-1976 constant dollars

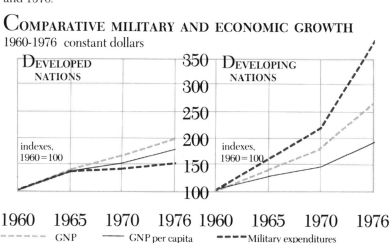

| DEVELOPED NATIONS | | | | DEVELOPING NATIONS | | | |
| indexes, 1960=100 | | | | indexes, 1960=100 | | | |

350
300
250
200
150
100

1960   1965   1970   1976   1960   1965   1970   1976

------- GNP   ——— GNP per capita   - - - - Military expenditures

The impact of military spending in underdeveloped countries is even more severe in taking away from civilian investment, in contributing to loss of economic growth and therefore to higher unemployment, and in putting even more strain upon labor resources and energy resources such as petroleum.

High military spending contributes to the gap between rich and poor countries. Countries with high populations and high population growth rates, with high illiteracy rates and lack of schools, with high unemployment and little economic development, especially need capital. Yet the richest countries of the world divert their resources to military expenditures and make a pittance of a contribution to capital development in poor countries. Between 1960 and 1976 total world economic aid was only $162 billion, only 4.8 percent of the total military expenditures which were $3,325 billion.[43] From 1960-1976 the economic aid received by developing nations averaged $3.50 per person. The United States spent in the years 1960-1976 .4 percent of its GNP for economic aid or $16.80 per capita, whereas it spent 7.4 percent of its GNP for military purposes or $347.10 per capita.[44]

Much of the aid that has gone to third world countries has been military aid. The U.S. and the USSR have sharply increased their arms exports as they compete for influence. Another dimension of this military aid to third world countries is that, as we have already pointed out, it is used often by elites within countries to repress their own people and prevent needed structural changes in these countries. Argentina, Nicaragua, Iran, South Korea, and many others have used U.S. weapons and the training of military personnel in the United States to repress their own people.

Ruth Sivard summarizes well the issue of priorities in her book, *World Military and Social Expenditures 1978:*

> The message conveyed by world budgetary allocations today is that military power is the primary preoccupation of governments. Although there are significant national and regional differences in the relative allocation of funds, in the overall global picture the priority is clear: no other social objective or official responsibility receives as much financial support from the public budget as the military function. The results suggest some curious twists in the world's scaling of priorities, for example:
>
> The average family pays more in taxes to support the world arms race than to educate their children.
>
> Governments as a whole spend 60 percent more to protect their populations against the possibility of military attack than against the

everyday ravages of illness, disease, injury.

One-fourth of the world population, concentrated largely in the northern tier of industrialized nations, has four-fifths of all funds available for the public services of education and health.

Developing nations, with over 1 billion people living in extreme poverty, invest more public revenue in military forces than in education and health combined.

In two days the governments of the world spend as much on national military forces as on a full year's cooperative effort through the United Nations to deal with world peace, unemployment, energy, health, and the range of other social problems that are universally shared.[45]

The nations of the world are trusting in the illusory security of arms and thereby sacrificing their real security in terms of human health and well-being. When will the citizens of the earth cry out in anger? When will they say enough? When will people realize the absurdity in the fact that two U.S. Trident submarines (14 are planned), which cost approximately $3.42 billion, and simply add to the U.S. overkill capacity, cost the same amount as the total federal funds appropriated for elementary and secondary education?[46]

These high military expenditures worldwide have a significant impact on the global economy and have an indirect effect in contributing to social conditions which inhibit human development and well-being. The effect of high military spending is fourfold: (a) it increases inflation; (b) it uses up scarce material resources; (c) it absorbs a large portion of the earth's scientists and engineers, inhibiting them from making contributions to other basic human problems; (d) it diverts capital from poor countries who need that capital to solve basic social and economic problems.[47]

Inflation is a crucial issue because it directly cuts into people's standard of living, especially poorer people on fixed incomes who cannot afford to pay more for basic necessities like food and housing. Military spending is inflationary in several respects. Governments pour money into the economies of the world in order to produce or buy guns, tanks, ships, missiles, and other hardware. But these goods have no useful economic purpose. They are neither capital goods, like trucks and factories, nor are they consumable items which contribute to the standard of living, so the economic demand for these goods is not the same. Because all this government money is poured out for military goods which do not produce a corresponding production of goods and services, demand is an excess relative to the supply of goods. This tends to put pressure on prices so as to cause them to rise and thus turns out to be one of the major inflationary pressures on the economy.

The production of military goods also absorbs scarce resources like copper, tin, and petroleum. Because demand for materials is increased, these scarce resources tend to rise in price, thus producing an additional inflationary pressure of the economy. In an age of energy shortage, this increased demand upon energy supplies by the huge world-wide military establishment is a crucial factor in robbing badly needed petroleum for fertilizer, heating, electricity, and transportation. Though I have never made the calculation, I expect that the amount of petroleum used by the U.S. military in Vietnam, particularly in the thousands of bombing missions over North Vietnam, would be an astronomical figure, and might even partially explain why there was an energy shortage in the late seventies rather than a decade later.

Though the information is extremely difficult to get, Helge Hveem of the International Peace Institute in Oslo, Norway, has attempted to estimate the mineral consumption by the U.S. military:

> In terms of "energy consumption," one source estimates the direct energy consumption of the U.S. military system worldwide to be 2460 trillion BTU's in 1971. In that same year, the "military-related" consumption, that is the energy consumed by those industries which supply the military system with goods and service, was 1870 trillion BTU's (Mow and Ives, 1974). This means that between 4 and 7 percent of the total U.S. consumption of energy by industry and by utilities producing energy, is consumed by the military-related sector. By comparison, the U.S. direct military consumption of petroleum equalled ⅔ of all of Africa's total consumption in 1974. If private and governmental consumption of energy is included in the total, the direct military consumption of energy accounts for some 3 percent of total energy consumption in the United States (early '70s) or 7 percent of total consumption of oil (Westing, 1977). If "direct military" and "military-related" consumption of energy are added, they then would probably account for some 7-8 percent of total energy use in the United States. For particular end uses, the percentage is much higher. One third of all jet fuel consumed in the United States is reportedly consumed by the military (Sivard, 1974).
>
> As far as non-fuel minerals and other raw materials are concerned the military is a particularly important consumer of cobalt and bismuth; it accounts for 13 percent of national U.S. consumption of these minerals.
>
> . . . Almost equally high shares have mica sheet (12) and thorium

(11 percent) (1973 data). The military-related consumption of some of the economically less important minerals is even higher; thus 42 percent of thallium and 28 percent of germanium consumption in the United States in 1972 was military-related (Hughes et al., 1974).[48]

Internally within a particular country, other factors can produce inflationary trends. In the United States the military procurement practices are a key factor. All the major defense contracts in the U.S. are "cost-plus" contracts. That means that the contractors have no incentive to keep prices down. The military knows it has only one customer and that customer will pay whatever a weapon costs plus a margin of profit. In the nonmilitary component of the economy a producer of a good must balance quality and cost. Though a very high quality product could be produced, consumers will pay only a limited amount in a competitive market where a product of slightly less quality may be considerably less expensive. Since a military contract has only one customer and a profit is guaranteed, there is no incentive for efficiency. As a consequence military contractors can afford to bid up the prices for both labor and resources which in turn affects the rest of the economy. In Wichita, Kansas, for example, where a large number of persons are employed at Boeing, a major defense contractor, other plants in the nonmilitary sector of the economy have decided not to locate in Wichita because they cannot compete for the labor force. This in turn means a loss of civilian jobs for Wichita and makes the economy even more dependent upon military spending.

High military spending also absorbs large numbers of the earth's scientists and engineers in the development of weapons systems rather than in the solution of other human problems such as alternative sources of energy, more efficient transportation systems, or increasing agricultural productivity. "By one crude and conservative estimate nearly one third of all the engineers and scientists in the United States were engaged in defense related work as of 1967. Assistant Secretary of the Treasury Murray Wiedenbaum had earlier put the figure at 52%."[49] These trends continue in the 1980s.

We can respond to this crisis in military spending at several levels. Most basic is to try to find an alternative system of security that need not rely so exclusively on military power. These issues are addressed especially in chapter seven. At a second level we need to seek to influence public policy, especially in more developed countries, to devote a greater portion of their GNP to economic aid for the purpose of solving social problems. At a third level we need to work to restructure the civilian economy so that it is no longer so dependent upon military appropriations to provide employment and economic well-being. In the long run the economy would prosper from a conversion from military spending to other kinds of programs such as health and education. Government spending for social programs generally produces more jobs than the same amount spent for military purposes; it has a significant positive multiplier effect in the economy as a whole. In the short run, however, cutbacks in military spending and shifts in priorities can be painful. But it can be done with careful government planning to help people retrain and relocate for other employment.[50]

d. Development that Helps the Poor

This chapter ends with a brief treatment on a vast topic of research and controversy. We cannot begin to enter into a thorough discussion of the complex issues in this arena. What constitutes appropriate development that genuinely helps the poor? I can only remind the reader what we said earlier: the important question that Peter Berger asks of any development strategy is: Who benefits and who decides? Development strategies are not neutral, but implicitly contain commitments about the future one is working toward and how future benefits will be allocated in a society.

In this arena the church can become an actor in the international system in its own right in furthering development that genuinely leads toward greater social justice. Churches can provide models of development which restore dignity to people by enabling them to help themselves. These models can then serve to shape development work on a broader scale.

Edgar Stoesz defines development as "the process by which both persons and societies come to realize the full potential of human life in a context of social justice, with an emphasis on self-reliance; economic growth can be seen as one of the means for carrying forward this process."[51] One must be careful not to assume that Western forms of technological progress and economic growth are the way to development. Merrill Ewert defines development as "the process of self-realization—the result of people gaining increasing control over their environment and destiny."[52]

Development is a social, economic, political, and cultural process, not just economic. Too often development has meant transplanting modern industry into a more primitive culture. Production does not come before people. The goal is self-reliance, a situation in which people can make their own decisions, control their own resources, have access to the productive resources of society, and increase their level of living. This process begins where people are at, not with the change agent. The people themselves must be ready for development; it can not be done for them. Simply giving people more technology often makes them dependent rather than self reliant.[53]

Development strategies must be multi-level. Grass-roots rural or community development is essential. Yet it cannot be divorced from the overall concern about the basic structures of a society that provide the general political and economic environment within which people function. Thus an adequate Christian development strategy must concern itself as well with social policy. Too often the efforts of a small minority of church workers overseas are simply canceled out by the practices of the majority of church members in that same denomination in their own country.

So we return to where we began. If we are to have any impact at all upon issues of social justice at the international level, we must be able to see the interconnectedness of factors that affect people's quality of life. We cannot be content to do only one thing, but must work on these massive and complex problems at many different levels simultaneously. That does not mean that individuals or smaller groups might not need to concentrate on specific aspects of a problem. But when that is done, we must also understand how each small effort fits into the larger whole.   O

6 NONVIOLENCE: NORMATIVE PRINCIPLE OF SOCIAL CHANGE

Justice is always far from perfect, and it is often threatened. What means are appropriate in bringing about justice or preserving a justice that is threatened? This raises very difficult and complex questions about the nature of power, the use of force and coercion, and whether violence is sometimes justified in bringing about or preserving justice. In this chapter I want to: clarify terms like violence, nonviolence, and power; elaborate briefly on the nature of nonviolence as a political strategy; critique the theory of justified violence; and conclude with some reflections about the possible cooperative relationships between pacifists and nonpacifists.

A. CLARIFICATION OF CONCEPTS

Terms like "power," "force," and "violence" are often not clear. It is often difficult to reach a commonly accepted definition because the nature of the ethical questions themselves are often at stake in the very definitions and distinctions used. The key concern in defining terms is to get at the real issues we face and not evade or obscure the issues.

What do we mean by violence? In order to clarify the ethical debate revolving around this term, a number of distinctions must be made. First of all, we need to distinguish between the moral quality of agents and the rightness or wrongness of the actions of agents. Sometimes we refer to persons as violent; and sometimes, to acts as violent.

Violence as an act can be defined either with reference to the *source* of the violence or with reference to the *recipient* of the violence. When we examine what it means to be a recipient of violence, we get at the fundamental ethical meaning of the term. The word "violence" is rooted in the Latin verb "to violate" which is the same in Latin as the verb "to rape." The word basically means to violate the dignity or integrity of a person. Many things, of course, can be violated such as laws, customs, promises, or property. In ordinary discourse, the word *violence* is often extended to include these kinds of violations. During the civil rights and Vietnam War protests the news media often used the term *violence* indiscriminately to cover all acts of disruption, destruction of property, and violation of laws. However, as an ethical term, the word means the violation of a person.

Because people do invest their lives, labor, and resources in various objects, and attribute deep meaning to objects of various kinds (art, books, religious objects), the destruction of property can be an act of violence in the root sense of the term. But not all violation of laws or destruction of property are necessarily violent acts. The pouring of blood on draft card files during the Vietnam War, even though it destroyed property, did not necessarily do violence to people, but was instead a protest against the violence of the war. Such actions certainly border on violence. Pouring blood on files is unduly insensitive to what the draft files mean symbolically to certain persons. Such action also probably fails to lead to any productive or redemptive outcome. It more than likely just alienates persons and prevents a genuine encounter with the issues which draft files represent. However, we must also say that though many people may have been offended and angered by this action, the subjective feeling of being offended is not sufficient to establish that violence has been done to persons.

If an act of violence means to harm or injure a person, then the term *violence* should not be restricted simply to physical or bodily harm. Violence is an attack upon the dignity of the person in his or her psychosomatic wholeness. Disrespect for another person or verbal abuse of another are violent acts.

We can distinguish between three levels of violence to a person. On one level a violent act is one in which a person's dignity or self-esteem is harmed or damaged. On a second level, a violent act is one where a person's bodily integrity is violated so as to cause physical harm to the person, when for example, one either does damage to his body or withholds from him the necessary life support systems for physical health (i.e., withholding of nutritious food). In other words, violence is not just the commission of an act, but may be present where acts are omitted that are necessary for life. Such physical or psychological damages may be either temporary or permanent. When injury is permanent such that it has a harmful effect on the rest of a person's life (i.e., lack of protein that causes permanent brain damage, or a blow that cripples a person for life), then the violence is ethically more violent than, for example, a physical injury which may heal in a short period of time. At a third level, violence is present when life is taken. This is the most extreme form of violence and is ethically the most serious violation of a person because of its finality. When persons are alive, even when they are damaged permanently, it is still possible to express care for them, to bring some measure of healing to their wounds. But once life is taken, the necessary conditions for the person to pursue any other value have been permanently destroyed. Thus, the taking of human life is almost a difference in kind from the other levels of violence.

Though the root meaning of violence concerns a violation of a person, the term is also sometimes defined from the standpoint of the source or agent of the violation. The following outline summarizes types of violence as defined by its source:

I. Institutional Forms
 A. By virtue of the way a society is structured: unjust conditions which violate people

 B. Organized forms of intentional violence
  1. Those legitimized by the legal system
   a. Police (internal)
   b. War (external)
  2. Those not legitimized by the legal system
   a. Resistance (terrorism, etc.)
   b. Revolution
   c. Military and police actions not legitimate by law

II. Personal Forms (I will leave this area undifferentiated as my main interest is in organized forms of violence as relevant to political institutions)

Violence can have as its source individual persons, organized forms of direct or overt harm by institutions as in capital punishment or war, and indirect harm that results from the way a society is organized or structured. The key terms here are *direct* and *indirect*. Scholars have used the term "structural violence" to refer to the violation of persons that indirectly comes to people by virtue of the way a society is structured (I.A. in outline).[1] While the word *violence* can appropriately be used to describe harm that comes to persons from structures, I think the terminology adds to the confusion. I do not think ethical discernment is aided by the use of this term because it extends the one word *violence* to cover too much.[2]

Some use the term *structural violence* in a polemical way to argue that since there is structural violence, we are thereby justified in using other forms of violence to eradicate it. But this is, of course, the very ethical question that needs to be debated. We have another good word to cover what is meant by structural violence, the word "injustice." In effect I have already dealt with the substantive issues which the term *structural violence* seeks to raise in my discussion of justice. Once we recognize that injustice is present, the old debate still remains. Is violence (I.B. above) justified in order to eradicate injustice? For purposes of greater clarity, we can talk about two kinds of harm that come to people: injustice and violence. Since the concept of justice covers the term *structural violence,* I shall restrict the word *violence* to refer only to the other institutionalized forms of violence. What characterizes all these forms of institutionalized violence is that they are deliberately organized and planned for, and that they are used with the deliberate intent either to threaten harm or to do harm to persons.

In the basic minimal sense, the term *nonviolence* is the opposite of violence. As I pointed out earlier, that includes not only killing or physical injury, but psychic damage as well. Pacifists must be careful not to limit the term *nonviolence* only to physical harm, lest they overlook many other subtle forms of violence in which they may be participating without being fully aware of what they are doing. Both Mohandas K. Gandhi and Martin L. King emphasized that their followers should have a very broad understanding of nonviolence. Martin L. King said that nonviolent resistance

> avoids not only external violence but also internal violence of the spirit.... The nonviolent resister would contend that in the struggle for human dignity, the oppressed people of the world must not succumb to the temptation of becoming bitter or indulging in hate campaigns. To retaliate in kind would do nothing but intensify the existence of hate in the universe. Along the way of life, someone must have sense enough and morality enough to cut off the chain of hate.[3]

It is easy to confuse here certain psychological effects our action may have on others (such as offending them or making them angry) with violence. For example, King was accused of violence when he engaged in civil disobedience in Birmingham because he precipitated violence. He argued that such reasoning was illogical. He said that would be like blaming the property owner for having property available for a robber to steal, or blaming Jesus because his behavior precipitated his crucifixion.

King discusses this nonviolence of the spirit as rooted in the concept of love. In effect he equates the two notions when he says, "At the center of nonviolence stands the principle of love."[4] I think King makes a mistake in equating the two terms for several reasons. First, we need to distinguish between the moral qualities of agents and the rightness or wrongness of actions. It is conceivable for a person not to be loving and yet be nonviolent. And some Christians would say that it is possible to be loving and still participate in violent acts.[5] Nonviolence is simply a term which means the opposite of violence, that one ought not to injure persons. Insofar as the moral disposition of love entails certain kinds of positive actions, it goes far beyond nonviolence. It is one thing to assert that we have a duty not to injure others. It is quite another to say that we are obligated to do good to others and seek their welfare. Love, in other words, entails altruistic behavior that seeks to work for the good and welfare of others. In this sense one of the requirements of love is to seek justice.

It must be kept in mind in this section that we are seeking to define norms that are relevant to political institutions. To be loving and expect persons to carry out altruistic behavior is an appropriate expectation of the Christian community of faith, but it is an unrealistic expectation of the political community where people do not share the common assumption of commitment to God's love in Jesus Christ. Within the political community, the most that can be expected is that political institutions follow the general norm of nonviolence not to do harm or injury to persons, since the basic function of political institutions is to serve the common good. Because King failed to make this distinction, some rightly criticized him for expecting black people to love white people before they had the moral resources to do such. King, in effect, assumed a common commitment to the gospel on the part of the entire black community. He failed to distinguish adequately between the motivational source of some blacks rooted in the church and others who were in the movement for largely political reasons.

Though King's expectations of nonviolent love for the political community are too idealistic, another aspect of his concept of nonviolence is highly relevant to political institutions—his notion that nonviolence must seek to "cut off the chain of hate." The ultimate goal of nonviolent action (in contrast to violence) is to achieve some kind of positive solution that leads to reconciliation or friendship. While genuine friendship or reconciliation may be too idealistic, certainly the importance of a positive solution to a conflict where all the parties are able to realize some measure of justice is the only genuine basis for lasting peace. Political institutions would do well to search for such solutions, for in the absence of more lasting solutions to solve political problems, only a more deep-seated enmity is created, and eventually more violence becomes necessary.

We also need to distinguish between *power* and *violence*. The root meaning of the word *power* is the capacity or ability to do something.[6] To say someone or some group has power is incomplete until one says *what* it is they are able to do. To assume one knows what is meant when one says someone *has power* is to beg the question of *what* it is they are able to do.

Bernard Loomer argues that this root definition of power involves two dimensions.[7] It involves the ability *to produce an effect*, i.e., to bring something into being, to actualize or to maintain what has been actualized against the threat of nonbeing. Second, power is the *ability to undergo an effect,* to be open and receptive to knowledge or to someone's request or need. Loomer argues that the second part of the dimension of power has been ignored, but this dimension is essential for the kind of harmonizing process to occur in our social institutions and in relationship to the natural world.[8]

Most definitions of political power build upon the first dimension. For example, Hans Morgenthau says: "When we speak of power, we mean man's *control over* the minds and actions of other men. By political power we refer to the mutual relations of control among the holders of public authority and between the latter and the people at large."[9] This definition tends to equate power and violence, since one basic meaning of holding public office is that those in authority have control over the instruments of force. But this is surely not a sufficient definition of political power. Control over the minds and actions of human beings may be accomplished by brute force in exceptional cases, but that only can happen if the people who are controlled allow that to happen.

A political system is not able to last very long if it does not gain compliance by those it seeks to control. It cannot do this unless the large numbers of people a political system controls view to a large extent the political system as beneficial to them, or at least as sufficiently benefical that it does not pay to resist. Even the most brutal systems cannot achieve control over people if it is not fundamentally responsive to those it seeks to control. We quoted Karl Deutsch earlier who says: "The voluntary or habitual compliance of the mass of the population is the invisible but very real basis of the power of every government."[10]

This leads me to suggest a quite different understanding of political power than that advanced by Morgenthau. Instead of defining power as dominance or control over others by the holders of public authority, power can more appropriately be defined as the ability of groups and persons from below to shape and control their environment.[11] This does not mean that people in key positions of public authority do not also have power. As individuals they have significantly more power than ordinary individuals not in public office. But their power is often overestimated when one considers the potential collective power of ordinary people when that is organized. It is the organization of the masses into collective power that underlies nonviolent social action, and that explains why it can often be effective even against physical violence. Gene Sharp views the power of nonviolence as twofold: (1) a people's capacity to do what they are not expected or required to do and (2) the withholding of consent from what they are supposed to do. Governments depend on habits of compliance by people. Their power is pluralistic and fragile because governments depend on many sources for reinforcement.[12] In the past several decades we have seen the growing consciousness by many groups (minorities, women, poor, and oppressed) of the real source of power. One of the central tasks of those working for justice is to empower the poor and the oppressed to become aware of their capacity to shape and control their environment.

A definition of power is also incomplete unless it recognizes that power involves not only the ability to shape and control one's environment, but also the ability to undergo an effect. People power, too, must be responsive to the world, open and flexible, able to change and receive new information, and able to adapt to changing conditions. When one examines the political action of persons like Martin L. King and Gandhi, their accomplishments are due to their recognition of these two dimensions of power. Though their power resided in the people's willingness to act contrary to the expected patterns of compliance, both men were able to remain open to new information, to modify strategy, and to adapt to the social structure they sought to modify.

B. NONVIOLENCE AS A POLITICAL STRATEGY

The power of people can be expressed violently or nonviolently. As a nonviolent power, people can bring about change or resist oppression by doing things not expected of them or by not doing the things expected of them, yet without inflicting injury (violence) on those they are resisting. Under a variety of political systems throughout history people have waged this kind of power to achieve change and resist oppression without the use of violence. This history is largely unknown, partly because historians have focused largely upon the phenomenon of violence in history, and partly because people have been dominated by the assumption that the way to achieve revolutionary change or the way to resist oppression is through violent means. In the past several decades, probably especially because of the impact of persons like Gandhi and M. L. King, people have gradually become conscious of a tradition of nonviolent change and resistance. In the past twenty years scholars have begun to study that tradition more seriously. [13]

It is especially noteworthy that people have often waged nonviolence successfully without being aware of a tradition of nonviolence and with little or no training in the technique of nonviolent social change. The 1968 Czech resistance to the Russian invasion continued for nearly a year, yet it developed rather spontaneously. The people of Iran overthrew the shah largely through nonviolent means, yet without a tradition or training in these techniques. It is now possible, given what we know about nonviolence, to train people much more self-consciously in the strategy and technique of nonviolent resistance and social change. It is not surprising, therefore, that some Scandinavian governments are spending some of their defense budgets for research into nonviolent civilian defense.

Since the exercise of political power depends to a degree on the consent of the governed, people can by withdrawing that consent control and even destroy an opponent's power by nonviolent means, even when that opponent's power is exercised in an extremely repressive and violent way. Nonviolent action is a technique of struggle. It assumes the opponent will resist, and that those who employ nonviolence must expect suffering and death. A common misconception of nonviolence is that it presupposes the inherent goodness of people. Rather, as Martin L. King puts it in his book, *Why We Can't Wait*, "We know through painful experience that freedom is never voluntarily given by the oppressor; it must be demanded by the oppressed." He draws upon Reinhold Niebuhr's insight in *Moral Man and Immoral Society* that privileged groups seldom give up their privileges voluntarily. Individuals may tend to act morally, but groups tend to operate more out of self-interest and tend to be more immoral.[14] Pressure must be brought to bear upon privileged groups so that change will take place. Later we will discuss the distinction between using pressure or force and violence.

Assuming that nonviolent action will involve suffering and death, the same standards should be used in determining whether a nonviolent campaign is a success or failure as when one is assessing a war or revolution. A double standard of judgment is quite common. One often hears persons judge as successful violent action that has involved the loss of thousands of lives at the same time judge as unsuccessful a nonviolent campaign which has involved minimal loss of life. I suspect the root of this misunderstanding is a false assumption about nonviolent action, the assumption that nonviolence expects to redeem the opponent without struggle and loss of life. Some pacifists have held this optimistic view, contributing to a misunderstanding. Though one of the goals of nonviolent action is to achieve reconciliation and friendship with one's opponent, one also expects resistance from the opponent.

Resistance from the opponent and suffering by the nonviolent actor, while an essential part of nonviolent action, does not mean that nonviolent action is ineffective and cannot achieve political change. Why and how nonviolent action works is based on the concept of asymmetrical actions.

The use of nonviolent means against violent repression creates a special asymmetrical, conflict situation, in which the two groups rely on contrasting techniques of struggle or weapons systems. To have the best chance of success, the nonviolent actionists must stick with their chosen technique. An extensive, determined and skillful application of nonviolent action will cause the opponent very special problems, which will disturb or frustrate the effective utilization of his own forces. The actionists will then be able to apply something like jiujitsu to their opponent, throwing him off balance politically, causing his repression to rebound against his position, and weakening his power. . . . The nonviolent actionists deliberately refuse to challenge the opponent on his own level of violence. Violence against violence is reinforcing. The nonviolent group not only does not need to use violence, but they must not do so lest they strengthen their opponent and weaken themselves.[15]

Sharp elaborates extensively about the nature of this nonviolent weapons system and the dynamics of nonviolent change.[16] Nonviolent action makes use of force, both persuasive and coercive. The key ethical question is whether coercion is inherently violent, or whether a distinction can be made between violence and coercion. Scholars have debated this question for some time and have not achieved much clarity. William Miller, who has written extensively on the subject of nonviolence, at times distinguishes coercion and violence. He says that:

> Physical force is a factor in violence, but not a determining one. There is an area of considerable ambiguity in which questions of proportion and legitimacy arise to distinguish between acts that are clearly violent but morally justified and those that are not justified, and between those that include physical force but not violence.[17]

Yet later in the same book he seems to speak as if all forms of physical force include some measure of violence.

Reinhold Niebuhr also at times acknowledges the validity of the distinction between force and violence when he says:

> It is possible to justify the use of such force [he is here referring to Gandhi's boycott of Britain, the Chinese boycott against the English in Hong Kong, and the strike of the industrial worker] without condoning violence of any kind. The distinction between violence and such other uses of force as economic boycotts is not only in the degree of destruction that results from them but in the degree of redemptive force that they possess.[18]

At other points, however, where Niebuhr contrasts his vision of the pure anarchistic and political nonresistant agape love of the New Testament with a politically oriented nonviolent strategy of social change, he says violence and nonviolence are not fundamentally different morally because both violence and nonviolence are coercive.[19]

Violence and force can be distinguished only if we keep in mind the root meaning of the word "violence," injury to persons. The following continuum between persuasion at one end of the spectrum and coercive physical force at the other end can help clarify the difference between force and violence.[20]

I. **Persuasion.** These are actions that try to affect the action of the other without denying their freedom to accept or reject a point of view.

II. **Coercion** (threatened or actual).

A. *Pressure.* These are actions which put pressure on a person to act in a certain way rather than another because of likely sanctions against the person ranging from disapproval, social ostracism, and estrangement from others, political defeat, to strikes and economic boycotts. Pressure permits persons to continue to act according to their desires as long as they are willing to take the consequences of their actions. Forms of pressure have been accepted by pacifist groups such as the "ban" or "shunning" or other forms of church discipline to pressure persons into repentance and reconciliation with the community. This is not simply persuasion because the costs to the person who is not reconciled are clear, such as ostracism or severance from the community.

B. *Physical Force.* These are actions which physically restrict persons from continuing to do what they have been doing, or make them do something that they would not otherwise do. These forms of physical coercion range all the way from certain forms of punishment of children, to the physical prevention of suicide and criminal acts, to the use of drugs and other forms of psychic manipulation which make it impossible for the person to behave any other way.

I maintain that any of the above (including persuasion) can be violent, and that all of the above (including physical coercion) may be nonviolent. The key issue is whether the persuasive or coercive acts are violations of the person. It is usually assumed that an act of physical coercion is a violent act. That is not necessarily the case. One can readily imagine a situation in which someone is about to commit suicide and one physically intervenes to prevent that person from killing himself. The justification for such an action is based actually upon the principle of nonviolence. Because of respect for the value of another person's life, one intervenes to prevent injury to the person. One does this under the assumption that were the person in rational control of himself, he would not want to injure himself.[21]

One may also justifiably use physical coercion to prevent a violent criminal act. On the one hand, one should do what is possible, short of violence, to intervene and restrain someone physically in order to prevent them from injuring another person. One may justifiably restrain persons engaged in or about to commit criminal acts of violence also for their sake. Physical restraint protects persons from doing irreparable damage to themselves. Persons who commit violent acts against others do damage to their moral conscience and may feel deep remorse later because of their action. They may severely damage their future life prospects because of eventual long-term incarceration and loss of freedom. Thus police use of physical force that is properly restrained and aims to protect and preserve the life of both the community and the criminal for the purpose of the enforcement of a just law is not necessarily violent. Some here might object and say that any loss of freedom is a violation of a person. I think such a view fails to understand the meaning of our social identity and entails an overemphasis upon individualism. (I refer the reader to chapter three where we discussed our social nature as beings "pressed by" or coerced by others. To assert that unless we are totally free we are being treated less than humanly is in fact a denial of our humanity as social beings. It is in being "pressed by" others that we become more fully human.)

We should also not assume that all forms of persuasion are nonviolent. A person who goes into another culture with the Christian gospel and preaches in such a way as to utterly condemn another culture and its way of life may violate the dignity and self-esteem of such persons. Even though persons of this culture can freely decide for or against the gospel, the injury can be done to people by verbal condemnation. Thus persuasion and violence can coexist. Persons who claim to be nonviolent because they are not being coercive or physically destructive can be violent through verbal abuse or other kinds of symbolic action. The destruction of a group's symbol (i.e., a flag), or the violation of a community ritual (like not saluting a flag) can be violent acts. Such actions, therefore, require just as careful and conscientious justification as an act of physical coercion. This does not mean that just because an act is subjectively offensive to another person or group that it is a violent act, though I would acknowledge that it is often difficult to draw the line between something perceived as violent and actual violence.

In summary we can say that both persuasive force and coercive force can be used either violently or nonviolently. The key question is whether the force used harms people (in which case it is violent) or whether it initiates a *process* that can lead to the restoration of human beings and eventually to reconciliation. The methods used by King and Gandhi brought coercive pressure on their opposition to change, but these methods usually set in motion a process that had the *potential* for a positive outcome.

However, we must be clear that the use of nonviolent strategy does not guarantee success. The key issue is not whether the outcome is accomplished, but whether the process provides for the possibility of wholeness and reconciliation without injuring persons.[22]

We also need to clarify the relationship between the ethical principle of nonviolence and nonviolence as an effective political strategy. Nonviolent action is not right only for pragmatic reasons—because it works and is effective. The ethical justification of nonviolent action arises out of two moral principles: the obligation to work for justice and the obligation not to injure persons in the process. These two ethical principles underlie nonviolent action as *a political strategy*. That nonviolent action is also a workable political strategy is not an argument that it is morally right because it is effective. It is morally preferable to the use of armed force because it enables us to pursue justice without injury to persons. It also happens to be the case that it is often effective as a political instrument.

What is the role, then, of judgments about political effectiveness in Christian ethical thinking? At one extreme are those who operate by essentially pragmatic or utilitarian standards. I have argued that we ought not violate the principles of justice and nonviolence for the sake of what works, for the sake of what we believe will produce a better future. At the other extreme are those who reject "effectiveness" as a category altogether, who argue that Christians are simply called to be faithful to the crucified and resurrected servant Lord and not try to "look for the right 'handle' by which one can 'get a hold' on the course of history and move it in the right direction."[23] John H. Yoder, who takes this latter position, does so for three reasons.

1. The problem with effectiveness reasoning is that for the sake of a good cause, one is able to justify "the sacrifice of the life and welfare of one's self, one's neighbors, and (of course!) the enemy."[24] Yoder rejects effectiveness as a moral yardstick which permits us to sacrifice these other values.

2. Second, Yoder rejects this position because he believes that we cannot predict very well the effects of our actions. He supports his view with Reinhold Niebuhr's notion of "irony": "that when men try to manage history, it almost always turns out to have another direction than that in which they thought they were guiding it."[25] The basic reason for this is that a host of other free agents also act with similar assumptions about managing history.

3. Third, Yoder argues that effectiveness thinking is basically behind

the denial of the relevance of the New Testament for social ethics. Since the New Testament does not speak in terms of managing history but in terms of faithfulness, then we moderns, if we want to manage history, will need to get our standards for social ethics from other sources. The New Testament affirms, says Yoder, that history is meaningful, but its meaning is to be found in the statement of the book of Revelation: "The Lamb that was slain is worthy to receive power."

> John is here saying, not as an inscrutable paradox but as a meaningful affirmation, that the cross and not the sword, suffering and not brute power determines the meaning of history. The key to the obedience of God's people is not their effectiveness but their patience (13:10). The triumph of the right is assured not by the might that comes to the aid of the right, which is of course the justification of the use of violence and other kinds of power in every human conflict; the triumph of the right, although it is assured, is sure because of the power of the resurrection and not because of any calculation of causes and effects, nor because of the inherently greater strength of the good guys. The relationship between the obedience of God's people and the triumph of God's cause is not a relationship of cause and effect but one of cross and resurrection.[26]

I agree with Yoder that the meaning of cross and resurrection points to an inherent connection of means and ends. For the sake of some good end we are not justified in using immoral means. Martin L. King summarizes my position with his statement: "Constructive ends can never give absolute moral justification to destructive means, because in the final analysis the end is preexistent in the means."[27]

I also agree with Yoder that the belief that we can manage history to make it come out our way is a serious illusion, one of the signs of human sin. Such a position fails to take seriously human finitude and sin. Many other actors with many different motivations and values help shape the direction of history and it is simply beyond our power to manage. The illusion that we can make history come out right leads to the kind of fanaticism that uses destructive and violent means. The assumption that we can bring in the kingdom within history through our own effort fails to take seriously the eschatological tension we live under. Faith in the Lord who transcends history means we can abandon fanaticism because we wait patiently for the full realization of the kingdom which is still to come through God's miraculous power.

But in the context of eschatological expectation we are expected to be faithful within history. At this level Yoder's language about the illegitimacy of judging an action in terms of its effects is misleading. How can I make any moral judgment about an action if I do not know how it will affect another person or a situation? How can I make any judgment at all about how to choose between alternative courses of action if I do not have some capacity to predict what the consequences of my action will be? An action cannot be judged violent or not if I do not know how it will affect other persons, whether it will injure them or not.

The Christian is called upon to work for justice for the poor, to defend the fatherless and the widow, to be a minister of reconciliation in the world. Compassion for the poor implies that Christians must have a concern for laws, policies, social structures, and general environmental conditions that are destructive of human health and well being. We need to be able to assess how alternative laws, actions, policies, programs, and institutions will affect people in order to know how to act in their behalf with compassion.

Sometimes problems are created when naive, well-meaning Christians believe they are acting out of love in obedience to their Lord, but fail to assess carefully what they are doing, why they are doing it, and what the likely effect of their actions will be. At this level the question of effectiveness and the careful social scientific inquiry which tries to predict the consequences of a course of action are absolutely essential in enabling a Christian to fulfill the Christian ethic of discipleship. In this respect the probablistic studies of social scientists have an important bearing on Christian ethics. Since John H. Yoder argues that the church should act compassionately in the world in such programs as mental health or overseas development, I doubt that he would disagree with me. The problem is that his language confuses the issue as if he were rejecting effectiveness altogether.

Faithfulness to Christ cannot be fulfilled without attempting to measure one's effectiveness and predict the consequences of one's actions in the specific and concrete decisions one makes in the process of acting in the world. The more Christians become involved in the transformation of structures, the more they will need to concern themselves with the effects of their actions. This is appropriate so long as two principles are kept in mind: that means and ends are interconnected, that a righteous cause cannot lead to the use of immoral means; and second, that Christians have an attitude of humility and patience recognizing that the ultimate fate of history is not in their hands but in God's. Abraham Heschel expresses in a profound way the proper perspective:

> We are continually warned lest we rely on man's own power and believe that the "indeterminate extension of human capacities would

eventually alter the human situation." Our tradition [Judaism] does not believe that the good deeds alone will redeem history; it is the obedience to God that will make us worthy of being redeemed by God. . . . Yet the Hebrew tradition insists upon the mitzvah [obedience to God, the good deed] as the instrument in dealing with evil. At the end of evil days, evil will be conquered by the One; in historic times evils must be conquered one by one.[28]

C. AN ASSESSMENT
OF THEORIES OF JUSTIFIED VIOLENCE

Most societies agree that the principle of nonviolence or non-injury of persons is a general moral obligation. The disagreements about the ethical significance of nonviolence between cultures and within religious traditions arise from two factors: the meaning of peoplehood and conditions under which violence may be justified. If, for example, a fetus, a retarded infant, a criminal, or one's enemy are not regarded as "persons," or are not essentially included within one's meaning of peoplehood, then an act of violence is not a moral violation, since one has not, in effect, violated a person. The Christian faith radically extends the meaning of "person" and peoplehood to include the weak and sick, the helpless, the stranger, and even one's enemy. Christians have no basis to exclude any human being from the community of persons.

Because the Christian faith has so radically extended the meaning of person and peoplehood, Christians have generally agreed that any act of violence must be justified. The general obligation of Christians is nonviolence. The burden of proof, therefore, lies on those who would justify violence. The ethical theory of W. D. Ross is helpful here to clarify this point. Ross distinguishes between *prima facie* obligation and *duty proper*, or one's actual duty. By a prima facie obligation Ross means the general moral principles of obligation as contrasted with one's particular or actual duty in a concrete case. We are forced to weigh these principles. One principle may be violated at times in order to fulfill another. Our duty proper is our actual moral obligation.

A simple illustration is harboring a person who is being hunted by police because he has violated a law. Let us assume the law, by all minimal standards of justice, is obviously unjust. If the police come to my door and ask me if my friend is in my house, I would be justified in lying to them. To tell them the truth would cause my friend to lose his life in the name of an obviously unjust law. This does not mean that the principle of truth-telling has been abandoned. It is still my general moral obligation to tell the truth.

Thus, if I lie, I must have good reasons why I lie. The "burden of proof" is upon me to justify the lie.[30]

The same kind of reasoning applies to the violence-nonviolence debate. The burden of proof is on those who would justify violence, since the general moral obligation of Christians is nonviolence toward everyone. Unfortunately, in practice the burden of proof has often been placed on pacifists to prove that nonviolence is appropriate. Most Christians usually have assumed that when their country asks them to participate in war, they should participate. Christians, rather, should assume that they should not participate in war and, if they do, then the burden of proof is on them to show that violence is required because of other overwhelming moral considerations.[31]

Some have argued that when a legitimate authority (the state) makes a decision to use armed force, then Christians are generally obligated to participate in the war, unless they can show why the war is clearly unjust. This then puts the burden of proof upon the person who objects to war.

This position has serious problems from the standpoint of Christian ethics. The assumption that a war is likely to be just if made by a legitimate authority is simply not the case, given what we know about the self-interested behavior of nations. In the modern period the *claims* of a state to have a just cause have in effect amounted to the ability of any state to engage in war whenever it wants to. Given a Christian view of human sin and particularly the idolatrous presumptions of nation-states, Christians should be quite skeptical about one nation's claims to have a just cause in war. The fact that a decision has been made by a legitimate authority to go to war in no way should put the burden of proof on the Christian to show why the war is not just. From a Christian ethical standpoint, the burden of proof is on the state. The general presumption is against violence.

Some might argue for the general presumption of obedience to the state, and that disobedience to the state is an exception. While that is usually true, I would argue that this presumption does not apply in war. When states go to war we should rather presume that they have most likely overstepped their bounds as a state. It is thus incumbent upon the state to bear the burden of proof when it asks citizens to participate in organized violence against another country. That prevents the state from too easily using war as a means simply to further its own selfish interests, which is what war almost always involves. In the context of this general presumption against organized state violence, Christians have developed a theory of justified violence to try to limit the conditions under which violence might be practiced by Christians. A long and deeply rooted tradition of thought justifying violence under certain conditions goes back to Ambrose and

Augustine. In more recent times this ancient tradition has been applied not only to wars between states but also to revolutionary violence.

Despite the fact that Christian masses over the centuries have utilized the various theories of "justified violence" as essentially an ideology to legitimate what the state requires them to do, increasing numbers of Christians have taken the theory seriously and have used it honestly to critique and oppose conscientiously wars they consider unjust. The honest application of just war criteria has led to a practical pacifism. For example, Emil Brunner writes:

> Some decades ago war may have been an instrument which, although it was brutal, could be used to resolve intolerable international tension; but today, owing to the fact that it cannot be controlled, it has lost even this shred of utility.... It has become so colossal that it can no longer exercise any sensible function.[32]

The nuclear pacifism which arose after World War II and the opposition to the Vietnam War which led many to refuse conscientiously to participate in that war are two examples of the honest application of just war criteria.

When just war theory is interpreted in its best possible light, the theory exists because of the recognition of the prima facie obligation of nonviolence. One can resort to violence only under the most exceptional circumstances, circumstances that must meet certain criteria and require one to give reasons for the violence. An honest adoption of just war criteria requires that one defend one's action in the arena of public debate. One cannot participate in a war just because a state has commanded it. It should be assumed that all Christians should be conscientious objectors to war unless they can prove they should in a particular case participate in a just war. The particular case, however, is the exception to the general rule.

Two general sets of criteria have been used to determine whether a war is just: those principles which seek to regulate the resort to war (the *jus ad bellum*) and those principles which seek to regulate those acts that are legitimate in the conduct of the war (the *jus in bello*).[33] Since numerous discussions of these principles exist elsewhere, I shall here only seek to evaluate the place of the theory as a whole in Christian ethical thinking.[34]

Just war theory has intuitive appeal to me for two reasons: (1) Using the just war criteria seems to be a realistic way of relating moral factors to the public policy realm where the availability and use of armed force is considered by persons in public office as a necessary instrument of protection against unjust attack by an external aggressor. (2) The principles of just war such as proportionality, last resort, just means, and others have a kind of internal logic to them. In other words, these are moral categories that seem appropriate to use when evaluating public policy. Nevertheless, I would like to raise seven problems with the theory.

1. I have already alluded to the tendency of the theory in practice to legitimate most wars most of the time. An honest and serious application of the theory would mean that resort to war is an exceptional case. Thus, it is surprising that not till quite recently have serious attempts been made to build a moral and legal foundation for selective conscientious objection to war. However, if one follows the internal logic of just war reasoning, then even the language of "selective conscientious objection" does not go far enough. Assuming that the general obligation of Christians is nonparticipation because of the general obligation not to injure others, then the logic of this position should lead to a definition of the conditions under which there can be *selective* conscientious *participation* in war. The language of selective conscientious objection sounds as if objection to war is the exceptional case, whereas, in fact, the theory says that participation should be the exceptional case.

2. A tendency in just war thinking in the modern period has been to distort the traditional criteria and to reduce principles for the justification of war to only one or two principles. A much larger number of criteria, essential in making a determination of whether war is justified, have often been ignored. James Johnson, a proponent of just war theory, says that "there are six elements in the classic *jus ad bellum,* and all of them must be satisfied before there can be an affirmative answer to the question whether it is allowable to go to war."[35] These six elements are: just cause, right authority, right intent, proportionality, the end of peace, and last resort. In addition, two criteria which define the *jus in bello,* proportionality and discrimination, must be met.

The problem of determining whether a nation has a just cause to resort to arms is compounded by both nations making such claims and there is no third party who can make an impartial adjudication of the competing claims. Because of this problem, Johnson points out that Vitoria argued in the sixteenth century that "both sides should be treated as if they had a just cause, and both sides must consider themselves scrupulously bound by the limits of the *jus in bello* (the law of war).[36] This in effect means that any nation may claim under any circumstance to have a just cause. The principle of just cause is reduced by Grotius to the formal principle of "belligerents to declare their intents and claims formally for all to see and judge."[37] This is a distortion of the just war theory principle of just cause, for under Vitoria and Grotius, just cause can essentially be claimed by any warring party. This distortion of just war theory is evident in Paul Ramsey who essentially reduces just war thinking to a consideration of questions of *jus in bello,* "how shall modern war be conducted justly."[38]

At the opposite extreme are those who use primarily the principle of just cause but ignore the other criteria which define the *jus ad bellum* and the *jus in bello.* The analogy of an innocent third party that is being attacked unjustly has been used as *the* typical test case to justify violence if that is the only way to protect innocents against attack. This kind of reasoning is often applied to various situations: the need to use violence for liberation against injustice and oppression where innocent people are suffering; or World War II in which people justified using violence against the Nazis because of their violence against innocent people. The more sophisticated proponents of just war thinking would argue that in order to use armed force one is required not only to have a just cause, but also to meet the criteria of just means, proportionality, last resort, and others.

Furthermore, the above test case can be criticized on the grounds that the reduction of the criteria to just cause (the obligation to defend by armed force an innocent third party against unjust attack) reduces moral thinking to an absolutism of one principle ethic. The intent of the case is to refute absolute pacifism, to show that principles other than nonviolence are obligatory. In fact, the case appeals to the priority of another principle which is seemingly absolute, the justification to defend an innocent third party against unjust attack with armed force. But upon what grounds does the principle of defending someone against attack take precedence over nonviolence?

Michael Walzer argues that the use of force is justifiable where there is a clear act of aggression. Aggression is not only a violation of rights; it also involves a decision to put human life in jeopardy. Walzer says, "Aggression is a singular and undifferentiated crime because, in all its forms, it challenges rights that are worth dying for."[39] But is the moral blame of aggression clear cut enough in the behavior of nations to be as certain a determining factor as Walzer seems to indicate? Where is the line between aggression and legitimate defense when a nation can argue that the other nation is at fault because it is simply responding to grievances provoked by its enemy. Also, are we to assume that always and in every situation armed force should be used where a cause is just? Is the justification of the use of armed force affected at all by the means that are used, whether the use of armed force is a last resort, whether the chance of victory over the aggressor is reasonable, whether the good to be gained is greater than the evil likely to result, or whether other innocent persons will be injured? Just war theory in the best and most sophisticated sense would hold that all of these factors, and others, are morally relevant in the justification of violence.

3. Theories of justified violence often illegitimately generalize from cases of personal defense against unjust attack or from the justification of police violence against criminals to the situation of war. The reason for just war criteria, especially *jus in bello,* is that war is *not* a simple extension of personal or police violence. Because war is an exceptional form of violence is the reason why the principles of the *jus in bello,* proportionality and discrimination, were developed.

Paul Ramsey, for example, extends the story of the Good Samaritan by asking what one should do if one were to come upon the situation of the traveler being attacked by the robber. One's obligation, he says, would be to defend the innocent party against unjust attack. "It is the work of love and mercy to deliver as many as possible of God's children from tyranny, and to protect from oppression. . . . When choice must be made between the perpetrator of injustice and the many victims of it, the latter may and should be preferred—even if effectively to do so would require the use of armed force against some evil power."[40]

It is surprising to find this kind of argument in Paul Ramsey's defense of just war theory since he generally regards war as a function of the power of nation-states in pursuit of what they regard as the good for their *own* people. For Ramsey the international system is an arena of move and countermove which is God's providential way of coming to terms with a sinful world. Eight problems can be identified with applying to war the image of personal intervention in behalf of an innocent third party.[41]

a. The image assumes that justice is primarily on one side. That is rarely, if ever, the case in war. Even in World War II the Germans had certain just claims which grew out of the unjust peace settlement after World War I.

b. The image assumes that a nation is such an impartial observer that it can determine where justice lies. Within a nation-state the court system provides means to adjudicate competing claims of justice. In a war a nation becomes judge, jury, and executioner all at once.

c. The image assumes that a nation is so altruistic that it behaves in the interest of a third party. This assumption cannot be sustained by the facts. Reinhold Niebuhr warned often about the pretension of nations who cover up their self-interest with appeals to high-sounding moral principles. For example, *ex post facto* justifications of United States involvement in World War II having to do with the preservation of Jews or the protection of innocent nations do not explain why the U.S. did not enter the war until it was attacked by Japan—long after Jews had been slaughtered and other "innocent" nations had been subdued by Hitler.[42]

d. In the case presented by Ramsey the guilty party alone would be the object of one's defensive violence. In war many innocent parties fall victim, and because of the exceptional nature of war, we have a special need for the categories of *jus in bello*. In war the violence cannot be directed only at the guilty. Not only do innocents suffer, but the destruction of war extends to property, the environment, and social institutions so that war generally disrupts the total way of life of a people. War also produces long-range damaging effects that are much more extensive than the self-contained direction of violence against a single individual aggressor.

e. In the case presented by Ramsey the violence ends once the unjust aggressor has been immobilized. However, the decision to use armed force entails an escalation of violence that is not so easily controlled or ended. Furthermore, because of military necessity in war, the techniques used by one's opponent tend to govern the violent means one uses oneself. This leads to an escalating spiral of violent means, which is not reflected in Ramsey's case.

f. In Ramsey's case one has an *ex post facto* procedure through the court system to review whether a personal defense against attack has been justified. War has no procedure of review to determine whether a nation has exceeded the legitimate use of preventive force.

g. The geographical conditions of Ramsey's case assume a common home territory where a defender has legitimate authority. In war things are rarely this clear cut and defense rarely stops on domestic terrain.

h. The preparation and weapons required to defend an innocent third party against unjust attack are fundamentally different from the amount of resources, advance preparation, and organization required to prepare and mobilize a nation for war. "A gun in the house need not change the family relationship. War preparedness changes the character of a nation."[43]

These points lead me to conclude that the use of armed force in war is not merely different in degree from the uses of armed force in personal defense against attack; the two cases are different in kind. In order to make a moral judgment in any case one needs to know *what* one is talking about. Ramsey's image obscures and seriously oversimplifies the *what* in the case of war. In war one has to justify violence assuming that war is a kind of violence that requires massive preparation and organization that affects an entire nation. It is not subject to judicial review and control. The violence of war usually escalates into a spiral that is not easily ended or contained. In war violence inevitably leads to the destruction of innocent people and massive damage to the physical environment, property, and social institutions. When one justifies war, one inevitably justifies all of this, an image quite different from defense of an innocent victim of unjust attack.

4. The purpose of just war theory has been to serve as a guide to both

Christians and policymakers. When it is used to guide Christian behavior, its main purpose is to answer the question: How can I as a Christian, given the general presumption against violence, participate in war in good conscience? When used to guide policymakers, the theory functions to acknowledge the need and right of the state to have recourse to armed force, and at the same time to put moral constraints upon that legitimate right. These two uses of the theory are not easily harmonized, however. The tendency of the thinking of just war advocates is dictated by the needs of policymakers. Policymakers *must* always have legitimate grounds for a possible use of armed force; but because the technology of warfare continues to advance, the criteria of what constitute conduct of a just war (*jus in bello*) are continually adapted to meet the new situations of political and military necessity. Often weapons and war procedures once considered unthinkable because of their violation of the *jus in bello* (weapons or tactics, for example, that involve the massive loss of life of noncombatants) are eventually considered and then approved.

For example, the principle of double effect has been used to justify large-scale aerial bombing where civilian loss of life is not the intended effect but only the secondary effect of an action whose intent is to destroy a military target. This is a sophistry. If one knows what the consequences of one's actions will be, even if one does not intend these consequences, then one is just as responsible for these consequences as for the intended consequences. Those who justify aerial bombardment as a legitimate act of war must do so knowing full well that, even in the pursuit of military targets, large numbers of innocent civilians will also lose their lives.

Michael Walzer has sought to correct the potential abuse of the principle of double effect by adding to the principle that once an actor is aware of the secondary evil effect of an action, he should seek to minimize it, accepting costs to himself. Thus in a situation where civilians will likely be killed as a result of striking a military target, Walzer argues that soldiers should seek to minimize that evil effect, including taking more risks for themselves in order to save civilian life.[44]

The issue of how to evaluate morally nuclear weapons and the terror of nuclear deterrence also illustrates the way in which military necessity, from the standpoint of the policymaker, dictates the understanding of the moral criteria of the *jus in bello*. Whereas at one time it would have been unthinkable that nuclear weapons could have ever been morally justified in war, once nations have these weapons, then the question is under what conditions could the possession or use of nuclear weapons become morally licit. The manner in which military and political necessity dictate the constant adaptation of the *jus in bello* criteria is evident in Paul Ramsey's thinking.

In 1965 he wrote an essay in which he suggested "a series of policy decisions which seem to me imperative at this hour for the free world's security."[45] Ramsey argued against the nuclear pacifists, because that position does not speak to the political and military realities of the modern situation. Earlier in his thinking he had condemned the *possession* of a nuclear deterrent because of the threat of violence to innocent life. Later he condemned as morally illegitimate the intention to *use* nuclear weapons in counter city warfare. He rephrased the moral question as follows: "whether possession of massive nuclear weapons is reducible to the crime of planning to use them over civilian targets." This leads him, according to Charles Curran, to "develop in detail the type of deterrence that is morally permitted without becoming immoral through the intention to engage in counter population or counter city warfare."[46]

5. Insofar as just war theory is dominated by the concern to be relevant primarily to the immediate policy considerations of policymakers, then Christian political ethics is essentially an adaptation to the status quo, to the structural conditions of the present international system. How does the Christian faith bring any kind of fundamental prophetic or critical stance to bear on the situation? What role does Christian ethics play in judging the way in which the international system itself is structured? How does it relate to actors other than nation-states in the international system, actors who may have a role in changing that system so that it is in more accord with peace and justice. Here I refer the reader to issues raised in chapter two. How does Christian ethics function as "salt" and "light" in the world, and keep from being reduced in its political ethic to a least-common-denominator set of principles dedicated to political and military necessity?

6. Though war is an exceptional case which needs to be justified, the eventuality of a just war commits nations to prepare for that eventuality. An advocate of the just war position is thus committed to support the preparations for war, not just a particular war when it breaks out. This has three serious problems with it:

a. Those who must prepare for the eventuality of war tend not to invest the same kind of human resources and energies in the structures and creation of conditions that prevent warfare or provide for alternative means of settling international disputes short of war. The massive investment of human energy in preparation for war leads to the assumption that war is the normal pattern of international relations, and international peacemaking is the exception and abnormal situation.

b. Human resources (knowledge and talent, money, physical resources) are diverted from the solution to human needs and peacemaking structures. One of the major causes of war is lack of distributive justice, a fact made more likely when nations divert human resources to armaments. Knowledge and talent are diverted to thinking up more ways to destroy other human beings and to settling disputes through an arbitrament of arms; precious little is invested in exploring and creating international institutions for dispute settlement, techniques of dispute settlement, nonviolent forms of defense, or cooperation on superordinate goals, such as the development of solar energy. Christian ethics clearly calls for Christians to be peacemakers, to devote themselves to a ministry of reconciliation in the world. The commitment to a just war position subverts that ministry.

c. The preparation for an eventual just war means that the military structures and arms are actually available to conduct war. The availability of arms increases the illusion of power. While the prevailing myth is that military strength preserves the peace, data indicate the opposite. Research done by Alan Newcombe and James Wert of the Canadian Peace Research Institute shows that in 1961 nations over a certain critical tension ratio (which they define as the ratio between GNP and military expenditures) "were 6.55 times more likely to go to war within five years than the nations in the 'under the critical value' set." When they applied this critical value to the years 1950-1960, they again found that "countries over the critical values were still about six times more likely to go to war in the next five years than countries under the critical values."[47] Their conclusions are that

> over a period of 16 years those nations which spent more than 4.63% of their GNP for military purposes in a given year were 6.61 times more likely to go to war in the next five years than the nations which spent less than 4.63% of their GNP for this purpose.... We do not have a mechanism to explain this phenomenon. Gandhi said that the personality of a man changes after he acquires a gun; we suspect that foreign policy of a nation changes when it becomes too heavily armed so that in reaching foreign policy decisions certain peaceful alternatives are ignored because the military might to produce a decision by violent means is ready and able to be used. One conclusion that was forced upon us was that if you prepare for war you get war. This conclusion is different from the Old Roman saying, "If you want peace, prepare for war."[48]

Some might object here that cause and effect are confused. Because nations have conflicts with others they spend more on arms, not that their spending more on arms causes them to get into armed conflict with others. Actually, probably both happen. Nations do arm because they are in conflict with others, but once they are armed, they are also more likely to solve their conflict through armed force. The statement "if you want peace, prepare for war" is oversimplified, as is also the notion that the availability of arms alone leads nations to war.

7. My final criticism of just war theory is that a number of the categories by which to make judgments as to whether a war is just or not are so vague and imprecise as to be practically useless. The principles of last resort and proportionality are particularly difficult to apply.

When is resort to war clearly a last resort? The existence of a set of criteria which justifies war under certain conditions tends usually to undermine alternative ways short of war to make peace. With the availability of arms and a legitimating ideology, it is too easy to resort to war before it is a genuine last resort. Furthermore, how is this category relevant to the actual military condition in which one side, anticipating that its opponent may resort to arms, tries to get a jump on the adversary through a first strike. Is resort to arms a last resort if one resorts to arms first in anticipation that one's opponent might get a head start? Contemporary international law says that one may resort to war only in case of self-defense. James Johnson says that "a number of authors, myself included, have commented on the injustice of this formula, which favors aggressors by disallowing defensive use of force until the initial attack is launched, and which also favors nations able to subvert others by propaganda, spying, and covert activities of military means."[49]

Just war advocates such as Paul Ramsey have recognized the vagueness of the category of proportionality. Ramsey says:

> It can never be right to resort to war, no matter how just the cause, unless a proportionality can be established between military/political objectives and their price, or unless one has reason to believe that in the end more good will be done than undone or a greater measure of evil prevented. But, of all the tests for judging whether to resort or to participate in war, this one balancing an evil or good effect against another is open to the greatest uncertainty. This, therefore, establishes rather than removes the possibility of conscientious disagreement among prudent men.[50]

Because of Ramsey's skepticism about being able to make judgments about proportionality, he tends to focus on the *jus in bello* rather than the *jus ad bellum*. Charles Curran is severely critical of Ramsey at this point.

> This, in my judgment, is an undue limitation which has disastrous consequences in terms of real limitations on warfare. . . . He [Ramsey]

takes away from the competency of ethics as such a very great area of the prudential or the teleological. . . . I would maintain that ethics can and should say much more about the area of the proportionality, even though on such specific questions it cannot claim to have such certitude as to exclude all fear of error.[51]

I agree with Curran that the removal of the category of proportionality from the principles of just war thinking has serious consequences, in that it tends to lead too easily to the justification of war in the first place. On the other hand, I am deeply bothered by the kind of speculative calculus about consequences that would lead us to justify violence in the first place. On what grounds could we be certain enough about the likely quantity of good proportionate to the quantity of evil that would lead us to justify the resort to war?

In his book, *A Christian Method of Moral Judgment,* J. Philip Wogaman asserts that the presumption against violence can be broken only if it can be shown that a greater evil can be averted or a greater good come about through the use of violence.[52] Yet one searches in vain for any precise guidelines as to what this means. What would count as evidence that a greater good is likely to come about? How would one come to know that? One suspects that intuition here replaces what otherwise has been a carefully developed method of reasoned ethical thought. Wogaman's method allows for an unquestioned rationale for violence to slip into ethical argument without sufficient justification.

D. CONCLUSIONS AND ECUMENICAL IMPLICATIONS

Ultimately just war theory involves making some kind of calculus about the likelihood that more good than evil will result from the use of armed force. It is at this point that I have my deepest theological objections to the just war theory as a whole.

From the perspective of faith, the "Lamb that was slain" is the Lord and master of history. Means and ends are integrally connected. The cause of justice can be obtained only ultimately through nonviolent means. The meaning of history is not based upon a utilitarian calculus about the likelihood of good or bad results that may issue from the use of violence, but in a principled commitment to the use of nonviolence as the only way in which true liberation can come about. The cross symbolizes the refusal of Christ to sacrifice the dignity of others for the sake of a just cause.

To a certain extent what we have stated above can be empirically verified. The way of violence, even when pursued for a good cause, leads to further destructive violence. For example, the rise to power of Hitler was rooted far back in history, but most immediately in World War I that was supposed to be the "war to end war." The irony of history is that out of the "war to end war" came the evil of Nazism. Out of the war to end Nazism came the even greater terror of nuclear weapons and the possibility of annihilation of the human race. The war to save Western civilization produces in the long run the very weapons that are now a threat to all of civilization. This is simply a working out of the inherent connection of means and ends.

To a certain extent one can also demonstrate empirically that faithful obedience to the Lord, even unto death, by the prophetic minority has led to resurrection and life, to renewal and new vitality in the historical process. The monastic order created by St. Benedict became a source of renewal for the church and an institution for the preservation of the best of culture. The faithful obedience of Anabaptists, even unto death, provided the stimulus for later institutionalization of the principle of freedom of conscience in matters of religion and the principle of separation of church and state. The vision of the Quakers was eventually translated into efforts to abolish slavery, and into many other creative institutional innovations.

Ultimately, however, empirical demonstration is partial and inconclusive. Finally at stake is what kind of *faith* one has with respect to the future. Does one believe that in the cross is resurrection or not? Is one able to endure, to bear one's suffering patiently, even when the evidence of success is not available? Though one can show that nonviolent action is an effective political instrument, the logic of political argument is finally not sufficient. Just as strong an empirical case may be made for violence as an effective political instrument as for nonviolence. But when the case is made for violence, this too is a commitment of faith. I call this another "faith" perspective because it cannot be demonstrated in the long run any more convincingly that violence "pays." The commitment that good may come about through violence is a leap of faith.

But people are sometimes persuaded that violence is the only way to be politically effective. Then the Christian will need to take a stand against the stream. No empirical verification is final and absolute. Those who do not believe that the one who took upon himself the cross is the Master of history will try to manage history toward the good through violent means. But from the standpoint of faith in Christ, in the long run, death and destruction lie at the end of the path where violence is used, even in the most righteous causes. Here the Christian stakes his or her life on a different future.

At the point where violence seems to be most justified, the Christian must not yield to temptation. In just these crises the Christian must risk his life for the cause of justice by using nonviolent means. The Christian who in these crises remains faithful to the way of nonviolence in the long run contributes to the way of life and justice. Had Christians in Germany over the years been faithful adherents to this principle, an Adolf Hitler would never have emerged. Hitler is a sign of God's judgment upon the church. Though Christians who refuse to take up the sword against an obvious evil like Hitler appear politically irresponsible and irrelevant in history, para-doxically, the Christian who stands against the stream is most relevant and responsible because of the conviction that in the long run obedience to the vocation of discipleship contributes what history really needs. If Christians leave their nonviolent vocation to participate in the violence of the world, then who will witness to the meaning of history based in God's action in Jesus Christ through the cross and resurrection?

This perspective requires faith. To be "in Christ" means to be set free from the dominant patterns of utilitarian political calculus that lead to the use of immoral means for the sake of a supposed good end. The Christian is set free to imagine alternatives to violence and take risks for justice through nonviolent means. The path of violence is an old and well-worn path. Many have traveled down that road. It takes little imagination to justify violence, and in that sense it takes little risk to give one's life for a violent cause. To-day we have a crisis in imagination and courage. Few are willing to think daringly and take risks for nonviolence.

Though one can see reasons for the theory of justified violence, the overwhelming weight of theological, ethical, and factual considerations leads me to reject violence as legitimate moral behavior for Christians. Christians are called out of obedience to their Lord to serve their fellow human beings in the cause of justice through nonviolent means. Christians are called to use their imagination in the cause of peacemaking. This means to use their imaginations to break the cycle of violence by searching for non-violent methods of defense and nonviolent alternatives of social change. Structures and methods are available which Christians should seek to argue for and help to create within the arena of public discourse. In this arena Christians should try to show why and how the methods and structures they propose can be successful and can lead to better consequences. Though many persons in the public arena will disagree with these judgments be-cause they will not be convinced of the political viability of nonviolence, nevertheless Christians are remiss in their calling if they fail to make this case.

But even when Christians cannot make their case in the public policy arena, they are not speechless. At this point just war categories have limited validity within Christian ethical discourse. The categories have limited validity as a form of address to a world that insists armed force still has an appropriate place. For those persons and policymakers who insist that violence must sometimes be used, the Christian can insist that at least this violence be justified in the arena of public debate, and that this violence be justified according to certain principles. In this public debate the moral logic of just war reasoning still has a legitimate place. As we, along with others, assess policies, we can appropriately ask questions about just cause, last resort, proportionality, and just means. The tendency of a pacifist contribution to this debate will be to press for much more stringent restrictions on both the *jus ad bellum* and the *jus in bello* criteria than customary. Pacifists can still make a contribution to the political arena even when they refuse to participate in violence. Once pacifists have first attempted to demonstrate the political viability of nonviolent means of defense and social change, they can then also urge that violence meet certain moral restraints if policymakers still insist on using it.

What are the ecumenical implications of my position? The dialogue can take place on three levels. At one level those who take a pacifist position must continue to state what they conscientiously believe to be a faithful statement of the Christian faith. Other Christians believe conscientiously that a just war position is a more faithful statement of the faith. Both positions must learn from and be corrected by each other. I am not sure we will ever resolve these differences completely. However, I am also equally convinced that a methodological relativism which assumes at the start that the two equally valid positions can never be resolved will cut the nerve of genuine dialogue. We can only have genuine dialogue with someone when we seek to test our position in terms of a common search for truth. For Christians this is found in Christ. In him we have our unity, and if that is the case, we cannot exclude the possibility of actual unity in the church on this issue.

At a second level we should recognize that a great deal more unity exists than we often think among those who have conscientiously considered the issues of war and peace. When it comes to specific policy assessments and to ethical judgments about specific wars (Vietnam being an example), I often find myself in agreement with those who have applied the categories of just war thinking conscientiously. The application of just war thinking in effect leads to a practical pacifism today for many Christians, since resort to war has become clearly an exceptional case. Thus pacifists and just war theorists will often be standing together against particular wars. I had this experience during the Vietnam War when I felt closer to Christians of just war persuasion who opposed the war politically than I did to some pacifists who stood by in smug silence.

At a third level of dialogue Christians will also find themselves working together as peacemakers in the world, creating those structures and methods that can lead to nonviolent resolution of conflicts and the use of nonviolent means of social change for the cause of justice. We shall often be standing side by side as we seek to leave this witness in our world. Here the civil rights experience in the U.S. under the leadership of Martin L. King is an example of where persons of just war persuasion could join a movement committed to principled nonviolence.　　　　　　　　　　　　　　　　○

7 THE POSSIBILITIES OF PEACE AND THE PREVENTION OF WAR

In this chapter we want to show how the ethical principle of nonviolence can be applied to the actual international situation. What are the political possibilities of positive peacemaking, for working toward the prevention of war and the creation of a more peaceful world?

To some persons this chapter will seem too utopian, as in the pages that follow I question the place of military force in achieving human security. I challenge both the so-called realists who believe military force must be available to prevent war or conduct war in certain tragic situations, and some Christian pacifists who, while holding that they as Christians cannot support war, believe it is necessary and proper for the state to possess military force. Underlying both these positions is the assumption that sin requires us to maintain military force and the institution of warfare to provide a measure of security. The reader should also keep chapter two in mind, which challenges the notion that war is an inevitable expression of human sinfulness.

Another underlying issue separating my position from those I am challenging is how we look at the future. I start from the premise that global security is increasingly threatened, that the prospect of nuclear war is increasing. The general policies which rely on military force for security, particularly those pursued by the superpowers, are outmoded and dangerous. These security policies are held tenaciously because they are regarded as realistic, as the only way to respond to the tragedy of the human condition. This argument is no longer emotionally nor intellectually compelling. In fact, it is utopian in its own way in that it consists of a deeply held faith about how to secure the future.

The current policies of the Soviet Union and the United States are really a "bet" about the future. They both hope that leaders of each nation will remain perfectly rational, for deterrence assumes that the leaders of nations are not so irrational or unstable that they would risk the damage of a nuclear war to their society. They also hope that their communication technology which warns of possible attack or that triggers response to threat will not malfunction from technological or human error. All of this they count on in an atmosphere of mutual hostility, where almost every day they throw barbs at each other or try to win at propaganda warfare. This approach by the superpowers is a bet on the future which requires considerable faith, a faith that through it all peace will be preserved.

I simply am no longer a believer in this scenario for world security, and there are growing numbers of people who want to live together on this planet who also have doubts about it. At the deepest level these issues are matters of faith, for each side can marshal their data and arguments, but when it comes down to it, we do not know for sure what kind of risks to take, given the uncertainty of the future.

I would like to invite readers to use their imaginations to consider an alternative set of risks. This chapter, therefore, is an exercise in the use of the imagination. Not every detail may necessarily be defensible, but I want to suggest a way to envision and think about an alternative future. The chapter is a challenge to those who think military force is an essential ingredient in security. It seeks to envision a world in search of alternatives to military force as a way to solve international conflict. That is utopian indeed, but so is the course we are now pursuing. The only difference is that the current course we are on has already been proven wanting, yet we stick to it as if it were inevitable. The direction I am suggesting has seldom ever been tried.

We actually know very little about what the factors are that lead to stable peace and the conditions that are likely to lead to war. A number of theories give various explanations for the causes of war. Kenneth Boulding is, however, quite skeptical of these theories because they give an *order* to the world of international relations that is in fact not there.[1] These theories often tend to distort reality and lead us into dangerous illusions about what produces peace. Some of these typical theories are captured in such phrases as "peace through strength," "the dangers of appeasement," "maintaining a balance of power." Both the left and the right are quite sure they know what produces peace and security, but more likely they do not know. We must begin this analysis with a frank acknowledgment of our ignorance and a measure of humility about our claims on what produces war or peace.

Boulding urges us to think of the problems of war and peace in terms of the concepts of strength and strain. A piece of chalk has a certain strength, but it will break when too much strain is put on it. To keep the chalk from breaking we can either increase its strength or reduce the amount of strain applied to it. We can think of the movement from peace to war as similar to the breaking of a piece of chalk.[2]

Rather than thinking in terms of specific causes of war, we should rather think in terms of probabilities: what conditions are likely to lead to the breakdown of peace and engagement in war and what conditions are likely to prevent war and maintain a stable peace. Social systems move in phases from war to peace and back again and we want to know what produces these conditions so that war is less likely to break out. A peace-making policy would be one that would seek to identify those conditions that would minimize the strain on a society which leads it into war.

We really do not know very much about what conditions bring about war. Most theories are quite speculative, and very little knowledge has been confirmed by careful scientific observation. Nevertheless, most human be-ings do make assumptions about conditions that will bring about peace and prevent future wars. Even though we do not know much about this ques-tion, it is necessary for us to make an inquiry into the conditions that are more likely to produce war. We often do not know what causes a disease. But we have developed ideas about nutrition, exercise, and environmental conditions that are more likely to sustain health rather than disease. Simi-larly, we want to explore those aspects of human behavior and social systems that are more likely to produce peace than war.

It is extremely difficult to sort out myth and reality. War, perhaps more than any other human institution, is cloaked in mythical and con-ceptual systems of self-deception and illusion. This is probably due to the nature of war itself. One can hardly think of a greater human evil—yet this same institution has been morally justified, celebrated, and even glorified. The ugliness of war, which involves such deep sacrifices and suffering on the part of so many people, is enveloped in myths and rituals which hide its hard realities. Margaret Mead says:

> The deeds of warriors are immortalized in the words of our poets; the toys of our children are modeled upon the weapons of the soldier; the frame of reference within which our diplomats work always contains war. If we know that it is not inevitable—that it is due to historical ac-cident, that warfare is one of the ways in which we think of behaving—are we given any hope by that? What hope is there of persuading na-tions to abandon war, nations so thoroughly imbued with the idea that resort to war is, if not actually desirable and noble, at least inevitable whenever certain defined circumstances arise.[3]

It is most difficult to separate myth from reality when war is justified by moral idealism. Lyndon Johnson masterfully hid the *reality* of war when he justified the U.S. invasion of the Dominican Republic in 1965:

> Over the years of our history our forces have gone forth into many lands, but always they returned when they were no longer needed. For

the purpose of America is never to suppress liberty, but always to save it. The purpose of America is never to take freedom, but always to return it; never to break peace but to bolster it, and never to seize land but always to save lives.

One month ago it became my duty to send out marines into the Dominican Republic, and I sent them for these same ends.[4]

While nations often say they go to war to further certain moral ideals, as Lyndon Johnson suggested, these ideals are also intertwined with the desire to defend or enhance power and further the national self interest. Though nations say they go to war because of their deep regard for the interests of others, they also go to war for very different reasons. John C. Bennett and Harvey Seifert warn against the temptation "of a nation to enlist exalted moral idealisms in its own behalf." George Kennan also warns us about the egocentrical nature of an embattled democracy. "It soon becomes the victim of its own propaganda. It then tends to attach to its own cause an absolute value which distorts its own vision on everything else. Its enemy becomes the embodiment of all evil. Its own side, on the other hand, is the center of all virtue."[5]

War is not usually a rational policy. It may happen against human will in the context of severe tension and as a result of misperception or failures in communication technology. Many think that if there is a nuclear war, it will likely have an accidental cause.

An environment, however, is created by human beings that provides the context for the possible outbreak of war, including an accidental war. War is made possible by: (1) a deep level of unresolved conflict between two or more societies; (2) a system of thinking legitimizing the preparation for and resort to war as an occasional and appropriate means for handling unresolved conflict; (3) a set of institutional structures that can implement the war (arms, armies, a bureaucracy, etc.); and (4) an absence of or failure of institutions to resolve the conflict peacefully.

To use Boulding's analogy again, when all four of these factors are present the international system may, like a piece of chalk, be put under such severe strain so that it, like the chalk, will break. To make war less likely, then, would be to reduce the strain by modifying any or all of these factors: to find ways to resolve conflicts peacefully, to develop institutional structures designed to resolve conflict, to delegitimize the institution of war, and to dismantle the institutional structures for the implementation of war. In the pages that follow we shall examine each of these four areas.

A. CONFLICT ANALYSIS AND RESOLUTION

Lewis Coser makes an important distinction between two types of human conflict: realistic and unrealistic conflict. By realistic conflict he means conflicts in which the antagonists have rival ends. They may want the same objects they both cannot have, or they may have fundamentally different values, both of which cannot be fully realized so long as they live in the same environment. By unrealistic conflicts he means conflicts that may arise as a result of stereotyping, misperception, or miscommunication. The parties are not competing over some object or real value, but they have barriers between them which are more psychological than real. Conflict between nations can fall into both categories. Sometimes nations do really compete for the control of territory, resources, or power over people. At other times conflicts between nations arise because of fear, stereotypes, misperceptions about the intentions of others, or inadequate or distorted communication. Many conflicts between nations involve a combination of both dimensions, and these are the most difficult to assess and resolve.

The current struggle between the United States and the Soviet Union is such a complex conflict. The two countries have real value differences and a real competition for power and prestige in the world. But the two also misperceive each other greatly. The United States' fear of the Soviet Union is based upon a real threat to the security of the United States because the Soviet Union believes in using military force to extend its influence. (The Soviets fear the U.S. for the same reasons.) But this fear is also based upon a fundamental misperception of the Soviet Union. Is the Soviet Union really interested in military control and conquest or rather in the defense of its own country against what it perceives as a threat from the West? The conflict between the Soviet Union and the United States is a combination of realistic and unrealistic conflict. As a realistic conflict, one kind of strategy for conflict resolution is required. Hard bargaining and negotiation must occur. As an unrealistic conflict, means for removing the barriers of communication and misperception are required to increase the level of trust between the two nations so that bargaining and negotiation can take place.[6]

Adam Curle provides a typology for analyzing types of conflict in his book, *Making Peace*.[7] Though this typology applies to all kinds of human conflict, we are interested in applying the typology to issues of war and peace. He distinguishes between three sets of variables. The one variable, which he calls a "balance" and "imbalance" between two parties, refers to the relative equality or inequality with respect to the power of the parties engaged in conflict. The conflict between the Soviet Union and the United States is a balanced conflict, whereas that between the Palestinians and Israel, or the recent conflict between the United States and Nicaragua is relatively imbalanced, particularly if we look in these cases at the military power at their disposal.

The second variable is the degree to which the parties are aware or unaware of the nature of the conflict. At the international level most people are usually very much aware of balanced conflicts. In unbalanced situations a lack of awareness of the situation may prevail. One nation or group within a nation may be severely repressive of another nation or group without sufficient awareness of that repression. This is the so-called happy slave mentality. In the twentieth century we have seen a fundamental revolution in awareness of the peoples of the so-called third world vis-à-vis their status in relationship to the former colonial powers of the West.

Third, Curle distinguishes between peaceful and unpeaceful relationships. He defines an unpeaceful relationship as one in which the conditions of a relationship impede human development. This notion of peace, of course, implies certain value commitments. We can define a peaceful relationship between two nations or groups within nations not merely as the absence of overt conflict or war but as the existence of a relationship in which full human development is possible. That means conditions which provide for the basic necessities of food, health, and shelter for a meaningful existence; equality of opportunity for all concerned regardless of race, sex, or creed; and the freedom to believe and practice a philosophy of life so long as that does not threaten the freedom or existence of other persons and groups. Where these conditions of peacefulness are not met, there is always the potential that conflict will erupt into violence.

We can diagram examples of these relationships (see next page).

Curle then defines the processes of peacemaking that are appropriate for each type of conflict. In a low-awareness imbalanced relationship, education for consciousness-raising may be the first step toward a peaceful resolution (what liberation theologians have also called "conscientization"). Once that has happened, then various forms of confrontation may be required to enable the weaker group to put the issues before the stronger party. A peaceful orientation would seek to find nonviolent means of confrontation so as to avoid violent confrontation. It is in this context that the advocacy role of a third party may be helpful. The ultimate root of terrorism is the inability or unwillingness of weaker parties to find nonviolent ways to confront more powerful parties against whom they have grievances. The international community and the machinery of international organizations should enable that confrontation to occur so that terrorism becomes unnecessary. Though other means may suppress terrorism for a time, the violent repression of terrorism without an empowerment of the terrorists to

	UNPEACEFUL RELATIONS		PEACEFUL RELATIONS
	Low awareness of conflict	Higher awareness of conflict	
Balanced		Soviet Union/ United States Syria/Israel	European Common Market
Imbalanced	Colonial people prior to independence Blacks prior to civil rights struggle	Underdogs who are confronting groups with more power Palestinians, revolutionaries in El Salvador	State/federal government France/Monaco

be heard only encourages more terrorism in the long run.

Conciliation is a word to describe those processes which lay the psychological foundations for bargaining and negotiation to take place. Conciliation seeks to change perceptions and reduce tensions so that the rational processes of bargaining can take place. Though conciliation is probably necessary in some stage of almost any kind of conflict, it may be helpful only at certain times. Particularly in situations of unbalanced and unaware conflicts, conscientization and confrontation (advocacy in the case of third party intervenors) must take place first in the peacemaking process. In fact confrontation may produce reactions that are the opposite of conciliation by creating conflict and hostility between the parties.

Hostility is not necessarily bad if it is part of a total process where the issues are confronted by the parties in a conflict. At some point, then, conciliatory processes will need to be utilized to move the peacemaking process toward resolution. If the conflict is an unrealistic conflict, then conciliation will resolve the conflict. Once the parties have been able to communicate effectively with each other, they will find no grounds for further conflict.

If the conflict between the parties is a realistic conflict, then bargaining or negotiation is the next stage in the peacemaking process. Bargaining is the process in which two hostile parties try to reach an agreement in which they maintain their own most important values without excessive concessions to the other party. This stage of the peacemaking process assumes some kind of balance between the parties (at least the recognition of each other as appropriate negotiating parties who have crucial values at stake). It assumes a relative degree of rationality. Third parties may play a key role here as mediators between the two parties, to foster communication and to enable the parties to find options and reach agreements.

A great deal of experience and literature about the role of third-party mediators has become available in the past several decades. Unfortunately, not enough of that experience and knowledge is being used by persons working at the resolution of international conflict.[8] In chapter eight we will say more about several practical peacemaking methods available to policymakers who genuinely desire to resolve conflicts.

The final stage in the peacemaking process is what Curle calls "development." By this he means restructuring the unpeaceful relationship along positive or peaceful lines. This is now the new structure of relationship, the new agreement between the parties that removes the old structure and puts a new one in its place. Curle says that development can take many forms, but he regards one principle as fundamental to the restructuring of relationships in the developmental sense.

> This is principle felicitously named "autonomous interdependence." According to this principle, development signifies a relationship between groups, states, governments and communities, or groups within communities—in which each recognizes and respects the autonomy of the other, its right to organize itself according to its cultural and political preference; and at the same time each admits its dependence on the other for such matters as trade, communications, the sharing of scarce resources, the exchange of skilled persons, security, weather forecasting, and so on.[9]

This is, of course, not where many nations begin with each other. This is the goal toward which they must move if they want to live together peacefully.

Too often governments use only the very primitive methods of threat and counterthreat. Most people believe that the posture of threat and use of force demonstrates strength. This thinking must be reversed and the fallacy that underlies it exposed. The resort to threat and the use of force is, of course, a sign of the weakness of a nation. It no longer knows how to solve a problem with its neighbor. It has lost its ability to solve problems peacefully. It is unable to get its opponent to do what it wants them to do. Threats also often reinforce the stubbornness of one's opponent. The teacher who must constantly resort to threat and force in the classroom is one who does not know how to control the students in other ways. Most parents know that when they get angry and hit their children it is because of weakness, their inability to get their children to do what they want them to do. Similarly a nation which uses a posture of threat and force as its primary mode of operation in the world is a nation that is demonstrating a lack of imagination, its weakness at solving problems. We ought to be immediately wary of politicians who campaign on platforms of threat and force, because obviously they are incapable of using their minds and imaginations to accomplish the purposes of government, to solve problems with one's neighbors by engaging in the conflict resolution process that will end up in the structuring of a peaceful relationship.

B. THE LEGITIMATION OF WAR AS AN INSTITUTION

In the movement from peace to war, a fundamental change in behavior takes place for large numbers of people. Behavior which is normally taboo—such as the killing of human beings, including innocents, and wholesale destruction of property and the physical environment—suddenly becomes acceptable behavior. This dramatic change in human behavior could not take place without psychological, social, and religious legitimation that come into play under certain conditions. One important area of research is to explore the conditions that lead to these massive shifts in behavior by whole societies. What are the systems of legitimation which provide support for war behavior?

Most societies have a wide spectrum of views on the legitimacy of violence. At one extreme are the militarists who are ready to engage in violent conflict at the slightest provocation. The seizure of a spy ship by the North Koreans or the presence of missiles in Cuba may be sufficient cause for such persons to be willing to plunge a nation into war. Foreign policy for this sector is similar to the policies of a Wild West gun slinger. If challenged or threatened, one is called upon to demonstrate one's machismo by using violence. To fail to act violently is a demonstration of weakness or cowardice. Such persons may even go so far as to glorify the violence of war. The American Legion and the Veterans of Foreign Wars have their identities strongly tied up in the glorification of heroic exploits in past wars. The patriotic fervor of Memorial Day or Fourth of July celebrations seeks to foster and sustain this identification with the nation's heroic struggles of violent conflict.

At the opposite extreme are the various types of pacifist ideologies which attempt to maintain an absolute taboo against the resort to war. Between these extremes of the spectrum are, of course, a variety of positions. Traditional just war theory, which in the past practically always legitimated the particular war one's own country was fighting, has more recently sought to take a more critical stance toward war. Many just war theorists who do not have an absolute taboo against war doubt whether it is possible for a just war ever to be conducted given the nature of modern warfare. Though absolute pacifism has never been the official policy of the Roman Catholic Church, Pope John XXIII came close to it in his encyclical, *Pacem in Terris*, when he said:

> It is hardly possible to imagine that in the atomic era war could be used as an instrument of justice.[10]

John Bennett, who has also upheld the just war position in the course of his career as a commentator on Christian ethics and international relations, says that:

> The burden of proof is now on governments that engage in war, since even those who are not absolute pacifists are driven to the conclusion that any modern war is likely to be unjustifiable. The burden of proof has also shifted to those Christians who believe it appropriate to use international violence.[11]

It is my contention that one of the main causes of war is the various systems of legitimation (especially religious-ethical justifications) that break down the taboo against organized violence. Because war is an institution that is legitimized, it is more likely to be utilized than if it were thoroughly discredited by a society.

Margaret Mead, in arguing against the ethologists who regard war as an extension of human aggressive and territorial instincts, develops the thesis that war is a social convention, an invention of human beings similar to

> writing, marriage, cooking our food instead of eating it raw, trial by jury or burial of the dead. Some on this list any one will grant are inventions.... But whenever a way of doing things is found universally, such as the use of fire or the practice of some form of marriage, we tend to think at once that it is not an invention at all but an attribute of humanity itself. And yet even such universals as marriage and the use of fire are inventions like the rest.... At some point in his social development man was undoubtedly without the institution of marriage or the knowledge of the use of fire.[12]

She argues that the case of war is even clearer. War is defined by Mead as "the recognized conflict between two groups as groups, in which each group puts an army (even if the army is only fifteen pygmies) into the field to fight and kill, if possible some of the members of the army of the other group." Some societies even today have no warfare as she has defined it. She cites two examples (others could be given): the Lepchas of Sikkim described by Geoffrey Gorer in *Himalayan Village* do not have warfare, not even defensive warfare; and the Eskimos who do not know the institution of warfare even though they are a passionate and sometimes violent people.[13]

Mead argues that the existence of the institution of warfare among peoples is a cause of war. She uses the analogy of the duel. So long as the institution of the duel was seen by persons as the way to settle disputes, that form of conflict settlement was utilized. Dueling became much less prominent when it became defined as murder; it eventually disappeared altogether when other forms of dispute settlement were invented (i.e., litigation in the courts). That does not mean people still do not kill each other. It does mean, however, that the particular institution of dueling as a way to settle grievances has been abolished.

So simple peoples and civilized peoples, mild peoples and violent, assertive peoples will all go to war if they have the invention, just as those peoples who have the custom of dueling will have duels and people who have the pattern of the vendetta will indulge in vendetta. And conversely, peoples who do not know of dueling will not fight duels, even though their wives are seduced and their daughters ravished; they may on occasion commit murder, but they will not fight duels.[14]

A similar kind of argument is developed by the international relations scholar, Werner Levi. He says that war cannot be explained in terms of various psychological theories of human nature. He argues that there is a missing link in these theories about how one gets from a general theory about humans to the actual specific outbreak of war. Levi argues that whatever destructiveness and aggressiveness may be part of human nature, "it is not part of his native behavior to combine these into strategy and tactics, into armies and sea power and air forces, all controlled for the purposes of the state."[15] Whatever we might say about group behavior (nationalism) and group tension, we still need to explain how these characteristics are translated into war. Levi concludes that war can be explained by the fact that war is deliberately regarded as an instrument of policy.

That decision-makers take war into their calculations at all will remain true as long as war remains as an institution.[16]

He then uses an analogy from the behavior of groups and individuals from within societies to illustrate what will need to happen in international affairs.

> The relative peacefulness within states was not achieved by changing human nature, altering human psychology or eliminating conflict. It was not even achieved by eliminating hatreds between groups, discrimination, false stereotypes, prejudices, bias, rivalry, or competition—all of which continue in some of the most peaceful (internally) states with an intensity matching that of nationalism. Only the use of violence as a normal and accepted pattern of social relations has disappeared. To the extent that it has so disappeared, it did so by the addition of new behavior patterns, that is to say institutions, leading to the integration of hitherto separated groups into a community.[17]

Levi's statement suggests that three factors are likely to decrease the chances of war: first, the addition of new behavior patterns, that is, new institutional structures for dispute settlement at the international level; Second, the integration of hitherto separated groups into community, or the increasing interdependence and communication among peoples of the world; third, the lessening impact of religious, psychological, and social systems of legitimation of warfare.

It is in this connection that pacifism becomes a practical necessity. Pacifism is the only system of thought which effectively delegitimizes war as an institution. All of the other positions hold in reserve the possibility of war, and therefore are bound to keep in place those institutions which support the preparation for and administration of war. Having said this, we must guard against a common misunderstanding of pacifism. We are under no illusion that one can suddenly ask for the nations of the world to put down their arms and announce pacifism. What we are calling for is the development of a much larger and aggressive worldwide pacifist community of persons who will act as a challenge to nation-states, who will vigorously oppose resorts to armed conflict, who will research the conditions that make for peace, and who will help to create new institutions for achieving security and for settling international disputes. Such a community can apply leverage gradually on nation-states to reduce their arms and refrain from behavior likely to produce war. Such a community can provide a different image of the world, challenge commonly held assumptions, and unmask the illusions of national powers which naively resort to armed conflict as a way of exercising national interest. A worldwide pacifist community can act as leaven within many societies to gradually undermine the various forms of legitimation of war as an institution at the same time that it works at developing new ways to handle international disputes. This itself will enhance the probabilities for peace and reduce the strain which may lead to the outbreak of war. This is certainly a vocation of the Christian church.[18]

C. INSTITUTIONAL SELF-INTEREST AND THE PREPARATION FOR WAR

To understand what makes war more likely, we also need to look at two institutional factors: the internal structures of societies and the structures of the international system itself. A popular misconception is that war results primarily from the behavior of particular government leaders. John Swomley's analysis of Hitler's Germany exposes the weakness of this view.

> The idea that there is a symbolic or actual devil whose removal would solve a given crisis or end oppression, totalitarianism or war is a myth. There are always preconditions for oppression and totalitarianism. Dictators, for example, do not suddenly impose tyranny upon an unwilling people. "Hitler," according to Hans Frank at Nuremberg, "was the devil. Thus he led us all astray." To this a German writer replied that "a people must first be in a condition to be led astray before it can abandon itself to the totalitarian adventure."[19]

The rise of Hitler and totalitarianism in Germany can be better explained by several more general societal characteristics: (1) the far-reaching influence of the military and the habits of command and obedience which extend much further back in Germany history; (2) the general support of Hitler by economic and military elites who stood to profit by German rearmament; (3) the nationalistic and anti-Semitic attitudes of the German people which were susceptible to manipulation by Hitler and which were also deeply rooted in German history; (4) the general conditions of the Versailles Treaty which imposed restrictions and insults upon Germany, leading to resentment and the willingness, at the first chance, to throw off these humiliations; and (5) the nature of the international system at the time which involved a struggle between those powers which wanted to maintain the status quo of the Versailles Treaty (especially France) and those which refused to accept the status quo (Italy, Germany, and Japan). World War II probably would not have happened without a Hitler, at the same time Hitler would not have been possible without the above underlying conditions being present. We must therefore pay attention both to the internal structures of societies and the structures of the international system which make war more likely.

1. Internal Institutional Arrangements

Systems of religious and psychological legitimation of war sustain institutions for the preparation and conduct of war. In modern societies, such as the United States and the USSR, large numbers of people who are members of large institutions have as their dominating concern the preparation and readiness for war. These institutions and persons in them develop powerful vested interests in furthering their cause within the political arena.

Since World War II America has gradually become dominated by a corporate and military elite which furthers national foreign policies that make for war-proneness. Those in positions of authority who make foreign policy decisions have as their economic and political interest the development of a strong military posture by developing bigger and better weapons systems. Though the actual use of nuclear weapons has generally been a taboo, more recently some persons in these elites have sought to establish their credibility by advancing the idea that a nuclear war could be fought and won. They tend to regard war-readiness as an appropriate policy by which to further the national self-interest. Because of the huge allocation of money for military contracts, many in industry, labor, and the research community—whole regions of the country—have become economically dependent upon huge military contracts.

The military elite also has access to a huge public relations and advertising budget which they can use to elicit public support for their policies. The CBS program, "The Selling of the Pentagon," tried to demonstrate the presence and power of such a propaganda force in America. The installation of Reserve Officers Training Corps (ROTC) programs at the college level, and more recently the emphasis upon Junior Reserve Officers Training Corps programs at the high school level, is further evidence of the ways a particular elite tries to instill in the public an acceptance of a military oriented society ready to support the Pentagon and its policies, which are oriented by definition to military solutions to problems. The existence of registration and the draft are additional ways of militarizing the general public.

Once the public has been thoroughly propagandized by the militarist point of view, public opinion can be mobilized by politicians for their own political purposes. In the campaigns prior to presidential elections or in the debates about the Strategic Arms Limitation Treaties (SALT), politicians appealed to the fears and anxieties of the American people that had been generated by militarist propaganda. One can never be sure that the questions raised by these politicians grew out of genuine concern for issues or how much they are simply demagogues trying to gain votes. The so-called missile gap raised by John Kennedy during his election campaign strangely disappeared after he was elected, though in this case he may have relied on intelligence that was not accurate.

The Soviet Union probably has a similar military elite. Germany probably had such an elite that made it possible for Hitler to gain the power he did. Some would argue that arms sales to other countries contribute to the strengthening of military elites in these countries and their readiness to seek military solutions to problems.

If the development of strong militaristic elites increases the probabilities of war, then we must find ways in which societies can be restructured so that military elites do not have as much power. We must also find ways to reorient economies away from dependence on big military budgets. Arms must also be limited and controlled.

Resistance to military conscription, particularly peacetime registrations and drafts, is also important. So long as military elites and heads of state have readily accessible human power to engage in armed conflict, they are more likely to use these resources, since the inhibitions against engaging in war are that much less. Furthermore, the existence of a registration or draft is one further means in which this elite seeks to prepare a people psychologically for the event of war. If the registration and draft are not in existence, then an additional barrier needs to be overcome before armed conflict can be engaged in.

2. The International System and the Dynamics of the Arms Race

Powerful forces in the United States have a vested interest in continuing an arms race with the Soviet Union. These military strategists and policymakers claim that increased armaments are necessary for security. United States officials and groups like the Committee on the Present Danger would have us believe that the Soviet Union has surpassed the United States in military power. Underlying the present arms race is a very powerful myth, the belief that more and better arms will increase security and that the only way to solve the problems with the Soviet Union is through military power. Opinion leaders, politicians, and powerful governmental and nongovernmental organizations perpetuate this myth. Ultimately this is a myth, not based upon careful observation and reason, but upon fear. It must be unmasked and exposed for what it is, or the momentum of these forces of fear will inevitably lead to a devastating war. The myth must be unmasked at two levels: that increased armaments lead to increased security and that the only way to deal with the United States' fear of the Soviet Union is through military power.

Do armaments bring security or do they increase insecurity? The development of new sophisticated weapons—cruise missiles, the Trident submarine, the MX missile, the neutron bomb, and the stockpiling of nuclear weapons—increases the threat of nuclear war and human survival. The commonly held view that having these weapons prevents war is a myth. As the arms race escalates, and as nuclear weapons spread to more and more countries, the chances of nuclear war increases. "Defense" is a misnomer in the nuclear age.

Lloyd Dumas has written a penetrating article elaborating why increased armaments lead to increased insecurity.[20] His thesis is that though "the purpose of military systems is to maintain and improve national security, as they grow in size and complexity they become less reliable, vastly increasing the danger of death, destruction and the compromise of national sovereignty."[21]

Dumas gives four reasons why an inverse relationship exists between armaments and national security: (1) the possibility of accidents, (2) the possibility of accidental war, (3) limitations on the ability to control and safeguard inventories, and (4) the large and widening gap between offensive and defensive military capabilities.

(1) By accidents Dumas means the chance that some component of the military system will malfunction unintentionally so as to threaten or destroy human life. Though Dumas points out that this potentiality is veiled in secrecy, sufficient public information is available to document the threat. He cites the following incidents as examples:

Palomares. On Jan. 17, 1966, a B-52 bomber crashed near Palomares, Spain. Four hydrogen bombs of 20 to 25 megatons each fell out of the plane. One landed undamaged, the conventional explosives in two others detonated, scattering plutonium over a wide area of fields requiring eventual removal of 1,750 tons of radioactive soil and vegetation; the fourth fell into the Mediterranean and was recovered intact after an intensive, nearly three-month-long underwater search.

Thule. On Jan. 21, 1968, a B-52 bomber with four megaton class hydrogen bombs aboard crashed into Thule Bay, Greenland. Some bomb fragments were found, along with indications of low grade radioactivity; but the mass of the plane and bomb wreckage apparently melted through the seven foot thick ice and sank in the waters of the bay. Tons of contaminated snow were removed.[22]

He estimates that roughly 90 such accidents have occurred worldwide in a 24-year period from 1950-1973, or one every three months. The fact that more and more weapons are being made and are being scattered more widely throughout the globe, using many different kinds of carriers (planes, submarines, ships, missiles), increases the danger of accidents.

(2) By accidental war Dumas means an exchange of weapons of mass destruction not initiated with the intentioned calculation of governmental decision makers in authority. Dumas says two conditions could bring about an accidental war: a background condition of high international tension such as was present during the Cuban missile crisis of 1963 or during the Middle East War of 1973, and a triggering event which leads one nation to conclude that the other side is launching an attack. Dumas examines the public record to find that a number of triggering events could have set off a major war had the situation also been one of severe international crisis.

> BMEWS. On Oct. 5, 1960, the central defense room of the North American Air Defense Command (NORAD) received a top priority warning from the Thule, Greenland, Ballistic Missile Early Warning System station indicating that a missile attack had been launched against the United States. The Canadian Air Marshal in command undertook verification, which after some 15 to 20 minutes showed the warning to be false. The radars, apparently, had echoed off the moon.

> NEWC. On Feb. 20, 1971, the National Emergency Warning Center at NORAD headquarters transmitted an emergency message, authorized by the proper code for that date, directing all U.S. radio and TV stations to cease normal broadcasting immediately by order of the President. The message, designed for use only in grave national emergencies such as enemy attack, was not cancelled until 40 minutes after its nationwide transmission. The same NORAD headquarters complex is the point of transmission for messages to trigger nuclear retaliation in the event of enemy attack.

> SECT. On at least two occasions during 1971, Submarine Emergency Communications Transmitter buoys, accidentally released from U.S. Polaris nuclear missile submarines, signalled that the submarines involved had been sunk by enemy action.[23]

These events continue to happen. On November 9, 1979, the *Wichita Eagle-Beacon* reported that "military officials briefly believed the United States was under hostile missile attack Friday. The U.S. missile warning system suddenly went on alert, indicating the country was under attack, the Pentagon disclosed." In this case officials determined the alert was a false alarm and did not notify the appropriate government and military officials.

Pentagon officials said that "in this case, only middle level officials were involved and only a short period of time expired before it was determined that no actual missile attack was taking place."[24] Given the nature of modern technology one only has a few minutes at most to verify whether an actual attack has been launched. One wonders whether in a situation of international crisis countries would be able to verify a warning and thus accidentally start a major war.

(3) The third source of insecurity is inventory control. Dumas points out two problems: the protection of nuclear weapons from loss, theft, or damage; and the problem of detection, the knowledge of the location and status of inventoried items. He reports that the Atomic Energy Commission admits that it cannot keep track of all the plutonium all the time. Thus blackmail by someone who has stolen enough plutonium (only very small amounts are needed for a bomb) is a credible threat.

> Orlando. On Oct. 27, 1970, the city of Orlando, Florida, received a note demanding $1,000,000 and safe escort out of the country as the price for not blowing up the city with a hydrogen bomb. Ransom instructions, a workable bomb diagram and a note saying the fissionable material had been stolen from AEC shipments arrived. The AEC could not give absolute assurance that the material had not been stolen. The ransom was assembled and would have been paid but the blackmailer was caught. He was a 14-year-old honors student, with no apparent access to nuclear explosives.[25]

The other problem is the protection of nuclear weapons themselves from seizure by a terrorist group in the context of political unrest in some country which has nuclear weapons. The recent political unrest in Iran and the transition from a government favorable to the United States to a hostile government provided some concern for United States officials.

> In 1970, Senator Stuart Symington stated that on the basis of his actual experience and personal investigation, U.S. tactical nuclear weapons were not guarded properly "at least in some places" and could be seized.... Admiral La Rocque suggested that if the "host" country in which U.S. nuclear weapons were deployed became unfriendly to the United States, "we couldn't get those weapons out and we might have to fight our way in to get control."[26]

It becomes clear that the increase in the numbers of nuclear weapons and the proliferation of these weapons around the world poses increasing dangers to human security. Many are becoming increasingly concerned about terrorist attacks and the possible seizure of nuclear weapons.

> Following a 6-month investigation of security at U.S. nuclear weapons sites worldwide, Rep. Charles Long issued a sweeping five page statement which concluded that some U.S. nuclear weapons sites are in fact vulnerable to terrorist attack, and that they are sometimes located near areas harboring dissidents and sometimes are as far as hundreds of miles from the nearest American installation.[27]

According to the Jan. 1, 1983, *Wichita Eagle-Beacon,*

> America's nuclear weapons are so poorly protected at some European storage sites that experts fear that a handful of terrorists could storm a site and seize a nuclear warhead. Richard Wagner, top assistant on nuclear matters to Defense Secretary Casper Weinberger, said, "The whole subject keeps me awake at night—sometimes literally—because the stakes are so high. . . ." Wagner says security defects at those weapons storage facilities include: broken and rusted perimeter fences, inadequate—or no—lighting at night, wooden guard posts penetrable by small arms fire, a lack of electronic sensors to detect intruders, and forests so close to some sites that they offer ideal concealment for hostile forces.

(4) The fourth area of insecurity is the nature of the weapons technology itself. Here we get to the heart of the problem. People have used two traditional ways to secure themselves against violent attack: (a) a "defensive" defense, to try to protect a defended territory against attack by the erection of barriers or the destruction of the enemy forces when they attack; and (b) an "offensive" defense, the attempt to destroy all the enemy's forces before they attack, otherwise known as preemption. Deterrence is a more modern form of the first category, as it seeks to defend by holding in reserve unacceptable damage to the other side should they attack.

Defensive defense in the more traditional sense has become outmoded with the advent of the missile and nuclear age. Until the post-World War II nuclear era, it was still reasonable for nations to seek to defend themselves against the attack of another nation. Though the airplane had already changed the concept of defense after World War I, even during World War II it was possible for an air defense system to knock enough airplanes out of the air to make the attrition rate so high as to defeat an enemy. Dumas says that "an interception rate of no more than 10 percent of the incoming

Luftwaffe bombers was sufficient for defensive victory during the Battle of Britain."[28]

That has all changed with nuclear weapons and the missile. Kenneth Boulding says:

> The significance of the military revolution of the twentieth century is that there has been an enormous increase in the range of the deadly projectile and a very substantial diminution in the cost of transportation of organized violence of all kinds. . . . The range of the deadly projectile which covered only a few feet or at the most a few yards in the days of arrows and spears, a few hundred yards in the early days of gunpowder, a few miles in the beginning of the twentieth century, and a few hundred miles by the time of the Second World War, is now rapidly approaching twelve and a half thousand miles—that is, half the circumference of the earth. This is the end of a long historic process. It cannot go any further than this and be significant. This means that no place on earth is out of range, *and the missile and nuclear warhead have potentially made the conventional national states as obsolete as gunpowder made the feudal baron and walled city.*[29] (Emphasis mine.)

There is no way to defend against a nuclear attack. Let us suppose that even 90 percent of the incoming weapons were destroyed before they hit, (a very high percentage and thus an unlikely prospect). The 10 percent that would get through would bring about such devastation of the population, industrial capacity, and physical environment, so as to essentially destroy civilization. Even if one of these nations were to absorb a nuclear attack without getting off a single weapon, it would still have sufficient weapons left to strike back and destroy the other nation several times. For example, the new U.S. Trident submarine, which employs a long-range missile system with a range of 6,000 miles, can carry 24 missiles with eight warheads on each missile. That means that one Trident submarine will be targeted to at least 192 separate targets and be able to deliver 192 separate nuclear explosions. The Navy wants a fleet of over 30 of these submarines— enough to deliver nuclear explosions to over 5,760 targets! Though some submarines can be tracked, not all can be reliably.

The argument underlying this massive nuclear arsenal is "deterrence," the theory that one must have sufficient weapons so as to counter threat from an adversary with a destructive capability to inflict unacceptable damage. It is assumed that this threat to an enemy's cities and population, industrial capacity, and physical environment will deter it from launching an attack. Even if we assume for a moment the validity of the "deterrence theory," the numbers and kinds of weapons each side has are far beyond what is necessary deterrence.

Both the Soviet Union and the United States now have so many nuclear warheads that they can destroy each other several times over. The so-called defense of the United States rests now on the triad of aircraft (bombers continuously in the air carrying nuclear weapons), ground-based missiles, and submarines that can fire missiles. The missiles are loaded with nuclear weapons. A ten-megaton weapon exploded at 300 feet above the surface would produce a

> crater 240 feet deep and perhaps one-half to one mile across, with a huge rim of piled up wreckage for up to twice that distance. The blast wave would travel along the tunnels of any underground system and so kill people sheltering in them ten or twenty miles away. People out in the open up to twenty-two miles away would be burned fatally; fires would be started up to twenty-eight miles away.[30]

John Cox points out in his book, *Overkill*, that every military move has its counter move. Given the fact that incoming missiles with one nuclear warhead could be destroyed by another nuclear weapon exploded even as far as five miles away, the technology of MRV (Multiple Reentry Vehicles) was developed so that as a missile nears its target, it can split up into several warheads and not allow the defense to knock them all out. But since MRV was not very accurate, MIRV (Multiple Independently Targeted Reentry Vehicles) was developed. With this system each missile has on it a number of warheads, each independently guided to a different target. "It is now possible to pack ten or more MIRVed nuclear warheads on a single missile."[31]

Each side could reduce its arms substantially and still have the capacity to bring about unacceptable damage on the other side. What then are the reasons for the massive arms buildup by both nations?

Part of the problem is a psychological one. Both the Soviet Union and the United States want to have the capacity to influence the shape of world affairs. Each of them believes it will have more clout if it maintains military superiority. For years the United States was far the stronger. This past superior strength of the U.S. is now admitted by most persons, though some of those who now claim the Soviet Union is ahead are the same ones who also made the claim of Soviet superiority years ago. The U.S. was the first to develop the A-bomb, the H-bomb, MIRVed missiles, and other weapons systems. In the post-World War II period the U.S. had no motivation to work for arms control since the Soviet Union was no real military threat.

The Cuban Missile Crisis of 1962 was the great divide for the Soviet Union. After being embarrassed by being forced to back down and remove its missiles from Cuba because of the overwhelming military superiority of the United States, the Soviet Union determined to catch up with the United States. It has been engaged in catch-up ever since until relative symmetry in the power of the two sides was achieved (if that means anything in a world of overkill where having the capacity to kill your enemy ten times is hardly better than being able to kill him five times). Though it is very clear that neither wants a war, both sides want to maintain an image of strength so that they can have more clout in world affairs. Thus, in an important sense, the weapons systems may have very little to do with actual military security.

Though some say we would be much worse off without arms control talks, we should also be aware that SALT I and II have actually done very little in producing any kind of arms control. They have done nothing toward the reduction of arms. Both sides also must be able to sell the treaties to the public. This is much easier to do in a closed society like the Soviet Union, but one must not forget that they have their military planners too who lobby for the latest and best military technology. In the political process in the United States, in order to get the votes of hawks and especially the support of the military for the arms limitation treaties, promises have been made for new weapons systems that escalate the arms race to ever new levels. The SALT I talks, though they made the world safer by banning the anti-ballistic missile, failed completely to stop the most critical technological innovation in the arms race at that time, the development of MIRVs. This failure allowed the superpowers by the late 1970s to have many more thousands of weapons than a decade ago.

SALT II treaties have failed in a similar way to halt major new technological innovations in the arms race. Though cruise missiles were not to be deployed until 1982, so that they could be part of the negotiation process in the meantime, the failure to agree early to stop them has led to their development.

The cruise missile is small and can be launched from almost any vehicle on land, sea, or air, making them hard to count and control. It will be very difficult to devise any kind of enforceable agreement on cruise missiles. Thus, while the SALT process did improve the climate of cooperation between the Soviet Union and the United States temporarily and controlled some weapons, it has limited only that which each side did not wish to develop anyway. It has not controlled major new technological developments in arms.

Another ominous aspect to the failure of the SALT process that has not been sufficiently noticed by Americans because of their preoccupation with the Soviet Union, is the impact on nuclear proliferation. The Nuclear Nonproliferation Treaty has two aspects: (1) the agreement of the non-nuclear nations not to acquire nuclear weapons and (2) the agreement of the United States and the Soviet Union to reduce their nuclear arsenal. Third world nations can hardly be expected to refrain from acquiring nuclear weapons when the two superpowers not only do not limit their weapons but continue to escalate them to ever higher levels. Arms control will become increasingly more difficult as new nations enter the nuclear club.[32]

A more malevolent view of the reasons why arms control has not been successful is that, though the United States claims to be interested only in a credible deterrence threat, it is seeking to use nuclear weapons for political purposes. In addition, it is possibly trying to achieve the illusive counterforce strategy or a first-strike capability—that is the ability to knock out all the Soviet weapons before they are launched. Here we turn to what Dumas calls "offensive defense," the attempt to develop the capability to destroy weapons with weapons before they can inflict damage.

A counterforce policy is especially dangerous and increases the threat to security even more dangerously than the present overkill capacity. A nation which faced the prospect that its weapons could be destroyed before they are even launched would be even more nervous at the trigger. If it believed an attack were imminent or actually on the way, particularly in the context of a major international crisis like the Cuban Missile Crisis of 1962 or the Middle East War of 1973, a nation would have only minutes to decide whether to launch an attack itself. Under the deterrence theory a nation can absorb an attack. It can therefore afford to wait because it will still have the capacity to strike back. Counterforce strategy undermines that system and introduces an even more dangerous world in which fingers will need to be on the trigger to strike at a moment's notice. If such weapons systems are allowed to be developed, one can hardly expect to avoid a nuclear war.

In summary, we can say that the weapons systems that have been developed, intending to bring us security, have in fact increased our insecurity. Though we have taken many pages to document that thesis, from a theological perspective we could have expected that to be the case. Trust in the human weapons of mass destruction has inevitably brought us to the brink of destruction. We are reaping what we have sown. Those who trust in the sword will perish by the sword. We cannot escape this fact. It is God's way of bringing judgment upon the human race for its deliberate mistrust of the only basis for security, that is, the God who is the Alpha and Omega.

But is not a threat from the Soviet Union real? After all, we live in an imperfect world of sin, not in the kingdom of God. Must not a nation be vigilant against the designs and evil intent of other nations? Without the credible threat of nuclear annihilation by the U.S., would not the Soviet Union destroy the United States? We must now turn to a second level of analysis, a deeper analysis of the relationship between the superpowers themselves within the context of the recent international system.

The fear of the Soviet Union is reflected dramatically in a guest editorial in 1979 in *The Christian Century* by Michael Novak. Novak says that "the growing military might, in every sphere, of the Soviet empire . . . leads me to believe that liberty may very well not survive." He believed that the Carter administration was not vigilant vis-à-vis this threat, and he opposed SALT II because he believed it places "limitations on the U.S. at the single point of its preeminence, strategic weaponry." Novak goes so far as to say: "I do not believe that the issue between free nations and totalitarian regimes will be settled pragmatically, with negotiations. I believe rather that a great military struggle is impending." A one time opponent of the Vietnam War, Novak now calls for persons to "reverse the field" in order to defend liberty threatened all over the globe.[33] Novak's position is also reflected by the Committee on the Present Danger, a group of intellectuals and military leaders who believe the U.S. is in peril from the Soviet Union.

What is so striking about Novak's viewpoint is that it is simply a "reverse image" of the Soviet Union's view of the United States. Robert Kaiser has written an imaginative description of the nuclear arms race from a Soviet point of view. Below are just some of the quotations from Kaiser, statements written as if they were spoken by a Soviet policymaker:

> In the past five years, the enemy has added more than 3000 nuclear warheads to its intercontinental ballistic missile force. It has added alarming new technology to its major weapons systems. . . . The enemy is building a new missile-bearing submarine force that may be impossible to detect at the bottom of the world's oceans. They are considering construction—at a cost of billions—of a new system of mobile, concealed, land-based missiles. . . . The other side now has deployed 200 new tanks in central Europe that are demonstrably better than any others in the world.[34]

The Soviet Union is particularly alarmed about the deployment in Europe of the new Pershing 2 ballistic missiles, the first generation of ground-launched cruise missiles. The introduction of the Pershing 2 missiles was justified by the U.S. on the grounds that it needs a weapon to offset the 900 warheads on the Soviet Union's new SS-20 intermediate-range missiles.

But these are already offset by 64 warheads on British submarines, 98 on French land and submarine-launched missiles, 640 on four U.S. Poseidon strategic submarines assigned to NATO, and 75 on Chinese land-based missiles. According to Randall Forsberg the new Soviet SS-20s actually reduce the threat to Western Europe since the older missiles were sitting ducks in a preemptive attack and would have had to be used first if they would not be destroyed. Because the new Soviet missiles are less vulnerable (the Soviets depend much more than the U.S. for their security on their land-based missile system), they can be held back and used only if they are attacked.[35] This is one of the extraordinary paradoxes of the arms race. The more secure the Soviet Union, the more secure is the West. The more they feel threatened, the more dangerous for us.

The Soviet Union is not, of course, an innocent bystander in world politics. It does have its own interests. It is a military power. It does seek to influence world affairs to further its own interests. It does intervene in conflicts around the globe. But all of this can be said of the United States too, perhaps to an even greater extent. The United States has a ring of bases around the Soviet Union. It has a history of intervention into the affairs of other nations. The Soviet Union must indeed be worried about U.S. intentions. Thus the posture of both nations reinforces fear and defensiveness.

The Soviet Union must not only worry about the United States. Along one of its borders are nearly one billion Chinese who claim a large part of the Soviet territory as their own. To the South are well-armed and unpredictable Turks, to the West the nuclear-armed French and British, and the West German Bundeswehr. To the north, Norway, a North Atlantic Treaty Organization (NATO) member with a coastal submarine force watching the Soviet submarines.

A senate aide who studies the East-West confrontation observed recently that Americans might well contemplate the prospect that, say, Canada and Mexico were both powerful and well-armed enemies of the United States—a situation roughly comparable to the Soviets. "How would Americans react to that situation?" he asked rhetorically.[36]

Novak's perspective not only fails to take into account the legitimate defensive fears of the Soviet Union, but he also fails to understand Soviet behavior in the light of *their* historical experience. The Soviet Union was devastated in World War II. They have a genuine fear that war could come to their country again. They particularly fear West Germany which the United States rearmed shortly after World War II. While it can be said that the Soviets also armed East Germany, it was also done in response to their fears of the armament of the West. So the two sides mutually feed each other's paranoia. Second, the Soviets were humiliated during the Cuban Missile Crisis when they were forced to back down and remove their missiles from Cuba. Many would interpret the Soviet arms buildup as a reaction to that humiliation, a concern of the Soviet Union never to be put in that position again.

Novak interprets the issue as a struggle for the preservation of liberty. The Soviet system is undoubtedly repressive of human rights. It is a relatively closed system, though much more open than during the Stalin era. No doubt the Soviet understanding of society will continue to be in competition with Western-style democracies. Novak, however, confuses the internal structure of a society with its conduct of foreign policy. Both superpowers, the United States and the Soviet Union, seek to influence world events in a way that is favorable to their own prestige, power, and economic self-interest. The connection between an internal ideology about the nature of society and the conduct of foreign policy is very loose. That explains why the United States has supported dictatorial and anti-democratic regimes over the years in Iran, Spain, Taiwan, the Philippines, Greece, Vietnam, the Dominican Republic, and many other countries. It also explains why the United States helped to destroy the democratically elected Allende regime in Chile and replace it with a more repressive system. In all these cases, foreign policy is dictated by national self-interest, especially economic interest, and very little by the ideology of liberty. The struggle between the Soviet Union and the United States from a more objective viewpoint is a fairly traditional power struggle between two competing forms of national self-interest. It is by no means, as Novak sees it, a struggle between liberty and totalitarianism.

There is, therefore, no future in furthering this dangerous game by enhancing the military power of either of these giants under the illusion that one country is on the side of light and the other on the side of darkness. The only way of avoiding the "impending military encounter" is to further détente, to encourage the Soviet Union and the United States to back off from a military confrontation as the SALT process began to do in a very small way, in order to move the relationship between these two giants into more peaceful arenas of competition in the areas of economic and cultural life.

The way to break the impasse is for the U.S. to take significant unilateral initiatives in a peaceful direction rather than to continue to threaten the USSR, thus reinforcing its hostility and paranoia. While most politicians believe the Soviets will only bargain under the pressure of threat, the history of the arms race shows the Soviet Union will respond in kind to what the U.S. does to them. Why cannot we take real initiative (in act, not just words) to show them our sincere intentions for another direction? The U.S. can afford to take such initiatives without even beginning to undermine its massive deterrence capability. It is time a new approach is taken to break the current cycle of an escalating spiral of armaments.

D. ALTERNATIVE STRUCTURES OF CONFLICT RESOLUTION

Since conflict is inherent in the human process, conflict resolution will always be needed at the international level. The key issue is whether human beings can begin to create more effective institutional structures that can be readily available to meet this human need for conflict resolution. The chances of war are made more likely by the absence of or weakness of international structures of various kinds—international law, international organizations, international structures for dispute settlement, and international peacekeeping forces.

Some persons have proposed some kind of system of world government. I think these proposals are both unrealistic and dangerous. The concentration of power in one monolithic structure is not desirable, both because of its possible abuse, and because it is contrary to the trend toward the dispersion of power in the international system. More and more actors of different types are increasingly having an effect on the overall shape of international politics. It is simply unrealistic to organize the world under one monolithic system. Also, international laws and structures cannot be imposed unless the world first has a sense of community. Many argue that first a sense of peoplehood must develop before structures of dispute settlement can be created on a worldwide scale.[37]

This does not mean, however, that we cannot work to design functional international organizations to help meet problems that are global and transnational in character. To this end models about how to restructure the international system are helpful. One should view these approaches as conceptual experiments about alternative futures which can signal new directions for working out very limited and specific policies and proposals to be implemented as first steps toward a gradual change in the international system as a whole. In order to do this, one must have a long-term perspective, if considerations in this realm are to have any relevance at all.

Two dimensions in the development of such a world order model are: (1) a projection of a carefully described world order model that one can envision as desirable and also attainable within the next thirty or more years and (2) a description in as much detail as possible of the transition by means of which one can expect to get from the present system to the future projected system. These two steps, say Betty Reardon and Saul Mendlovitz, "may be termed the use of relevant utopias." The ultimate goal of a world order model according to Mendlovitz and Reardon is:

> an international system so revised as to prohibit nation-states from employing organized violence against each other, either in the pursuit of national goals or in the redress of national harms. Such a system requires the establishment of a world authority equipped with legislative bodies for making laws against international violence and, in addition, agencies to enforce these laws, keep the peace, and resolve conflicts.[38]

The present system is inherently unstable because each nation tries to protect itself unilaterally through arms, thus continuously setting off spiraling arms races which could, given the existence of the dangerous weapons now available or projected, lead to a war of annihilation. The assumption behind the world order model is that no political elite of any nation-state will abandon concern for its own security in the absence of an alternative security system. Disarmament, therefore, is meaningful only in the context of the development of some kind of alternative collective security system where serious disputes can be handled without resort to arms.

World order models can be particularly helpful in envisioning international structures for the settlement of disputes between nations, even as societies use the court system internally as a means for settling conflicts within the framework of law. Kenneth Boulding has suggested that governments should adopt a "peace policy" aimed at strengthening world political organizations, particularly intergovernmental organizations.

> The great hole in the structure of world political organization is the absence of any organization for negotiating disarmament.... A United Nations Disarmament Organization, which would have the delightful acronym of UNDO, could act as a kind of marriage counselor in flitting back and forth among various decision makers, clarifying understandings, widening agendas, and removing obstacles to agreement. It could also play a role in policing, in inspecting agreements once they are obtained, and in monitoring the whole world war industry, as the Swedish International Peace Research Institute does now in a small way.[39]

The reason for this type of a structure is the enormous difficulty of accomplishing much in bilateral negotiations. The Soviet Union and the United

States have made very little progress in the SALT negotiations. A third party structure could provide a more stable framework for actual movement in the direction of disarmament.

Some say that nations will not abandon any of their sovereignty to entrust their fate to others. As the current system works, that is for the most part true. But the current system has also led us to the brink of disaster. Will we continue to remain rigidly locked into the utopianism of so-called realism, or is it not time to take some risks in another direction?

To return to the analogy with which we began this chapter, if too much strain is placed on a society or the international system as a whole, war is likely to occur. No one factor, necessarily, *causes* war. Rather, a variety of factors, particularly when all of them together are operative, increases the chances that the system will break from too much strain. The task of peacemaking, therefore, is to work simultaneously on the variety of fronts outlined in this chapter to envision an alternative future in order to decrease the probabilities of war. ○

PART IV
ACTING
IN THE WORLD

8 THE CHURCH AND SOCIAL ACTION

How does one put into practice the vision of peacemaking I have previously described? In the introductory chapter of this book, I said my audience is composed of ordinary lay Christians, the average citizens who are not necessarily in a position to make government policy, and certainly not in a position to manipulate the systemic arrangement of international relationships. What can be the role of the churches, of ordinary Christians who are often far removed from the centers of decision making that determine whether nations go to war and whether they distribute goods and resources justly?

Given the gradual breakdown since medieval times of the close alignment of ecclesiastical and political power, the Christian church no longer has the same direct access to political decision makers nor the power by itself to change the behavior of political elites (except perhaps still in some Latin-American countries). Yet the church seems to make pronouncements on a whole range of political, social, and economic relationships as if its word alone had an impact on decision makers. Indeed, some individual Christians are in decision-making positions where significant peace and justice questions are decided. We must go beyond pronouncements, however, to think more carefully about how ordinary Christians can contribute to social change.

We should think of the church itself as an actor in world affairs. As one of many nongovernmental organizations in the world, the church is an actor in world affairs not primarily or only by means of *Christian* policymakers who really shape world events, but the church itself is a shaper of the world. In the pages which follow we will outline five levels on which the church can act to influence world events.

A. FIVE LEVELS OF ACTION
1. Ethos: Help Shape the Character of Society
In the preceding chapters we made the point that one of the basic causes of war is the belief system which legitimizes war, justifying war as an acceptable means for resolving disputes and an inevitable outgrowth of the behavior of nations. Churches have played a major role in legitimating the institution of war. The church has also often legitimated the basic structures

of society, structures that have sometimes been extremely unjust.

It is, therefore, possible also for the church to delegitimate the institution of war, and to prepare people attitudinally to support nonviolent forms of conflict resolution aimed at creating a more just social structure. The church does help shape the ethos of society. It shapes people's views of the world and their basic values. It shapes the so-called public opinion to which policymakers must be responsive. As long as policymakers and the general public continue to consider war an acceptable means of waging conflict, war will continue to happen. A new ethos must be shaped in which the general public, and especially policymakers, recognize that war causes more losses than gains, that violence will continue to breed violence, not peaceful settlements, and that at this point in history the risks of great or even total destruction in a nuclear war constitute a grave danger which must be avoided. A new conflict resolution ethos must develop that leads people to no longer consider war and violence automatically as *the* legitimate means of resolving conflicts, but to search intuitively for other more peaceful means and methods.

The seeds of new possibilities for dealing with conflict must first be sown in the educational processes of society—in the family, schools, and the media. Parents can contribute to peacemaking by nurturing peaceful attitudes in their children. My wife, who is a second grade public school teacher, observes fundamentally different attitudes in children toward conflict growing out of their various home and community environments. Some children almost automatically resort to violence to solve their conflicts. Others intuitively seek more peaceful means of conflict resolution. Though these patterns are significantly shaped by the family structures from which children come, she finds that most children can be socialized quite quickly to nonviolent conflict resolution methods in the public school setting.

More teachers at all levels of the educational process need to teach students methods of conflict resolution. This teaching ought to be linked to the social science curriculum, giving children opportunities to think about the nonviolent resolution of international conflicts. Unfortunately, most public school education focuses upon the history of war and the outcomes of wars, leading children to expect that war is the normal and only way to solve international conflict. However, new curriculum and study aids for children are being written, and peace studies programs are beginning in universities.[1] The media, especially television, could do much more to educate and help shape public attitudes. Unfortunately, much television programming suggests that violence is the normal and only way to solve most conflicts.

Religious institutions represent probably one of the most important places where attitude change can occur. Religious institutions have been guilty in the past of sanctifying war and violence. Far more than they realize, they put policymakers at ease with their decisions for violence.[2] The churches have an important role to play here as an increasingly vocal voice against policies of violence and injustice. The church's teaching in many parts of the world still has a profound impact upon the family and what children grow up believing. Unfortunately, that teaching still biases persons to grow up to be content with unjust structures and violent means of conflict resolution. The churches in the United States have failed miserably to create among Christians an ethos of peace with justice through nonviolent means of conflict resolution, despite the fact that the Bible, especially the New Testament, is permeated with that ethos.

However, in the past decade that ethos has begun to change among some of the major denominations. In 1980 the General Assembly of the United Presbyterian Church passed a major statement affirming the role of the church in peacemaking. Riverside Church in New York City has played a very significant role in the past decade in stimulating a new commitment to peacemaking through its convocations and publications. All over the country churches in communities, large and small, have organized to educate lay people for peacemaking responsibilities. The 1983 pastoral letter of the National Conference of Catholic Bishops, *The Challenge of Peace: God's Promise and Our Response*, has had an enormous impact upon the public. Numerous other examples could be cited.

2. Example: Demonstrate Justice and Nonviolence in the Church

At a second level, the church, when it is being the church, will act out its own values to a degree that is independent of and in conflict with the general mores and values of the society around it. As a nongovernmental actor it may or should often exist in a state of tension with the political system or society around it just by being itself.

This nonconformity of the church often has deep political and social significance. In the 1950s the very existence of Clarence Jordan's Koinonia Farm in Georgia, where blacks and whites lived and worked together, was a visible sign to the society around it of an alternative way of life. The presence of this alternative model of black-white relationships served as a threat to the status quo which often resulted in acts of violence against Jordan's group.[3] In South Africa where apartheid is deeply entrenched, one of the greatest challenges to the present system is multiracial churches that worship and act together as blacks and whites. They are a constant visible symbol which exposes the lie of the apartheid system, and their very existence poses a threat to the current system.[4] The church's worship—prayer, preaching, and liturgy—can eventually sensitize people to their ethical responsibility. Worship can link them to their brothers and sisters around the globe, and thus begin to have an impact upon how they view and act upon public policy.

The church cannot forget that sometimes its most powerful witness may be made at the point where it is seemingly defeated by the principalities and powers. No one can ask another to suffer. Yet former El Salvadoran Archbishop Romero's assassination in 1980 may have spoken even more eloquently than did his life. Death and suffering, even when it does not lead to the temporal evidence of victory, is a sign of defeat for the state. For the church, suffering and death in the name of Jesus Christ is a sign of hope and resurrection. This kind of suffering is a political act, one that cannot be calculated in terms of temporal effectiveness, but one that nevertheless testifies to the power of the transcendent Lord who stands in judgment over all our paltry human schemes.

When Christians are obedient to the way of nonviolence and refuse to participate in the support of a war—refuse to allow themselves to be drafted, to register for the draft, or to support the military system of a country with their taxes—their actions, particularly when done visibly and corporately as a larger group, serves again as a visible sign of an alternative. Such actions are indeed perceived as a threat to the status quo, as usually the response is some form of repression. In some countries of the world, simply to show compassion or support for the poor becomes a political act subject to severe repression. We have already pointed out what a potent power and weapon nonviolence can be.

3. Service: The Organization of Institutions to Meet Human Need

At a third level the church is a shaper of world events in the way it organizes itself to do things in the world. The church often organizes itself to do tasks that aim to meet the basic needs of people. It is an organizer of institutions which are responsive to human needs such as poverty, ignorance, malnutrition, disease, and community disorganization. In this role the churches have been and continue to be the creators of numerous institutions—educational and health care institutions, programs for prisoner rehabilitation, agricultural and community development projects. Insofar as the root cause of violence and war are often to be found in the unjust and unhealthy structural conditions of the social order, these institutions and programs can function to create conditions so that violence and war do not need to break out. Along with new attitudes that support peace, we also need new social conditions that make peace and justice more likely.

Just as churches in the past have effectively met human needs, new institutions and programs can serve as models for others to emulate. Churches, for example, took the lead in the development of hospitals for the care of the sick. Some of the most innovative models of care for the mentally ill were developed in church institutions.[5] These new models of care then became widely adopted by public institutions and gradually some of the most barbaric practices in dealing with the mentally ill have been overcome. The concept of a voluntary association itself was only fully adopted by society after radical left-wing church groups in the sixteenth-century Protestant Reformation actually became models of voluntary organizations.[6]

Today some churches are experimenting with alternative ways of rehabilitating criminals outside the prison system. We know that the prison system simply breeds further crime. Perhaps the church will find a preferred model of rehabilitating persons so that the vicious cycle of crime is stopped. One of the new models is a victim-offender reconciliation program. Victims and offenders are brought together by third parties to make it possible for the offender to make some restitution for the crime and seek reconciliation with the victim. By such a process a genuine healing and transformation of the offender can occur that makes committing a crime in the future less likely.[7]

In chapter five we already mentioned third world development work. Churches can provide models of development which genuinely restore dignity to people by enabling them to help themselves. These models can then serve to shape development work on a broader scale.

The church can also become an innovator in the development of institutions for dispute settlement. Two churchmen who have been active in this regard are John P. Adams and James Laue. As a representative of the National Council of Churches, Adams played an active role in helping resolve the dispute between the U.S. government and the Indians of Pine Ridge Reservation in the conflict at Wounded Knee in 1973.[8] He was also active in advocating the cause of several of the parents whose children were killed or wounded in the Kent State shooting in May, 1970. He describes these experiences in detail in his book, *At the Heart of the Whirlwind.*

James Laue has developed a model of how people can become involved in community crisis intervention. In this role a church, or a group of persons within the church, or church members in alliance with others from a community, can become involved as third-party intervenors in order to help people in community crises creatively resolve their conflicts. A variety of roles can be played: activist, advocate, mediator, researcher, and perhaps even enforcer.

The activist works closely with a powerless or non-establishment party to help them further their cause. The church may often appropriately find itself allied with poor and oppressed people.[9]

The church can also be an advocate. Whereas the activist is completely identified with the group whose cause is being furthered, the advocate may remain a bit more detached by serving as an adviser or consultant to the group. The advocate supports the goals of the group, promotes that cause, and interprets the group's interests to the wider community.

A third role is that of the mediator. The mediator is less identified with the cause of any party in a dispute and is effective because all the parties in a dispute have some confidence in her role. She helps overcome communication barriers between groups, often serves as a liaison between groups, and helps groups bargain and eventually negotiate a position.[10]

The researcher can be helpful in dispute settlement because he is even further removed from the conflict. The researcher can gather data and provide analyses that may help parties in a dispute find a solution, a solution that is not based on illusion but on the realities of the situation.

Finally, the church might even have a place as enforcer of decisions which have been reached. While the enforcement of a decision is usually upheld in the courts and by police, churches can play a very significant role in the enforcement of agreements in more informal ways. Simply by keeping a close watch on a situation to see that persons abide by the rules they have agreed upon may serve to inhibit violations. The media often serve such an enforcement role because of the threat it will expose violations of agreements which would publicly discredit an organization or group. The church too can help enforce dispute settlements by legitimating the agreements, and by exposing and declaring illegitimate any violation.[11]

These forms of dispute settlement must become institutionalized, so that they can become models available to the larger community. It is the role of the church to become a builder of such models.[12] While the church is likely to be much more effective at building such models at the local community levels, these models are also adaptable to the international level. Perhaps indirectly, community models of conflict resolution, particularly the skills and techniques involved in negotiation and mediation, will influence the resolution of disputes at the international level.[13]

The major conflicts in the world today are and will likely continue to be in the third world—Latin America, Asia, and Africa. The church in these settings, insofar as it seeks to serve the poor, often has close contacts with those who have a stake in changing the unjust conditions in these societies. The United States government, on the other hand, in alliance with military and economic elites in these societies, often has a stake in preserving stability. Not only will the churches working with the poor increasingly clash with the foreign policy objectives of the U.S. government, but they will increasingly find themselves in positions where they are potential mediators between their own government and the people within a country with whom they have developed channels of communication. Traditional foreign policy has been conducted primarily through formal channels of communication between heads of state and their representatives, but many problems in revolutionary situations in third world countries cannot be resolved in this manner, for these conflicts involve actors who are outside the framework of traditional diplomatic channels.

The breakthrough in the Iranian hostage situation came, for example, when the United States recognized the inability of the official heads of state in Iran to solve the problem and began to work through a nongovernmental third party to reach those in Iran who had the power to reach an agreement. Some might argue that the Iranian situation is a special case because of the nature of power within that particular Islamic state. However, I think not. At present many conflicts remain unresolved because major actors in the conflict remain unrepresented in formal diplomatic negotiations. That is clearly the case in the Middle East, where the Palestinians remain formally unrepresented in the search for a peaceful solution to that conflict. Churches may play an increasingly important role in the future as third parties who can serve as mediators, particularly as informational and communication links between parties that otherwise have no contact with each other. Very little has been done or is known about how this process might work.

The church has a special task to perform in developing new models of conflict resolution and peacemaking. Unfortunately, the church has not been a leader in developing new models. Rather than taking risks in view of a vision of shalom, the church has been mostly a conserver of the status quo, an institution ready to justify one war after another rather than an agent leading the way to peaceful resolution of conflicts.

Setting up innovative institutions effectively demonstrates that alternatives exist to mainstream culture and institutions. They serve as experimental stations and models for the future, and they provide visible and concrete action around which to organize more people. In many respects the church is an alternative institution when its members live out a lifestyle of love, forgiveness, and peace, and through that example, witness to what could be, and convert others to that position.

The church, insofar as it lives by the vision of the kingdom of God, seeks to bring into being in the present those possibilities of the future. By demonstrating in the present what the future can be, the church becomes an agent of change. To act with vision requires that one take risks, that one act beyond any visible guarantees of past success. One of the callings of the church is that it acts by faith in this sense, that it be ready to take risks for the sake of the kingdom. It is then possible for the rest of the world to follow, once the possibilities of the future have been demonstrated.

4. Policy: Influence Public Policy

At a fourth level the church often self-consciously organizes itself to shape public policy and to influence elected or appointed officials in deciding policy.

Both pressure politics and electoral politics are important in trying to shape public policy.[14] Pressure politics means attempting to influence those people who already hold power. Through mass movements, protest meetings, letter writing campaigns, media coverage, and other means, politicians can successfully be influenced to revise their policies or take a specific stand. John L. Adams has documented the positive and decisive effect the church lobby, involving a wide variety of denominations, had on the passage of the 1964 Civil Rights Act and other legislation.[15] Since that time the direct effect the church can have on policymakers has become increasingly apparent. Most major denominations maintain offices in Washington.[16] They represent one interest group or lobby group among many. In this arena the church may be no more or less effective than any other interest group. Often church groups cancel out each other's influence, since on almost every public policy issue churches usually represent the whole spectrum of views.

When, however, the church's attempt to influence policy is closely linked to its experience and demonstration of effective efforts to meet human need through significant models (as outlined above), then the church's credibility with policymakers is strengthened and its impact often far outweighs its numbers. Sometimes church people are more effective because of their advocacy on behalf of others, whereas so often people engaged in pressure politics are furthering their own self-interest. Any given church should not necessarily try to speak to every peace and justice issue, but should selectively put its energies into those issues where it has already demonstrated active concern and some measure of success at meeting human need through its own efforts. Credibility can be reduced substantially when a public pronouncement or exhortation is made from the relatively secure confines of a conference meeting or church board setting, if it is not being acted out by that church's members in the world.[17]

While public pronouncements probably have limited value in terms of their impact on public policy, they nevertheless do serve to generate discussion and encourage theological and ethical discernment in the church. Pronouncements can mobilize the church to focus attention upon a crucial area of concern, and thus can become an important educational tool.

For most churches, most of the time what is done by the left hand is canceled out by the right. A very significant and creative program in a foreign country (such as a development project with the poor) can be carried out with great sacrifice and dedication by a few members of a denomination while the large majority of that denomination, by virtue of their own political and economic views and the manner in which they express them in their voting patterns, cancels out the very efforts made in that country. Trade policies and foreign aid policies or support of a repressive regime can be counterproductive to everything the church stands for in a foreign country, yet such counterproductive policies may be supported by most of its members. Thus one of the most important functions of the churches in working at policy formation is educating its own members at home and then enabling them to communicate their views to policymakers. The church needs a much closer link between its work abroad and the church at home.

The church at home must attend more carefully to helping its members vote more intelligently and conscientiously. The candidates we choose for public office do make a difference. So often church members, like almost everyone else, simply vote for a particular party out of habit or out of their own economic self-interest—whether *they* are better off under this president or that, whether *their* taxes will be raised, or whether their job is in jeopardy. In the course of the 1980 U.S. presidential campaign President Reagan asked people to ask themselves whether they were better off after four years of Carter. Though that is a valid question, it is not the primary question Christians ought to ask about candidates. We must ask whether a particular candidate's policies further nonviolent resolution of conflict and social justice. The question is not the image candidates portray, but what have they done or what are they likely to do.

Unfortunately, Christians often tend to relegate electoral politics to a sphere of life which does not come under the critical scrutiny of the Christian faith. Members of congregations give money for denominational social programs both at home and abroad that are more than offset by the policies of persons they helped elect to public office. I am not saying that the church should advocate certain candidates for public office, or that we should necessarily become too specific as a church in recommending particular policies. The church can aid discernment by identifying the ethical *Criteria* by which to assess candidates and their policies, though it should refrain from endorsing particular candidates or policies. Our political judgments are never a direct outgrowth of the gospel, as the candidate we support is influenced by empirical judgments about issues and our own human judgments about the candidates' personal qualities. Nevertheless, the Christian must bring to the voting booth an ethical evaluation of the candidate's policies. Though no particular party, or candidate, will necessarily be in full agreement with these ethical standards, in evaluating a candidate individual Christians will be able to make relative judgments about who, more or less, is likely to further justice and nonviolence.

Workers in the foreign settings can often play an important role when they return home and itinerate in the churches that sent them out. Richard Celeste, former director of the Peace Corps under President Carter, proposed that one of the most important functions of Peace Corps workers was the educating they do here at home. At that time he was preparing to propose funding for Peace Corps workers to spend a year in this country after their experience abroad just helping Americans to understand the situation in the world. It may be that Americans would actually contribute the most to the life of people abroad by the way they have an impact upon the policy of their own country.

It is important that the church enable its workers abroad to provide policymakers with a world perspective on issues that they would not otherwise have. How can the church, because of its special place in the world, provide government decision makers with insight they would not otherwise have by virtue of the barriers created by the very roles government bureaucrats play? How can the church especially be an advocate of the poor and those who do not get heard?

A typical case is the Middle East conflict. One of the fundamental root causes of that conflict—what to do about the Palestinians—has remained unsolved partly because no one has found a way to bring the Palestinians themselves into the negotiation process. The Palestine Liberation Organization (PLO) does not necessarily speak for them, Israel refuses to negotiate with the PLO, and the Arab states also do not speak for the Palestinians. To some degree church agencies (Mennonites and Quakers) have been able to make the voice of the ordinary Palestinian farmers and villagers heard by some persons in Congress. This activity, of course, has had its costs. A Mennonite Central Committee (MCC) worker, Paul Quiring, was not allowed to return to the West Bank specifically because of testimony he gave to the U.S. Congress concerning the plight of the Palestinians. According to Israeli officials, MCC was granted the license to do only humanitarian work on the West Bank. Quiring was accused of engaging in political activity (including being a voice of the PLO). The problem, of course, is that one cannot easily separate humanitarian and political activity. For instance, MCC works with West Bank Palestinian farmers. One of the scarce resources that these farmers compete for with the new Jewish settlements is water. That persons have water (a humanitarian concern) becomes a political issue on the West Bank.

The dilemma for the church is how much can it advocate the cause of poor or oppressed people within a country without jeopardizing its invitation to work in that country? This issue faces the church in country after country where advocacy of the poor before their own government may so jeopardize the church's relationship with the government where it is working that it is unable to remain in the country. The impact of the church in these situations is enhanced and its program is in less jeopardy where the U.S. church program is linked directly with the church in the local setting of the country. Such is the case with the Roman Catholic Church in many Latin-American countries where it has a strong program of advocacy for the poor in a particular country that can be linked to a transnational organization which can seek to influence U.S. government policy as well.

One of the most important things for the church to do is support voluntary organizations working for peace and justice. Many exist for the purpose of exerting influence on public policy and the national culture. By joining one of these voluntary associations the individual exercises a choice for the causes which the association stands for and gives the association more power by increasing its membership. James Luther Adams has written that these associations are of vital importance to society because they allow the individual to participate in decision making in some way. They provide a way of wielding power, of individuals banding together to exercise influence, of keeping minority opinion alive that would normally find no organized expression in government or society.[18]

Joining voluntary associations can play a significant part in the peace movement in two ways. First, as already mentioned, these associations can exercise influence and give more power to values of peace and justice. The Fellowship of Reconciliation, an interdenominational pacifist organization, publishes a magazine, sponsors peace education, and initiates peace-related actions. Clergy and Laity Concerned is a union of local groups from around the country that organized opposition to the Vietnam War on both a local and national level and now uses the same organizational structures to promote other peace and justice issues. Second, many voluntary associations transcend national boundaries and thus contribute to building international understanding and community. The more intricate, complex, and extensive the web of relationships that bypass national boundaries and governments, the greater the chances for peace.

5. Vocation: Working in Institutional Settings

At a fifth level, the members of the church work at tasks in the world in and through other institutions—business corporations, governmental structures, social agencies, schools and universities, and international organizations. In these vocations Christians can seek primarily to serve their own self-interest by gaining power, status, and material wealth for themselves. The work can be done primarily because it is a job to earn money and make a living. Or the task can be seen as an opportunity, a "calling," by which to try to further interests of peace and justice in or through the institutions where Christians work.

A person can be an innovator, one who seeks to create an alternative vision of how institutions can better serve human need: a business corporation that designs and markets products to meet basic human needs rather than superfluous products with the primary motive of profit, a lawyer seeking to defend the cause of justice or civil liberties or working in behalf of the poor rather than defending the special privileges of the rich, a teacher who teaches social science from a global framework rather than from a narrow nationalistic perspective, a social worker who helps to organize the poor to restore their dignity rather than simply cooperating with a demeaning social welfare system which dehumanizes people. These are just a few illustrations of how in our everyday work we can begin to think of ways to be creators of peace and justice in our world, rather than primarily supporters of the status quo. Of course, such action is risky. It requires that people act in terms of a future vision, to begin to act as if the kingdom of God is a present possibility.

Christians must recognize peace as a vocation. A vocation is the cause or objective—something ultimate—which a person orients his whole life around. Having such a vocation involves serving that cause or purpose in every condition, work, or relationship of life. Traditionally, in the history of Christianity, vocation has been associated with a call or calling to live in accordance with the divine plan.[19] The Christian monastic movements before the Reformation represent a good example. Monks held a goal to direct the mind so firmly toward God that every moment of life was not only determined by the thought of God, but where possible, completely filled by it. This was vocation—a complete orientation of life to something ultimate.

Before the Reformation, vocation in its highest sense applied only to monks, with the reasoning that only they could actually fulfill and carry out the complete incorporation of the divine into all of life. However, especially through the contribution of Luther, the scope of vocation changed so that it applied not just to monasticism, but to everyone. Luther saw vocation not only in isolated communities, but in the everyday events of the world and its work, when people took life upon themselves in its totality—pressures, disillusionments, oppressions, successes—and attempted to bring the divine Spirit of God into every moment.

The church must approach peace with this sense of vocation. Peace must not simply be the responsibility of isolated communities. Peace and justice must rather be the cause and objective that individuals, in the context of the church, direct every aspect of their lives toward fulfilling.

The concept of vocation definitively differs from the concept of occupation, profession, or job. The latter terms center around the individual and are not fully compatible with the goals of peacemaking because a peacemaking vocation implies pursuit of a pattern of life at odds with that which society encourages.[20] The individual specializes in a field like medicine, education, or industry, and that specialization can become a profession like being a doctor, teacher, or lawyer. The goal of this occupation or profession often means advancement in the field, increasing professional status, and a larger salary, and those goals are usually attained most easily if the individual does not rock the boat too much, but tries to sail smoothly among the established limits and rules of the prevailing society. Those goals may be hindered when the doctor leaves a growing practice to use her services in rural or third world development, or when a teacher involves himself together with his students in criticism of government policy, or when a laborer helps organize a movement to pressure her company into stopping armament production. In contrast, a vocation does not center on the individual. A vocation involves a social purpose concerned with such broad issues as peace and justice instead of individual advancement. A person structures his whole life pattern around that calling, not just eight hours a day and what constitutes success. The vocationally oriented person will want to be known more for her values than for her résumé or career standing.

A vocation spans all levels of society and a wide variety of areas. A vocation of peace cannot be written up in a ten-point job description, nor is it established in detail, easily definable, or comfortable in the sense that a person can expect the same thing day after day. The peacemaker may operate from outside the system, which involves attacking society's existing institutions and setting up alternatives such as free schools, underground newspapers, and revolutionary groups. A person may try to change or reform existing institutions through such groups as Common Cause or through political lobbying. Or a person may operate within an institution by helping to make policy. A peacemaker may work at the local level with community groups and church congregations, or at the international level of nations, diplomacy, and international organization. The peacemaker's action will vary all the way from simply writing letters to the editor of a local newspaper or publically airing his conviction, to nonviolent direct action that involves civil disobedience, the mobilization of large groups of people, and intense planning.

From whatever angle, a vocation of peace can clearly not be narrowly defined or contained by a single concept. Vocation broadly includes many styles of action and levels of operation that have a peaceful world as a goal. For the person interested in helping to create a peaceful world the primary consideration is not to decide what action to take, but to gain a sense of vocation or calling. The specific job is not as important as the values brought to it.

Lifestyle will become an important consideration in the pursuit of a peace vocation. The first question to ask, however, is not, "What is the proper lifestyle?" but "How can I best live out my peace vocation?" One correct lifestyle does not exist. The person choosing a peace vocation does not automatically have a moral obligation to live at poverty level, sell her car, stop eating meat, or quit paying taxes. Since many social-change jobs have only limited budgets, and since many peace actions may involve boycotts, tax refusal, or other types of self-denial, a peace vocation may well lead to a more austere lifestyle in order to be effective. Yet, jobs also exist, especially in leadership positions, that require owning certain things, traveling around the country, and circulating in a variety of social groups. Pursuing the vocation of peace takes precedence. A person's lifestyle should include whatever aids the vocation most effectively.

For the people who approach a profession from the standpoint of vocation rather than career, the professions offer a variety of opportunities to use their skills to further peacemaking. People skilled in media and communication can work within the established media world, challenging current practices, and inserting programming and articles that help to shape peaceful attitudes; or they can branch out into the alternative media or journalism; alternate television and radio programs, filmmaking, theater, free-lance writing, and publishing. Educators in universities, public schools, day care centers, and adult education programs can contribute by teaching attitudes of peace and methods of conflict resolution to their students. Lawyers and legal skills are needed to help people maintain civil liberties and human rights, to keep the government and other organizations accountable to the law, and to provide legal aid and counseling in both court cases and other legal matters to people working for peace at all levels. People skilled in economics, science, and technology can lend support to economic development in the U.S. and overseas, or they can use their influence to organize politically other professionals in their field.

B. CHOOSING A STRATEGY OF ACTION

Christians and the church as a whole must sort through a variety of peacemaking options and make a choice. How does one choose a strategy or method? Who is involved in carrying out these strategies? Whom does one want to change?

In this process of choosing a strategy, two considerations are of prime importance: first, that the strategy conform to one's principles of ethics, and second, that the strategy be effective. The tension between these two poles has been the subject of much ethical debate, and often surfaces in specific issues. Should the church support third world liberation movements in which the only recourse seems to be to use violence in order to achieve the ends of equality and justice? Should the church become a strong political force in order to be more effective in policy formation, or should the church witness to the state simply by "being the church"? Should I withhold my income tax from the government to protest military expenditures even though that action seems very ineffective?

At one pole seems to be the purely pragmatic position which would sacrifice anything to achieve an important end, and at the other end a position which considers only the means and may appear indifferent toward any ends. As has already been discussed in much more detail in the earlier chapter on nonviolence, neither position by itself is adequate. Principles of ethics should not be violated for the sake of what works. The means make the ends. If one's ethics place a high value on nonviolence, then obviously any action that includes violence is definitely out, no matter how effective it may seem. Likewise, however, even if an action meets all the tests of a person's ethics, it is of little value if ineffective in accomplishing anything. Once an action has met the test of ethics, it must be carefully assessed further to determine effectiveness. To these assessments, we now look further.

One must calculate and carefully reason through the proposed action.[21] Shouting in the streets to everyone in general but no one in particular may be legitimate, but it has little effectiveness in actually creating a peaceful world. Five questions need to be considered in choosing a strategy.

1. Resources

Who is acting and with what resources? A person must first assess whether he will act alone, in connection with few other people, or as part of a larger group. Once a decision has been reached on exactly who will take part in the action, the participants must determine their resources. First, who are the allies? What organizations or political figures will back the action? How many, and which people can be counted on for support? What groups and organizations are already working on this particular issue? What outside contacts do the participants have? Second, how much time and energy are the participants willing to invest? Full time? One day per week? Third, what expertise and talents do the participants have? Speaking? Organizing? Art? Previous education? Previous experience? Professional training? Fourth, how much power do the participants wield? What positions do they hold? What organization do they belong to? What people are they able to influence? What types of decision making are they responsible for? How much money do they control?

2. Who

Whom are the actionists trying to reach? The actionists make this decision from a wide range of possibilities. A person or group may choose to work from the local level to the international level. Where a person acts along this spectrum and whom a person attempts to reach is largely dependent on whether the person acts alone or with a group, and how those participants assess their resources as discussed above. If a problem is understood systemically (chapter five), then groups will act most likely with both the local and international level in mind.

3. What

Exactly what change is supposed to happen? The goal, object, or demand of an action must be specific and focus on a particular issue or event. Telling an opponent that we want a peaceful world will only frustrate the situation. The opponent probably knows no better than the actionists how to achieve that. The demand should be something concrete that the opponent is capable of doing, such as halting certain weapons systems, voting in a certain way, or making a certain concession. Concentrating on too many issues or too broad a spectrum spreads the actionists thin and increases the chance of failure. A better strategy is to work on one specific aspect of the struggle and experience success before moving on. Martin Luther King, Jr., and other leaders of the civil rights movement used this concept effectively. Each time they began a nonviolent action they had a specific demand that they wanted met.[22] In Montgomery they wanted blacks to have the right to sit anywhere on the city's buses. In Selma they wanted the integration of lunch counters and waiting rooms. In Chicago they wanted a fair housing law. Civil rights activists always worked for the larger goal of racial justice, but the demands were always specific.

World problems such as energy, food, health, need to be approached as superordinate goals that only can be solved cooperatively as many individuals and groups contribute resources and skills.

Muzafer Sherif, a noted psychologist, conducted an experiment in the 1950s with two groups of boys at a summer camp.[23] He arranged for conflict and rivalry to develop between the two groups. He then tried to resolve the conflict with various methods such as exhortation and preaching, and by sensitivity sessions where they shared their feelings with each other and sought to resolve their differences through communication. Finally, he decided to shut off the water to the camp. Through the experiment he discovered that the two groups resolved their rivalry best when they were forced to work together to solve a common problem, in that case a lack of water in the camp.

As applied to the international situation, this would suggest that nations may be drawn away from hostile rivalries that lead to war when they become engaged in a superordinate goal, solving a problem that could mutually benefit both of them. A superordinate goal is a common problem or goal that affects or appeals to members of all groups involved, but which no group can solve or achieve without the participation of the others. It may take the intervention of a third party to enable two nations in conflict to focus upon their common interest rather than those factors which are generating conflict. Examples of superordinate goals include development of solar energy, converting deserts to food production, pollution control, and expansion of medical and health services.[24]

4. When

When should the action be carried out, and in what length of time must the goal be accomplished? In the case of some types of action like building alternative institutions, or using professional skills for peace causes, "the sooner, the better" may be a better axiom than "act with a sense of timing." However, actionists should be sensitive to when their action will have the most effect and impact, and when people can be rallied around a cause. Another consideration is the eventual accomplishment of the goal. For their own benefit the actionists ought to know whether they consider their action as short range with immediate fulfillment or long range with few immediate rewards. Also, if the actionists make a demand of an opponent, both parties should be clear on when the demand must be met and what consequences will accrue if it is not.

Pacifists are often criticized by nonpacifists because they believe the pacifist position entails immediate and unilateral disarmament. To expect such to happen is, of course, politically unrealistic, given the types and amounts of arms the nations of the world possess. If one of the superpowers would immediately and unilaterally disarm, the world would probably become more dangerous rather than less. A realistic pacifist position would call for the initiation of a step-by-step process analogous to the way Gandhi operated on the issue of British imperialism in India and Martin L. King did on the civil rights issue in the United States. Though both had long-range goals, they sought limited and specific political objectives that moved them toward their goals. The arms race is like the disease of alcoholism. The alcoholic who has acknowledged his problem hopes to overcome alcoholism for life, but the way he solves his problem is by not drinking one day at a time. Though the pacifist hopes for disarmament in the long run, he works for those specific political decisions that can lead in the right direction one step at a time.

Such a method is available to governments. In his book, *Alternative to War or Surrender*, Charles Osgood has described the process of GRIT (Graduated Reciprocation in Tension Reduction), a process in which one nation makes a small but significant unilateral initiative, awaits a response from the other side, and then takes another initiative. Such a process can reverse the escalatory cycle of an arms race or cycle of violence. Osgood points out that this process worked successfully for a time during the Kennedy-Krushchev era. Anwar Sadat implemented this idea when he made his dramatic visit to Jerusalem. Sadat's visit did not establish peace between Israel and Egypt, but it did set in motion a process that over several years led to a vast improvement in the relationships between the two countries.

5. Why

What are the reasons for demanding the change? Why should the opponent consider the proposed changes as fair, morally right, and in the best interest of society? Everyone, including the people the actionists want to change—no matter how wrong they are perceived to be—are influenced by what they think is right. Careful thought must therefore go into the question: Is our demand justifiable? Will the demand seem legitimate in the eyes of the people we seek to change? In terms of morality and the past actions of ourselves and our opponents, how will the demand appear? A great deal of effectiveness can be gained if the actionists are able to convince their opponents that in terms of the opponent's own value system, what is being asked for is the right thing to do.

In summary, an individual or group interested in peacemaking has a wide range of methods to choose from. The criteria of choice is whether the proposed method fits with the individual's or group's ethics, and second, whether the method can be effective. To achieve the most effectiveness, those acting must carefully consider their own resources, and exactly what they want to accomplish, when, and why. These criteria are certainly not exhaustive, but they illustrate the importance of choosing action wisely and carrying it out intelligently and carefully.

The form which political action takes depends to a great extent upon a judgment of the nature of the times in which one is living. Personal and communal judgment is a necessary element in any decision to act that is not solely dictated by the rational calculations of theological, ethical, and factual judgments. Sensing what is the appropriate course of action in the moment of history in which one is living grows out of a complex web of factors. These include one's aesthetic sensibilities, one's sensitivity to the nuances of the historical process which can never be subsumed under rational categories—particular memories of the past which intrude upon one's consciousness of the present, deep associations and loyalties one has to other persons and groups, one's sense of capacities of time and energy, and one's interests and capabilities.

The words of Ecclesiastes that everything has a different time and season are apropos; so is the poetry of James Russell Lowell: "New occasions teach new duties, time makes ancient good uncouth." In the realm of prophetic social action, it seems that often a dialectic exists between times when societies are relatively open to change in the direction of a more just and peaceful society, and other times when societies are reactionary and repressive—situations where efforts at social change are resisted with violence and torture.

Persons living under Nazi tyranny in the 1930s and 40s experienced this violent terrorism when they tried to give witness to an alternative to Hitler. It was this situation which moved Dietrich Bonhoeffer to say:

> One may ask whether there have ever before in human history been people with so little ground under their feet—people to whom every available alternative seemed equally intolerable, repugnant, and futile . . . whether the responsible thinking people of any generation that stood at a turning point in history did not feel much as we do, simply because something new was emerging that could not be seen in the existing alternatives.[25]

At times every available political alternative may seem inappropriate or futile, whether electoral politics or movement politics, the expression of concern through one's profession, activity in a voluntary association, or nonviolent direct action. What then? Is the only alternative some form of violence or underground movement of resistance to try to subvert or overthrow the forces of repressive violence? One can certainly empathize with the frustration and rage that often erupts in violence in such situations. It would be quite inappropriate to condemn the actions of persons whose situation we cannot begin to comprehend from a vantage point of relative peace and security.

However, we would also be remiss if we did not point to the example of the thousands of persons who through the centuries have chosen another kind of response to repressive violence.[26] They stand as an example to us, as a model of action that should not automatically be excluded from our consciousness as a possible course of action for ourselves. Paradoxically, at times the only way to affirm life may be to accept death at the hand of a foe. Christ's sacrificial death was a model for the early church and it should not be dismissed as a possible model for us. Early Christians accepted death when they affirmed the living reality of the lordship of Christ and refused to bow down to the limited lordship of Caesar. In the context of Nazi Germany, to speak out for life and against the Nazi ideology of death was for some an act of affirmation, an act of freedom affirming meaning in the face of death. To respond to Nazi terrorism with violence would have been for them a sign that they had succumbed to the forces of evil and death. An affirmation of life is expressed in the acts of those who by helping Jews to escape to safety, faced a certain death when they were caught. In their dying, they still affirmed life.

Today in South Africa, as in the situation of Bonhoeffer, all the available options seem almost futile. What is the church to do in response to the repressive violence of the state, with its arrests and bans of individuals and organizations? Certainly the frustration and rage of violent reaction would be understandable. Yet even in that situation, one possibility which supremely expresses the vitality of the church's social message is the existence of the multiracial church—a living vital movement of blacks and whites who in their worship and work together give a constant and vital witness to the possibilities for a new way of life in South Africa. Violent reaction by blacks to the repressive violence in South Africa is certainly understandable, and can hardly be condemned from the relative peace and security of North America. Nevertheless, it may be that the nonviolent witness of the multiracial churches is precisely the way to express social responsibility in South Africa today, because it represents more the affirmation of life rather than the adoption of the methods of violence of the South African government.   O

9 SUSTAINING ACTION: SPIRITUAL RESOURCES FOR EMPOWERMENT

This chapter focuses on those who have recognized peacemaking as their vocation, who work as creators of peace and justice rather than guardians of an unjust status quo. These are the peacemakers who act under the conviction and inspiration of a future vision and begin to live with joyous abandon in the temporal reality of the kingdom to come. Peacemaking is vocation; it is the Christian vocation. Just as with Luther, the scope of vocation broadened to embrace not only the clergy and the cloistered, but all Christians in all walks and acts of life, so the vocation of peacemaking belongs not only to a token activist fringe, but to all who live and work under the lordship of the Prince of Peace.

We have traced the development of this vocational calling from the theological ground through the growth and fruition of active response. In this chapter, we will describe holistic men and women who have been touched by the transcendent and led by vision, acting in solo and in concert, and being sustained by hope.

The discussion on holistic men and women addresses these issues: What are the resources that nourish and cultivate a growing peacemaker? How is character formed? What goes into the individual story? What is the vision that convicts and inspires persons to become instruments of shalom? How does this vision empower and sustain peacemakers, both in solitude and in relatedness?

In the following sections, we shall describe in greater detail the means through which the transcendent speaks, both in the individual pilgrimage and in the communal life. Each person faces finitude alone, and experiences the moments of *kairos* in which the finite is touched by the infinite. What are the images that characterize the religious stories of peacemakers? How can individuals be sustained through prayer, nature, community, and the larger culture?

The ground of our being is one who works in history to bring together a people of shalom. How does the gathered community find sustenance and edification from that source and from each other? What are the structures and vitals, the functions and passions of the gathered community that sustain it as it goes about its work in the world?

Finally, we know that a life lived in faithfulness to the calling of shalom must often find expression independent of, and in dissonance with, surrounding society. Sons and daughters of God may be persecuted for the sake of righteousness. In the hours of silent darkness, whence comes the renewal of vision, the words to speak, and the dawn of hope?

A. HOLISTIC MEN AND WOMEN

In this section, the influences that mold and shape the human character will be discussed within the context of the theological perspective detailed in chapters three and four. In this perspective, God as Creator makes human beings in God's own image, endowing them with social, relational, and symbolic capacities which allow them to become co-creators of society and culture. God creates human beings as social beings, rather than isolated individuals, who come to full humanity in togetherness, rather than isolation.

Yet people as a reflection of the Creator are more than egregious animals. Humanity alone in creation bears the distinctive mark of the "imago dei"—the unique capacity to symbolize. Men and women can name, can assign a representative symbol, and the implications of that act leave them, as the psalmist says, little less than deified. It is this distinctive capacity that makes possible the miracle of language, the communicating of ideas and events through time and distance by translating them into symbolic form. Language keeps alive the past through remembrance. Language travels as sound patterns or marks on paper, relating a vision from eyes that have seen to eyes that have not seen. Language even makes possible discourse about things that no eyes have seen. Through memory and imagination, men and women can bind time, in past or future, accumulating and creating stories and ideas.

The capacity to symbolize, in both cognitive and affective dimensions, enables humans to become creators of culture. Abstract representation makes possible the creation of pattern and system in a variety of media: concepts and numbers, sound and color, wood and stone. The depth and breadth of passionate experience finds form in music and drama, art and story, ritual and custom. And man, both male and female, cognitive and affective, begat song and dance, art and architecture, disciplines and institutions, beliefs and mores—creations which bear the image of God as reflected in the human capacity to symbolize and bring into being a new thing.

The socio-symbolic nature of human beings means not only that they are creators of culture and social institutions, but that these institutions and culture shape them in return. For human beings exist in relation to their context, a context of society and culture, and through that context they realize their humanity in its fullness. Humans relate in context, and life for relational beings is a continuing dialogue of perception/integration/ response with that context, a rhythm of creating and being created. W. Somerset Maugham describes the condition of being created by creation:

> For men and women are not only themselves; they are also the region in which they were born, the city apartment or farm in which they learned to walk, the games they played as children, the old wives' tales they overheard, the food they ate, the schools they attended, the sports they followed, the poems they read, and the God they believed in. [1]

And, we might add, the stories they read in books or visualized in cinema and the arts, the heroes and archetypes they learned to esteem, the living force of their parents, teachers, and mentors—all such influences impress upon the imagination a course of action, a style of life, a way of response.

The message of shalom which calls people to become peacemakers is transmitted through significant encounters with events, people, and ideas. Notable examples include Mohandas K. Gandhi, whose idea of satyagraha, the truth-force which works through the channel of nonviolent action to effect the goal of justice and reconciliation, was inspired by the writings of Tolstoy (*The Kingdom of God Is Within You*), Thoreau (*Civil Disobedience*), and the New Testament, particularly the Sermon on the Mount. [2] Gandhi in turn provided inspiration for Martin Luther King, Jr., who combined Gandhi's method with Christ's ethic of love as the foundation of his civil rights activism. [3] Gandhi's writings also reached Trappist monk Thomas Merton in the solitude of Kentucky's Abbey of Gethsemani, touching the contemplative, social critic, and leading him to explore the mystical experience of the East. [4] Social reformer Danilo Dolci, who works toward cooperative organization, education, and economic improvement in Mafia-saturated Sicily, had not read Gandhi until a journalist likened Dolci's tactics to those of Gandhi. Dolci is now known as the "Gandhi of Sicily." [5]

Yet human beings are more than a sum of influences. We err if we project a picture of humanity as a mere product of social determinism. For men and women are not passive receptacles of sensory data; their minds are not blank tablets or blocks of wax upon which impressions are made. Rather, new data is continually processed through and integrated into a dynamic perceptual screen, and minds and feelings are coparticipants in this active process. Maturity is marked by the ownership of self, the recognition of responsibility for who one is.

Furthermore, humans are beings who experience themselves as acting, decision-making individuals with accountability to others for those decisions and acts. The autonomy of the individual is not negated but balanced by the influence of others. For example, the counsel of a group may be voluntarily sought or coercively transmitted, but in the moment of decision-making the individual stands alone. The freedom to give the ultimate Yes or No is both undeniable and inescapable. It is alone that we make decisions of ultimate concern, alone that we face our finitude and our Maker, alone that we experience awareness of the ground of our being. It is alone, says Dietrich Bonhoeffer, that we hear and answer the call to discipleship:

> Through the call of Jesus men become individuals. Willy-nilly, they are compelled to decide, and that decision can only be made by themselves. It is no choice of their own that makes them individuals: it is Christ who makes them individuals by calling them. Every man is called separately and must follow alone.[6]

Though the need to make decisions is shared, decisions are made by individuals. Though individuals may share the same culture and worldview, even the same parents and family life, their thought and personalities are never identical. Inasmuch as no two beings share the totality of their experience and thought, no two beings can ever understand each other in the depth and totality of their innermost being. In this sense, each of us is essentially alone, and yet we share enough so that we are not locked into the total confinement of solipsism. We recognize, communicate with, and influence beings other than ourselves. We could not be ourselves without them. So it is in a creative symbiosis that individuals are shaped and nourished by communities, and nourish and shape them in return. The experience of each individual, no matter how common, remains in some ways unique. No two autobiographies are alike.

B. TOUCHED BY THE VISION

A transcendent or eschatological vision is the ground, context, and source of all work for peace and justice. "Where there is no vision, the people perish" (Proverbs 29:18). It is indeed the vision of shalom that empowers and sustains peacemakers, as individuals and in community. This transcendent vision, which permeates men and women in every aspect of their being, is the power that redeems fallen creation and transforms it into instruments of shalom. This vision is manifest again and again in the historical drama of redemption. Integral to the vision is the unshakable conviction that ultimate reality is just and good in a universal sense; it recognizes in the universe a creative force that works to bring the disjointed parts into a harmonious whole, by whatever name that force is known. This vision avoids messianism, the worshiping of the particular over the universal, the "my god" of "my people" over the one lord of all. Rather, it calls us to worship the one, the universal, the Creator of all beings, the one in whom all being is valued. It is a vision of the oneness of humanity, and the interrelatedness and interdependence of all things.

This vision sees clearly that the implications of justice are economic as well as spiritual, and is not clouded by the delusion that evil can be overcome with violence. The pursuit of true justice is done in the manner of nonviolent love; only redeemed means can serve the end of redemption.

Throughout history, kindred hearts in different times and places have shared such a vision, in part or in whole. In Gandhi's satyagraha we recognize a parallel to the force of ultimate goodness and harmony. Etymologically, *satya* is derived from "sat" meaning "being," and implies love and truth. *Graha* means "firmness, force." Therefore, satyagraha is that force of truth and love which is one with being. The object of the satyagrahi (nonviolent warrior) is to convert, not coerce, the opponent into a change of heart.[7] Martin Luther King's deep faith in the future was rooted in the belief that the universe is on the side of justice. This faith, wrote King, enables the nonviolent resister to accept suffering without retaliation, and to recognize unmerited suffering as redemptive. Because she knows she has "cosmic companionship," the resister has strength to love the oppressor into a relationship of friendship and understanding.[8] Danilo Dolci, organizer of the first successful civil-disobedience satyagraha in Western Europe, began working outside of Sicily's Catholic Church when he found it to be an agent of oppression. Yet Dolci retains a sustaining religious faith in the community of all humankind, and the power of solidarity.[9] Non-Christian and nonpacifist leaders such as Malcom X shared a similar vision of oneness. Malcolm's pilgrimage to Mecca, where he witnessed thousands of people of all races and colors coming together in unity, proved to him the power of the one God, and the oneness of humanity under the oneness of God.[10]

Such are the elements of the vision that redeems and sustains peacemakers, in solitude and in relatedness. In the remainder of the chapter we will study the working out of this vision in these two dimensions: the solitary walk and the social, communal journey. We will examine in greater detail the various means and structures which manifest the drama of redemption, and impart the overflowing power of inexhaustible hope.

C. IN SOLITUDE

We begin by directing our attention on holistic, redeemed humans in their individual pilgrimage, and explore the means by which they are nourished in their solitary experience. The transcendent speaks to the individual in many ways: through the silence of a person before God, through the comtemplative, mystical experience, through regular meditation and prayer, through the appreciation of God's creation in nature, and human creativity in forms of art, music, and story. The possibilities of individual religious experience are as varied as individual beings, as limitless as the unlimited, and are known only through personal, solitary encounter.[11] Religion, says Alfred North Whitehead, is what a person does with his solitude.

1. Religious Experience

We limit ourselves here to the brief description of two contrasting ways of acquiring a religious story, and follow with a more thorough investigation of the experience most common to peace activists—that of the mystical/contemplative religious experience.

Many persons whose story from birth contains religious metaphors and images, cannot point to any specific place or time in which a particular religious story became their own. They are the ones who were bathed in the waters of religious experience, who breathed the air of sacred myth, whose maturity was a process of growing up in the faith. The inevitable times of doubt and questioning, and even temporary renunciation, could not separate them from that which was already a part of their being. For certain individuals the incorporation, acceptance, and public affirmation of formal articulations of belief may be pinpointed and dated, but their basic orientation, their faith perspective, remains a continuous, unchanging thread which runs through the fabric of their life.

For others, the individual religious life is marked by a "Damascus-road," "born-again" experience of conversion. The breach from the old life to the new is clear and distinct, and the agent of that change is a greater power who acts purely out of mercy, rather than in response to the worth or works of the recipient. William James has described the conversion experience in the following sequence of events: First, persons feel the grasp of a higher, controlling power and perceive themselves as empty, negated, or totally unworthy—if in fact they are even aware of themselves. Then comes the gift of salvation, the act of grace, which leaves the individual in a state of assurance. Worry is abandoned and replaced with peace, harmony, or ecstatic happiness. Internally, truths not known before are perceived and understood. In the external world, all of creation takes on an aura of newness. The conversion experience, according to James, leaves the individual with a changed attitude toward life, a new orientation which does not fade regardless of the extent to which religious enthusiasm may decline, or how much backsliding there may be.[12]

Often those who belong to one of the two types described above tend to view the other with suspicion, the one wondering if the other's experience was authentically regenerative ("Ye must be born again," you know), and the other dubiously questioning the longevity of commitment inspired by a more "emotional high." Such suspicions may or may not be unfounded. At any rate their validity is not for us to determine. We who neither possess ultimate truth nor sit on the throne of God may not stand in judgment of the relationship between an individual and God. Perhaps those who harbor suspicion are on the defensive, unsure of the status of their own religious experience.

Another double-edged error results when too much emphasis is placed on the receipt of grace in a once-for-all-time conversion experience. The one side argues that since grace is free and no one can earn it, some must be predestined to receive it no matter what they do. The other side maintains that some persons, by virtue of their personality, are more likely candidates for such an experience than others, so evangelical energy should be channeled into creating appropriate traits of receptiveness. Neither the deliberate calculating of receptiveness nor the seeking of refuge in doctrinaire predestination constitute the proper understanding of grace. Grace is a free gift, a gift given in different ways to different persons. As a gift it is unearned, yet the faith-response to that gift will necessarily be manifest in the life and works of the receiver. At times grace may be given in rather large doses, depending on the need, and it is given again and again, for like Paul we recognize that we too have sinned, have shortcomings, have need of salvation in ongoing instances. Like Paul we die daily and are daily renewed; like Paul we need reminders that "thy grace is sufficient." In the final analysis, however, grace remains mystery, and we need grace to accept that mystery. Often our zealous attempts to explain mystery result in some form of idolatry.

The experience of grace, of a gracious and boundless love which embraces all of being, is the enduring power which underlies a sense of worth and confidence in life. Without this confidence that being is loving and friendly, and that I as an individual person am of worth, a peaceful vision is difficult, if not impossible, to sustain. The redeemed community is free to love and accept others because its members have been loved with a boundless love, have been given unconditional acceptance by Ultimate Reality, have been declared okay by the grace of God. Because of such an unshakable psychological grounding, the eschatological vision of shalom becomes a viable way of living. Human beings depend upon the breakthrough of the infinite into the finite. God touches, human beings respond, and out of that interaction grows the possibility of shalom.

The experience of grace and love has its counterpart at the psycho-social level. Erik Erikson has shown how early experiences of a child can have a profound impact upon that child's sense of self-esteem that may set the tone for an individual's entire life.[13] Persons with an accurate self-concept and healthy self-esteem, with an inner locus of self-worth, are less likely to be threatened by differences, less easily put on the defensive, less prone to resort to violence in problem-solving. Self-acceptance makes possible the acceptance of others. Self-awareness makes possible awareness of others. Persons must know and respect themselves before they will be able to respect the personalities, rights, and differences of others.

Although self-concept is a dynamic entity, continually being shaped through the integration of experiential data, children's self-concepts are wellformed by the time they reach school age. Thus the dynamics of the early environment are of paramount importance. Healthy self-concepts are fostered in open, affirming environments characterized by free expression and ownership of feelings, two-way listening in dialogue, and friend-to-friend, rather than dominant-submissive relationships.[14]

Common to many persons who have become active proponents of a peace vision is a type of mystical or contemplative religious experience. We want to look briefly at several of the life stories of these individuals, some prominent and others less well known. What is interesting is that though these stories are expressed and interpreted in various cultural and social contexts, in their depth dimension these different stories are amazingly similar.

We begin with an experience of the prophet Isaiah, as told in the sixth chapter of his book. Isaiah's account may be described in four parts, as follows: First, the prophet is struck with wonder and astonishment at his vision of the Lord enthroned in glory, surrounded by seraphim. Second, the shaking foundations and billowing smoke bring forth Isaiah's response: "Woe is me! For I am lost; for I am a man of unclean lips, and I dwell in the midst of a people of unclean lips, for my eyes have seen the King, the Lord of hosts!" In Isaiah's experience, the initial sense of awe and reverence is followed by the recognition of unworthiness and finitude. Third, the Lord purifies and forgives Isaiah's unclean lips with the touch of a burning coal, and asks "Whom shall I send, and who will go for me?" Purification by fire and forgiveness serve as preparation for the call. Fourth, Isaiah answers, "Here am I! Send me." Having experienced ecstasy, emptiness, and cleansing pardon, the strengthened Isaiah then goes forth, bringing the message of the Lord to his people.

It is the paradox of purification by fire, strength in weakness, liberation through crucifixion, and new life through death that identifies mystical renewal. Themes of emptiness, renunciation, self-denial, and suffering unto death so that the old become new and the ultimate truth-force can be released in its fullness echo through the writings of mystics both past and present, East and West. The mystical experience, though temporary, has enduring implications, for the seed that has died then grows into new life and bears fruit. The journey inward is followed by the journey outward, the going forth into the world with a task to accomplish.

The relationship between this mystical emptiness and social action has been experienced and analyzed by James Douglass, university professor and exponent of nonviolent revolutionary tactics. In his book, *Resistance and Contemplation*, Douglass elaborates the thesis that contemplation and resistance are the complementary, yin-yang dimensions which combine to form the "way" of social protest. Neither can be affirmed at the expense of the other, for the "way" is both within and transcendent of the yin-yang dynamic. "In a revolution of truth-force, of the power of being," writes Douglass, "there is no way up except down, no way to power except through renunciation, no way to being except through nothingness."[15]

The contemplative way of liberation begins, according to Douglass, with the "shock of recognizing the bedrock poverty of one's self."[16] Or, as he quotes his wife, Shelley, "We must be strong in our acceptance of impotence before we'll be given any real power."[17] The results are yet to come, and they are the work of God's power, not people's. Douglass continues, "In the desert, on the sheer face of the mountain, man becomes God by renouncing power and becoming nothing. Now yin, now yang, and for a few hours man is transfigured on the cross and resists with the power of God: The world changes."[18]

The transformation that occurs is the work of a transcendent Being through the emptiness of the individual vessel. Individuals cannot calculate and determine the release of divine power by following the proper formula, nor can they take the credit for the work of that power. As Gandhi knew, individuals must act from the pure motive of seeking truth, and remain detached from the fruit of their action.[19] In this understanding, it is only through the renunciation of personal social/political effectiveness that effective change can occur. As priest-activist Daniel Berrigan once said, "I really despise the term *political*. I mean, either we are mystics or we are nothing, absolutely nothing."

A parallel but not identical experience is recognized in the life of the Sicilian Gandhi, Danilo Dolci. A promising student of architecture, Dolci began to question his direction because of the contrast between the comfortable society in which he lived and an indelible memory of rural Sicily's abysmal poverty which he had seen in his youth. When walking in the country, Dolci had a vision which led him to join a Catholic community, and later move in with the poor in Trappeto as a brother. Dolci describes his experience:

> I saw that when the leaves fall, only the seeds remain, that the seeds then return to the earth. I saw that in the act of wasting away they become reborn. And continuously the seeds fall and become fruit, ready for eating. And I saw all the seasons like this, from inside, as it were. I was the whole cycle of life. I *felt*—I didn't reason it—that Nature, that everything was a tragedy where the living devoured the dead. And then slowly I felt the need to be consumed, like the seeds, to become manure myself. And then I understood the value of communion, that everybody must be together.[20]

The need to be consumed and the drive toward universal communion are akin to Gandhi's understanding, although Dolci's tactics are more pragmatic, designed to embarrass the establishment, arouse public opinion and effect change, rather than convert the opponent.

Three additional stories will be mentioned in brief, those of a twentieth-century female philosopher, a Zen Buddhist, and a Trappist monk. Simone Weil, French, Jewish, Christian, and brilliant, was born in 1909, and began teaching philosophy at a lycée for girls in France at age 22. Her teaching career was interrupted by two intervals of factory work. Her writings, all published posthumously, reveal her multifaceted genius as a writer, philosopher, historian, political observer, and unorthodox mystic.[21] Weil's intellectual pursuit of truth, of a reality stripped bare of illusion, followed a mystical course of detachment, renunciation of desire, and unmerited suffering. She knew that "to philosophize is to learn to die," quoting that phrase in her journal, and said in her own words that "to love truth means to endure the void, and, as a result, to accept death."[22] Weil maintained that grace alone overcomes the gravity that pulls us away from God, and grace is received by the soul that is bare and vacant. "Grace fills empty spaces but it can only enter where there is a void to receive it, and it is grace itself which makes this void."[23] Her premature death in London at age 34 was hastened by voluntary malnutrition, a chosen expression of solidarity with the native French population subsisting on wartime civilian rations.

The drive to face truth, to perceive reality stripped bare of illusion and see with purified vision, provides the motivation for ethical response, because we can respond only to the world which we see. The reflective, contemplative experience must direct us toward reality, not away from it, and serve to broaden and clarify that vision of reality. The destruction of illusion implicit in purification of vision is not without pain and anguish. Yet the experience of one's nothingness is cause for hope because it reveals the source of sustenance—a being beyond oneself.

Zen Master Thich Nhat Hanh, nonviolent activist of the Vietnam War era, has written a manual entitled *The Miracle of Mindfulness* to help peace workers improve their vision.[24] Through his leadership of the Vietnamese Buddhist peace delegation in Paris during the war, and cochairmanship of the Fellowship of Reconciliation, Nhat Hanh brought to public attention the need for the meditative dimension in the peace movement. Zen does not teach, it points. Rather than offering a kerygmatic message or revelation, Zen communicates an awareness, a consciousness of the ontological ground of our own being here and now, in the midst of the world. Nhat Hanh's book offers exercises which help to enhance everyday awareness, for Zen meditation is not an activity disjointed from the mundane. Rather, every act of life is to be done in a meditative way. Similarly, there is no "way" to peace, peace is the way.

The contemplation of certain themes such as emptiness, detachment, and interdependence brings a great compassion to peacemakers, for they are able to identify with the sufferings and joys of others and enter into the universal harmony of life. In such a liberating experience, the heart is flooded with compassion, and the world is seen through the eyes of compassion. Peace workers who see with the eyes of compassion are able to respond appropriately to what they see, and are not blinded by despair.

It was in the depths of contemplative solitude that Trappist Thomas Merton found nonviolent compassion for all human beings. In solitude he recognized the evils of the world in himself, found forgiveness, and identified passionately with all living things. In solitude he discovered his vocation to unmask through writing the illusions of a violent society.

It may seem contradictory that Merton's response to the call led him to monasticism. The monastic life is often viewed as diametrically opposed to social activism, a withdrawal rather than a going forth, a retreat from an evil world into sheltered irrelevance. Merton speaks to that criticism: "Are monks and hippies and poets relevant? No, we are deliberately irrelevant. We live with an ingrained irrelevance which is proper to every human being...."[25] Such an irrelevance makes possible the awareness of the reality of God and others, from which follows the proper response.

For Merton, the way of authentic relevance was the way of prayer and contemplation. His life and work showed that monasticism is not a retreat from reality, for his sociopolitical criticism was the fruit of a compassion learned through a life of monastic ascesis and silence.

We have been describing general religious experience, beginning with two kinds of beginnings, and focusing on the common elements of mystical experience as traced through the lives of several peacemakers. Now we shall examine some specific means through which the transcendent offers sustenance to individuals: prayer, nature, and culture.

2. Prayer

Prayer is the fuel that renews, the energizer that flows from an inexhaustible resource. Prayer is the immersion of the self in God, becoming dead to the self and the world so that creative, fearless living can begin. Prayer changes the world by changing first those who pray. Says Henri Nouwen, "Prayer makes men contemplative and attentive. In place of manipulating, the man who prays stands receptive before the world. He no longer grabs but caresses, he no longer bites, but kisses, he no longer examines but admires."[26]

Through prayer we are born into new existence in Christ's kingdom, and are given the strength to begin living that kingdom with joy and hope in the midst of a destructive world. Through prayer we assert our allegiance to a higher authority, and find security in a higher power. Prayer becomes, finally, the revolutionary act, because it is the basis and source of all action. Without prayer, there is no faithful action.

The contemplative lifestyle is not, of course, the only way to reconcile prayer and vocation. Workers for peace and justice offer prayers or surround themselves with a "force-field of contemplation" while moving on buses and trains, in planes and marches, from platforms to podiums, and on both sides of picket lines and jail bars. "Pray at all times" is a mandate to be taken seriously, so that each act is done with an attitude of prayer, so that every act becomes a prayer.

Workers also testify to the sustenance received in the daily-scheduled blocks of meditation and prayer. Mother Teresa, whose life is a "living prayer," considers her time alone with God to be as important as her work on the street. A day with her Missionaries of Charity contains mass, half an hour of meditation, morning prayer, afternoon prayer, and a full hour of adoration in the evening. Says Mother Teresa, "You should spend at least half an hour in the morning, and an hour at night in prayer. You can pray while you work. Work doesn't stop prayer, and prayer doesn't stop work. It requires only that small raising of mind to Him. 'I love you, God, I trust you, I believe in you. I need you now.' Small things like that. They are wonderful prayers."[27]

Dag Hammarskjöld, an outwardly active and political man who gained prominence in Swedish politics and later died in a plane crash while trying to negotiate a cease-fire between United Nations and Katanja forces as Secretary General of the United Nations, left behind also a record of an inward man of prayer and contemplation. This record of Hammarskjöld's inner struggles he has described as "sort of a white book concerning my negotiations with myself and with God." One of his last prayers, written on July 19, 1961, reveals the close connection between a life of prayer and a man of the world working for peace between nations.[28]

> Have mercy
> Upon us.
> Have mercy
> Upon our efforts,
> That we
> Before Thee,
> In love and in faith,
> Righteousness and humility,
> May follow Thee,
> With self-denial, steadfastness, and courage,
> And meet Thee
> In the silence.
>
> Give us
> A pure heart
> That we may see Thee,
> A humble heart
> That we may hear Thee,
> A Heart of love
> That we may serve Thee,
> A heart of faith
> That we may live Thee,
>
> Thou
> Whom I do not know
> But Whose I am.
>
> Thou
> Whom I do not comprehend
> But Who hast dedicated me
> To my fate.
> Thou—

For workers outside the rigors of the cloistered life, the discipline of the daily devotional, done in a spirit of disciplined faithfulness rather than legalism, provides for regular spiritual nourishment. Popular children's author and librarian Madeleine L'Engle emphasizes the need for discipline in prayer, the need to "keep one's technique going." Telling of an instance when Serkin performed Beethoven's "Passionate Sonata," and played "better than Serkin can play," L'Engle says that that "moment of grace" happened because Serkin kept his technique going. "Prayer is like playing the piano," she says, completing the analogy. "You don't do it well every day, but unless you do it every day, you're never going to do it well."[29]

3. Nature

The creation of God as manifest in nature also provides a medium through which the transcendent touches the individual. The heavens tell the glory of God: the earth testifies to his grandeur. Alone in nature individuals feel an overwhelming insignificance, a humility before their Maker. At the same time they may experience a cosmic oneness, a part of the interrelatedness of all things, as they witness the rhythms of changing seasons, creation and consumption, birth and death. As in the life of Danilo Dolci, such an experience may mediate the understanding of God's call to go forth and be consumed.

I have found certain experiences of nature to have profound religious significance. Several years ago my wife and I hiked to a little Alpine lake, high in the Teton Mountains. I decided to go a bit farther and climb up to a ridge above the lake, hoping I might be able to look over to the other side. As I climbed and climbed, the ridge I hoped to reach kept eluding me. At each new level I discovered another and another ridge ahead. Finally, I stopped and looked back. I was now high above the lake. I was completely alone. I heard no human voices, saw no sign of human civilization, only the sound of the wind along the massive rock ledges of the rugged peaks. As I sat there trying to catch my breath I was simultaneously overwhelmed by two almost contradictory moods, a feeling of awe and reverence and a sense of wonder at the grandeur and majestic beauty of the mountains. I was also struck with fear, with a kind of terror, the vastness of the space and its power over against my weakness and insignificance.

Many of us may have had similar experiences in our lives—the vastness of space as we gaze at the stars, the expanse of the prairies in eastern Colorado, the grandeur of the Rocky Mountains, the huge thunderheads that build up in the plains and unleash their force and power, the sea expanding into infinity with its endless pounding upon the finite land. Paul Tillich drew basic images for his theology from the sea. In his book, *On the Boundary*, he writes that his concept of the infinite bordering on the finite supplied a metaphor for his thinking. I can remember sitting all day at

Scoodic Point on the coast of Maine watching the waves batter the shore. The swells would build and build until a massive wave would hit the rocks and send white spray into the air. Then the sea would subside, a sense of calm would prevail, until again the swells would build. This goes on and on. The sea is a symbol of infinity. It is a symbol of God—the Alpha and Omega. The land is a symbol of the human condition—finite, battered, and beaten by the waves, vulnerable and subject to erosion.

These images—the feeling of insignificance and aloneness in the vast space of the grandeur of the Teton Mountains, the infinity of the sea bordering on the finite land—these portray the human condition. They put reality in perspective. They express, I think, what Isaiah experienced in the temple: "Holy, holy, holy is the Lord God of hosts—the whole earth is full of his glory" and "Woe is me, for I am a man with unclean lips."

4. Culture

The creations of people manifest in various dimensions of culture may also serve as instruments of love and truth, because cultural creations are concrete "particulars," "incarnations" of universal experience. These creations function in a transcendent way when they point beyond their concreteness and particularity to the universal, the depth dimension of experience from which they came. Art can express the universal themes of human life, and bring these themes into the consciousness of the individual viewer. Good art confronts and affirms, convicts and inspires, and always demands response.

The graphics and sculpture of Prussian-born Käthe Kollwitz offer a prime illustration of the transcendent power of art, and how that power can further the cause of peace and justice. Through the selection of subjects she found beautiful—the workers, the poor, the patients of her physician husband—Käthe's art was a cathartic reconciliation of the universal themes of love and death, with her personal experiences of motherhood and grief (she lost a son in World War I and a grandson in World War II). Depicting only the oppressed, the victims of poverty and war, Käthe's works shouted out against social injustice, and denounced the brutality of war so strongly that Hitler's Third Reich labeled them "degenerate" and prohibited their exhibition.

As with art, so the individual encounter with music and story can similarly be a vehicle of transcendent transport. Music has long been dubbed the universal language, and conductor-composer Leonard Bernstein suggests that evidence in linguistic studies of children's songs may support that cliché. "Children the world over tease one another with the same sing-song, and play singing-games to remarkably similar tunes. A basic fabric of patterns and series (pentatonic, for example) can seriously and scientifically be called *universal.*"[31]

Further, the gamut of musical expression, from folk to classical, vocal to instrumental, contains aural imagery that reminds us of the vision of the unity of all being, of universal experience and universal worth. The blending of voices or orchestration of instruments into a harmonious whole is like the body with many parts. Variation and elaboration of a theme is the trademark of human culture; themes of human experience are the "one," the universals, standing in relation to the "many" particular expressions. And underlying the inevitable dissonance of chords or a meandering melodic line is the strong drive toward resolution of dissonance and return to the tonic, an image analogous to the truth-force which seeks reconciliation and harmony.

A pointed word of caution: analogies are useful tools, yet their efficacy is limited. To discuss music in words can at best bid us listen or create but can never replace the actual experience of listening or creating, for music exists to express in its own medium what none other can express. Music, like any other art, speaks in its own way, and with power. What individual can hear and not feel the pathos of folk music and spirituals? And who can remain unmoved by Beethoven's *Ninth Symphony* or Handel's *Messiah?*

Dorothy Day self-consciously incorporated art and music into the Catholic Worker movement. She believed the poor deserved the best, and so often musical groups or poets would perform at the Catholic Worker houses. The newspaper prominently featured the visual arts as a way of conveying concern for the poor—a medium as important as the written word.

The transcendent function of art, the power to "move," is equally operative in all the fine arts, such as literature and various forms of spoken and written word. These we categorize as "story."[32] Stories link patterns of events in time. Stories are the images and metaphors, the worldviews, which provide continuity and integration of a people's life and culture. Stories are imbedded with religious experience, and offer time-tested temporally translated answers to the great questions of human existence. Moral stories present principles in concrete context, providing a design, an orientation, for ethical action and response. Stories deal with the mundane and the extraordinary, the wondrous and varying themes of life. Each human life, too, may be described as a "continuous story." Thus every person can say, this is my story, this is the story of my people, this is What, How, and Why. In the words of Elie Wiesel, "God made man because He loves stories."[33]

By sharing stories we enlarge our experience vicariously, and gain increasing appreciation for different perspectives as we recognize universal elements in different stories. Says Annis Duff, an author who promotes good literature for children, "Once you have broken bread with people, even if it is only in a book, you are less likely to be intolerant of their customs and beliefs."[34] The sharing and real listening that can come about by telling life stories can have a profound impact upon the peacemaking process. Would that both Israelis and Palestinians could really hear each other's stories as narrated by Frank Epp in his two volumes, *The Israelis* and *The Palestinians*. These are stories of two people who have suffered deeply at the hands of others, now thrown together in the same land. Here they seem tragically fated to fight and struggle with each other, even though they share a common misery and pathos that could lead to empathy with each other's stories.

Earlier we mentioned the influence in writing of Tolstoy on Gandhi, and of Gandhi on King and Dolci. We could also list countless other instances in which individuals are convicted, inspired, and sustained by that which rings true in story, whether the story is encountered through drama, folk tale, great literature, or sacred text.

In summary, the peace vision can be imparted in a variety of ways through human culture. Art, music, story, and other forms can become vehicles through which human beings experience and are moved by the transcendent vision of shalom.

D. IN RELATEDNESS

We have chosen to illustrate the shaping and sustaining of peacemakers, the experience and working out of the shalom-vision, in terms of two dimensions: the solitary and the communal. The decision follows from the intent to illustrate that the two, each necessary and important, are not mutually exclusive. Rather, their relationship is one of interdependence, for the existence of the one depends upon the existence of the other. The qualities of experience, in solo and in concert, are interdependent, yet distinct. Each contains elements that are common and unique. Of the common elements, that which concerns us here is the shalom-vision. The experience and working out of the shalom-vision varies from solitary to group experience. The form and manner of individual experience have been described. Now we move to the discussion of the group experience. What are the means and structures which manifest the vision of redemption and hope in the communal experience? In that time together, how is the vision shared and worked out?

That which we call the social/communal experience encompasses many types of social interaction: from the close-knit religious fellowship which gathers to worship and discern together, then scatters to work in various capacities; to the vision-inspired social movement which calls persons to work and suffer together; to the task-oriented organizations whose members join together in order to accomplish a particular end. And, on each level or type of interaction, the creative capacities of holistic humans serve as tools of peace-work, and mediators of transcendent sustenance.

1. The Gathered Religious Community

We begin with a description of the gathered religious community. The ground of being for a religious community is the One who works in history to bring together a people of shalom. For it is in community that individuals find mutual forgiveness and support, common memory and vision, as they participate in the unfolding of a corporate history. The message of shalom and the experience of reconciliation are mediated to individuals through community. In community, the reconciled members become instruments which mediate shalom to the world.

This shalom-peoplehood is distinguished from other social gatherings in that it combines characteristics of community, ethic, and cult, all of which are a response to God's desire for shalom on earth. Such a community finds form in a pattern like that of the apostolic church, with its koinonia fellowship, commitment to radical discipleship and nonviolent love, and regular gatherings of worship and discernment.[35]

The kingdom of shalom on earth is a co-creation of God and those who respond in chosen obedience to the historical revelation of God in Christ. The resulting community is a fellowship of believers, drawn together voluntarily to commit their lives to each other in service of the kingdom. More than an institution, more than an instrument for the proclamation of divine work, more than a support group for individual pietism, this church is a koinonia, a fellowship, a loving-sharing community modeled on the early church as interpreted through the life and teachings of Christ.

Diverse groups from the time of the apostles to the present have taken the biblical description of early church communities as "having all things in common" to exemplify a literal mandate, and they structure their social and economic situations accordingly. An example is the Hutterian Brethren, a branch of Anabaptists whose colony format of Christian community originated in 1528 and functions to this day.[36]

In community, members find support and forgiveness. Members know each other by name, and love each other with Christ's agape love. The church sees that the various needs of its members are met, and in its fellowship exhibits to the world the love and peace which God desires for all beings.

Though the church lives in the midst of society and culture, its modes of belief and conduct should not be dictated by any surrounding authority. In the world but not of it, the church is marked by a glaring nonconformity, which results from the transforming work of grace. Grace makes possible a life of holiness, a holiness not relegated to the realm of inner piety. Neither is it diluted to denote sanctimonious withdrawal. Rather, holiness is to be realized in everyday aspects of life. In the peace church community, members call each other to holy and righteous living, and in their lifestyle model their eschatology—the present reality of the kingdom to come. They are salt and light for the world.

This church of peacemakers is fundamentally characterized by its visible practice of uncommon ethical response: a practice of radical discipleship grounded in nonviolent love, which is obedient even in suffering. Disciples are followers of Christ, the Prince of Peace, for faith in Christ implies following him in life. The frame of reference for disciples is the life and teachings of Christ, particularly the teachings of the Sermon on the Mount. The form of discipleship is implied in the person and work of Christ. In its concreteness, discipleship means mission, service, and active nonviolent love.

The vocation of mission, a response to the Great Commission, seeks to spread the kingdom of shalom to all people. An attitude of service follows from Christ's example of servanthood. Agape love, which Christ described as the sum of the Law and the Prophets, is the principle which determines the form of all action. Discipleship, then, describes the way of life which is the way of the Prince of Peace.

Moreover, this radical discipleship is a communal vocation, not a solo enterprise. The community functions to act radically in concert, to support individual members (financially, spiritually, emotionally, physically) as they encounter dissonance, and to discern together the appropriate forms of action and response.

At the heart of radical discipleship is the experience of grace and subsequent transformation. As it is commonly viewed, grace neither involves nor invokes, but is disjunct from, ethical action. In some traditions the receipt of grace is essentially participation in the sacraments. The Lutheran tradition focuses on the inner faith response to the gospel. The shalom church, however, recognizes both the inner and sacramental-symbolic aspects of grace, but goes beyond both to emphasize the resulting transformation and subsequent application of grace in all human actions and relationships. The implications of such grace are radical and costly.

Membership in such a community is, then, a mature *voluntary* decision, which has been symbolized in the form of adult baptism. This community views baptism as a covenant of complete commitment to the being and teaching of Christ. Baptism into Christ means being baptized with his baptism, which is a baptism of water, fire, and blood. In reference to his death, Jesus said, "I have a baptism to be baptized with" (Luke 12:50). The church which partakes in the baptism of the Prince of Peace may be called to suffer with him as well, even unto death on a cross.

The congregational life of a community of disciples must involve discernment, the process by which a congregation formulates its identity as disciples, and understands its ethical responsibility in the world. Put simply, discernment is ethical decision-making. The structure in which this activity takes place is not hierarchical, with decisions handed down by clerical pronouncement. Nor are decisions reached through forum discussions and majority vote, methods which arrive at a decision at the expense of a feeling of community, and which tend to polarize and alienate minority views. Rather, the congregation which practices discernment joins together in an atmosphere of mutuality to engage in a process of dialogical give-and-take, culminating in consensus. The drive toward concensus is like the drive of the truth-force toward reconciliation and harmony.

Yet more important than the end is the process itself which consists of discussion and illumination of biblical text, both under the guidance of the Spirit. In discussion, the most difficult task is often that of listening—of openness in mind and heart to hear and understand another's point of view, of openness to the word of God as spoken through another brother or sister. Faithful listening requires inner silence, and a confession that complete understanding belongs to none of us. Faithful listening also implies an attitude of honest searching—a willingness to understand, consider, and perhaps be changed. The Society of Friends, originating out of the radical wing of the Puritan movement in seventeenth-century England, has provided the best model of this form of discernment.

The interpretation of biblical texts in discernment should also be a communal venture led by the Spirit. Biblical scholars can help a congregation understand the original context, meaning, and purpose of writings in enabling the congregation to formulate the meaning and application for today. But the total enterprise is a joint effort. Together, members can share insights and counsel against unsound interpretation.

When the discernment process is completed, all should have had the opportunity to speak and to be heard. Each should have learned and grown. If consensus has been reached, the body can speak with one voice; if not, much has still been gained, for all have grown together in the process of dialogue, and the lines of communication essential to community health are still open. Commitment to communal discernment is essentially a commitment to ongoing conversation.

Another activity of the gathered community, in addition to discernment, is that of worship. Earlier we discussed the individual experience of the sacred; worship is the corporate experience of the sacred. The gathering for worship also serves to sustain vision by keeping alive the common memory. Experiences of the sacred and significant historical events are so important that men and women distinguish certain times for remembrance and celebration. Annual holy days and festivals mark the calendar, and one day a week is designated the Sabbath, the day of rest and worship. These occasions represent a separation from the everyday and the material things that fill the week and offer demarcation of holiness in time.

Judaism has much to contribute to an appropriate understanding of the Sabbath. Abraham Heschel, in *The Sabbath*, describes Judaism as a religion of time, not space. The Jewish Sabbath symbolizes the sanctification of time, so that the Sabbaths are the "great cathedrals" of Judaism. Ritual is characterized as the "art of significant forms in time," and the "architecture of time."[37] Twentieth-century men and women, subject to the fragmenting dominion of digital timepieces and sophisticated secularism, need reminders of the long-forgotten, yet fundamental, life-rhythm of ritual and holy times.

The Sabbath, then, is the holy time, the day of gathering for worship and sustaining common memory, celebrating the unfolding of corporate history. Vision and memory are inextricably linked, for it is the vitality of memory that provides vision for the future. Insecurity about a past, the question of identity, undermines security in the present and strips the future of conviction. A people needs to remind themselves of who they are; people of a vision must remind themselves of that vision. That end is accomplished by the sharing and repeating of corporate historical events in a variety of media—reading of sacred text, telling of historical stories, singing of hymns, saying of prayers, and the ritual nourishment of the sacraments.

Sacred texts set forth in written record the primary experience of the sacred, the moments of *kairos* and revelation in history, and the reading of that text serves to pass on the vision imparted in the original experience. The historical stories of people, the heroes and heroines of the faith, need to be told again and again, for education of the young and edification of the old.

When the Lord passed over Egypt, for example, slaying the first-born of the Egyptians in order to bring about the deliverance of Israel from bondage, he instructed the Israelites to mark their doorposts with sacrificial blood, and to eat unleavened bread and bitter herbs. He also instructed them to keep that day as a memorial day, and observe it forever.

Mennonites in the seventeenth and eighteenth centuries, harassed and persecuted, carried with them usually two books, the *Bible* and the *Martyrs Mirror*. The former was the only book which could neither be taken from them nor banned from circulation. The latter was a collection of stories of men and women who were faithful unto death. Supplemental to these two records was the *Ausbund*, which contained their hymns of faith. These were the documents, the "journals," that sustained the vision of the Mennonites by preserving the memory of their experience. To outside scholars of the time they must have seemed "only the mournful and credulous apologetic of a harried people."[38]

Rituals in the form of liturgy replicate the experience of the sacred, and provide specific forms to record the identity of a people. As voices blend in singing of traditional hymns, congregations unite in expression of solidarity and identity. In corporate prayer the body of believers unites in one voice or in silence before God.

The most important celebration of memory is the ritual of the Lord's Supper. This ritual is one of the most meaningful and powerful symbols of the Christian church. The testimony of many individuals attests to its richness in meaning, its edifying power in sustaining the shalom vision.

For Dietrich Bonhoeffer, communion was the culmination of the common life in Christ. Reconciled to God and man, the fellowship joyfully gathers and unites in the body and blood of Christ. "Here the community has reached its goal. Here joy in Christ and the community is complete. The life of Christians together under the Word has reached its perfection in the sacrament."[39]

Dorothy Day, cofounder of the Catholic Worker movement, finds the sacrament analogous to the nourishment a young child receives from her mother: "We drink milk from the breast of our mother. We are nourished while we are in the womb by the blood of her heart. From her flesh and from her blood we grow before we enter into this life, and so from the Body and Blood of Jesus we are nourished for life eternal."[40] Day finds that the original joy which first brought her to the faith is constantly renewed as she daily receives "our Lord at Mass."[41]

Mother Teresa, winner of the 1979 Nobel prize for her service to Calcutta's poor, depends on the nourishment of the sacrament for her work. She says:

> If we can see Jesus in the appearance of bread, we can see Him in the broken bodies of the poor. . . . When we have that deepening of contact with Christ and can accept Him fully, we can touch the broken bodies. We put it into practice straight away. . . . You feed yourself in the Eucharist and after you are fed you want to use that energy, to give

it out. That is why you see the Sisters run, they never walk. They call us a "running congregation."[42]

At the heart of the Roman Catholic mass is the sign of peace. Before the congregation shares in the bread together, the people express their love for each other and petition each other for peace and unity in the church and with all humanity.

The apostle Paul describes the breaking and eating of bread as a participation in the body of Christ, done in remembrance of his broken body. The drinking of the cup of wine is a participation in the blood of Christ, done in remembrance of his sacrifice of life (1 Corinthians 11:24, 25; 1 Corinthians 10:16). Bread, the universal stuff of human sustenance, so simple and so basic, when broken and shared in a group of people, becomes a symbol of nourishment, of solidarity, and of communion. The eating together of a common meal is an all-embracing gesture of friendship and love, understood the world over.

Followers of Christ in the shalom community break bread and drink wine to show that they keep him in their hearts and minds. The partaking of the Supper is also a sign of communal love and solidarity, for just as the grain becomes one loaf of which all partake, so all are members of one body (1 Corinthians 10:17). The Supper is an important ritual of nourishment and memory, maintaining the identity and fellowship of a body of believers.

2. Movements and Organizations

The church we have described is a people of shalom which gathers regularly to discern their course of discipleship, and sustain their memory through corporate acts of worship—prayer, song, ritual. Then nourished and edified, they scatter to work for peace in a variety of capacities, some in organizations created specifically to promote peace, others in secular vocations to which they bring a peace perspective.

Some groups, as noted earlier, combine their religious community with a social and economic community, and as such do not experience the rhythm of gathering and scattering. For others, such as the Catholic Worker movement, the daily work of those in the community is that of the *movement*.

New York's Lower East Side witnessed the birth of the Catholic Worker Movement in 1933, cofounded by French peasant and social philosopher Peter Maurin and leftist journalist-turned-Catholic Dorothy Day. Combining ideals of community, personal action, nonviolence, and voluntary poverty, the movement called for a "personalist revolution" in society, to be achieved through a synthesis of "cult, culture, and cultivation." The synthesis was embodied in the founding of urban communities which provided food and shelter to the unemployed, and rural farming communes which offered opportunity to those pushed out of the urban economy. There are presently about 50 of these communes scattered across the country.[43]

The voice of the movement is a newspaper, *The Catholic Worker*, which consistently advocates nonviolent pacifism and social reform. Those who have contributed to the *Worker* often feel they cannot write about the issues without experiencing them, and often join in protests and acts of civil disobedience. The purpose of *The Catholic Worker* is "not just to print news, but to create it," for, in the words of Peter Maurin, the *Worker* "was not just a journal of opinion, but a revolution, a way of life."[44]

Another type of communal structure is the Movement for a New Society (MNS). This structure, which grew out of A Quaker Action Group in 1971, erects living centers and projects which provide fellowship and support, and encourages simple lifestyle. Integral to MNS is analysis of political and economic conditions, collective work, and community involvement, and a vision of nonviolence which embraces political action as well as responsible, joyful living.

Other social efforts incorporating the vision of shalom embody neither the communal structure nor the church fellowship. Yet they work for a cause with religious fervor and inspiration. One example among many is the civil rights movement, championed by Martin Luther King. King's nonviolent movement began with his leadership of the Montgomery bus boycott in 1955, just a year after his move to Montgomery to pastor Dexter Avenue Baptist Church.

The Montgomery bus boycott is an excellent illustration of the importance of strategy, organization, and charismatic leadership. The city-wide boycott was implemented on Monday, December 5, only four days after Rosa Parks' historic refusal to give up her bus seat and subsequent arrest. King's group, calling themselves the Montgomery Improvement Association (MIA), arranged alternative transportation with black taxi cab drivers, who agreed to provide their services at the same rate as bus fare. When the police commissioner issued an order requiring all taxi companies to charge the regular fare, King and his organizers mobilized in only four days a car-pool system with routes and dispatch/pickup stations, employing over 300 automobiles.

The boycott lasted for a year, yet week after week crowds came together to sing and pray, renew courage, and hear the words of their leaders. At these meetings King's charismatic leadership shone through. His passionate commitment to the cause of justice and nonviolent love inspired hundreds of thousands to support the movement, and his words instructed masses on the philosophy and implementation of nonviolent tactics.[46]

Leaders must not only be able to strategize and inspire. They must also be able to keep their following united, and resolve possible divisive elements within the movement. King successfully averted a potential crisis in the later days of the bus boycott, when the recording secretary of the MIA, Rev. U. J. Fields, resigned and accused the leadership of seeking personal gain, misrepresenting the people, and misusing funds. Later, at Fields' initiative, he and King met to talk. Fields confessed that his accusations grew out of personal conflict with several board members, and that his charges of misappropriation were totally unfounded and made in a moment of anger.

Sentiment against Fields had risen rapidly in the black community, and King wanted to heal the rift and unify the movement in the spirit of forgiveness. At the mass meeting that evening, King expressed his faith in the structure of the MIA, and insisted there had been no misappropiation of funds. He then asked the assembly to forgive Fields in the spirit of the nonviolent movement, speaking the words of Jesus, "Let him who is without sin cast the first stone," and recounting the parable of the Prodigal son. When Fields asked forgiveness of the group, assuring them he had no evidence of misuse of money, he was supported with solid applause. A situation that might have destroyed the MIA, when handled by King in the manner of nonviolent love, consolidated the movement even more.[47]

Gandhi faced similar problems in his first year of action in India, when he had to cool the fires of anger that were ready to burst into violence at the least provocation. He relied heavily on the maintenance of order and discipline in order to prevent chaos. Gandhi also knew that good leaders must extinguish their own desire for power, and train their followers to continue in their absence. Gandhi's two-year imprisonment did not leave the movement in shambles, for his followers had learned how to proceed using his methods.[48]

A leader must also be capable of discovering and modeling the exemplary act, the symbolic action which will ignite a people's courage to resist injustice with their whole lives. George Lakey, strategist of the Movement for a New Society, calls these acts the "propaganda of the deed," the spreading of the message through the drama of action.[49] Gandhi was a master of the exemplary act. His initiation of the Salt March, through the simple gesture of bending over and picking up a handful of salt from the shore, began a nonviolent revolution which eventually won India's freedom from British rule.

The United Farm Workers Organization under the leadership of Cesar Chavez also manifests the important facets of organization and strategy mentioned earlier. Chavez insists on organization and flexibility:

> There has to be a real organization, a living organization . . . people in motion, and they have to be disciplined. . . . We're so flexible, yet there's so much discipline that we do things and don't even talk about them. . . . For instance, we can be striking today, and tomorrow morning or a couple of days later we can move the effort into a boycott without missing a step. We have motion and rhythm. That mobility makes a difference.[50]

Preliminary to effective organization and strategy is research, a thorough investigation of the situation. Chavez' successful organizing of the grape strike and international grape boycott began with an exhaustive investigation of local labor conditions and interviews with the workers. Then came the construction of an expansive network of committed relationships, the organizational skeleton of the movement.

At the base of any organization or movement is the solidarity of the common cause. Movements, too, perish without vision. The vision that led King's movement was one of cosmic justice, accomplished through the method of nonviolent love. Gandhi and his followers were led by satyagraha, the truth-force driving toward reconciliation. The common cause of the United Farm Workers was the life of poverty they all shared, including their leader, Chavez. That poverty, combined with community and the "truth of an uncontradicted cause," inspired the strength of Chavez' organization.[51]

Movements and organizations which work for peace and justice thus take varying forms. Some combine their goals with a religious impetus, others become primary social communities for work and faith. Others are task-oriented, volunteer organizations. Yet all require good leadership, organization, and vision, and all may serve as instruments of shalom.

The spreading of shalom in the social sphere is also accomplished through forms of culture such as music, visual communication, and printed word. Music, for example, has accompanied the rhythm of people's movements from their inception in human history. The history of the United States alone contains a rich heritage of folk music, people's music—from the Revolutionary and Civil wars, the pioneering of the Western frontier, the bondage of slavery, the struggle for unions and labor organization, the Depression, the civil rights, and anti-Vietnam War movements. There are union songs, suffragette songs, temperance songs, and parodies, ballads, and spirituals. Tom Glazer has collected over 160 of these songs and published them in a book called *Songs of Peace, Freedom and Protest.*

Singers and songwriters are visible. Think of Joan Baez, Bob Dylan, Pete Seeger. Their music spread like light across the land. Songs carry lyrics which record stories and convey pathos of experience. Theologian James Cone even suggests that the spirituals of the black community were an expression of black theology and eschatology: the "blues" were "secular" spirituals in that they refused to adopt a God-centered perspective.[52]

Singers also inspire and unite. Remember the mesmerizing fervor of Mahalia Jackson's charismatic spirituals during the Civil Rights movement. Gandhi too knew of the mass power of music, and lamented its absence in his movement: "Our great stumbling block is that we have neglected music. Music means rhythm, order. . . . I would make compulsory a proper singing, in company, of national songs. And to that end I would have great musicians attending every congress or conference and teaching mass music."[53]

Finally, music brings results: Paul and Silas sang and prayed through the night in jail, and at midnight an earthquake loosed their fetters and opened the prison doors. They chose not to escape, a choice which brought the jailer and his whole household to adopt the faith of Paul and Silas, who were later released (Acts 16:25-36). Nineteen hundred years later, in Greensburg, Pennsylvania, wives of striking coal miners were arrested for disturbing the peace. The women sang in jail, all night and all day, and so irritated the residents of neighboring hotels and private homes, not to mention the sheriff and his wife, that after five days the judge ordered their release![54]

Visual communication in the form of graphics, posters, placards, billboards, and even costumes spreads the message of peace in society. Artists can use their medium to illustrate injustice and oppression, placing issues before the eyes of viewers in such a way that demands attention and response. The work of Käthe Kollwitz comes to mind, as does Picasso's "Guernica," a vivid political statement on the horrors of war.

The power of the printed word to inform and remind is similarly a force to be harnessed. *The Catholic Worker,* for example, spreads its message on newsprint, illustrated with poignant woodcuts, to over 60,000 subscribers. The *Worker* prints social critiques and stories of poverty so that "we all may constantly repent and start over again, God help us."[55]

Social critic Thomas Merton penned precise, insightful social analysis and commentary, as well as profound theological writings, from the silence of his Trappist abbey in Kentucky. And the Sicilian Gandhi, Danilo Dolci, has authored several volumes of poetry, stories, case studies, trial proceedings, and documents, in his campaign to attract public attention, expose cankerous social ills, and break the conspiracy of silence which kept the Sicilian Mafia in power.

This has been but a hasty overview of the way in which art, music, and story can support social movements. Also worthy of mention are the forms of dance, film, theater, and numerous other human activities which can be used to further the shalom vision. All of them, when redeemed and transformed, can be instruments of the work of shalom in society.

E. SUSTAINED BY HOPE

The issue addressed in this chapter is the edification and sustenance of peacemakers, as individuals and in community. We have traveled the inner journeys as shared from individual experience, and worked and worshiped via the records of communal endeavor. Finally, we return to the vision which sustains and inspires both. We hear again of the power of eschatological hope. For life lived in faithfulness to the vision of shalom often entails dissonance with surrounding society. Disciples of peace, alone and together, may face suffering and persecution. The vision which they follow may appear tarnished or untenable. When utterly fatigued, especially after heady enthusiasm and initial naïveté have worn off, and ugly realities and personal pieties are faced head on, peacemakers are especially vulnerable to burnout, despair, disillusionment. In the hours of silent darkness, whence comes the renewal of vision, the words to speak, and the dawn of hope?

Needed are energies that renew, that replenish the burned-up supply, without demanding more energy in turn. Margaret Mead's statement about resources that do not demand energy may remind us of alternative sources: "Prayer does not use up any artificial energy, it doesn't burn up any fossil fuel, it doesn't pollute. Neither does song, neither does love, neither does the dance." Prayer, song, love, dance—these are sustenance, part of a daily balanced diet for peacemakers.

When futility strikes in the weak moments, it undermines the significance of small faithful acts, leaving a void of hopelessness. Dorothy Day, in her book *Loaves and Fishes*, recounts the story of the Catholic Worker movement, and offers these words:

> Young people say, What is the sense of our small effort? They cannot see that we must lay one brick at a time, take one step at a time; we can be responsible only for the one action at the present moment. But we can beg for an increase of love in our hearts that will vitalize and transform all our individual actions, and know that God will take them and multiply them, as Jesus multiplied the loaves and fishes.[56]

The greatest challenge of the day is: how to bring about a revolution of the heart, a revolution which has to start with each one of us? When we begin to take the lowest place, to wash the feet of others, to love our brothers with that burning love, that passion, which led to the Cross, then we can truly say, "Now I have begun."

Day after day we accept our failure, but we accept it because of our knowledge of the victory of the Cross. God has given us our vocation, as he gave it to the small boy who contributed his few loaves and fishes to help feed the multitude, and which Jesus multiplied so that he fed five thousand people.[57]

The key, as suggested in the above passages, is a faithfulness through the conviction that the work of shalom is the work of a higher power, which enables, energizes and sustains, and makes fruitful all action. For that power has provided manna in the wilderness, and has promised the Spirit to comfort and give words to speak in the hour of trial. The action of that power in history to initiate a kingdom of shalom, culminating in the person of Christ, makes possible the present reality of the kingdom. The risen Christ has assured the victory of his kingdom over the powers of death and destruction. Because of Christ, the kingdom is here, a present reality in the midst of the world! In Christ, the work is being accomplished.

Praise God that Christ can set individuals free before the society or even the church is ready. A family can start to live a simple lifestyle and give to the poor. A couple can refuse to pay war tax. A man can be set free from racial prejudice. A woman can be freed into power and confidence.... Christ has taught us how to love, in the midst of conflict. His Holy Spirit is among us to guide us and heal our brokenness. And He has promised us grace to overcome the world.[58]

The problem of sustaining hope in time of despair becomes less a problem, because the work of shalom is the work of God in history, and the victory has already been accomplished in Christ. Finally, in the words of James Forest, coordinator of the International Fellowship of Reconciliation, "It is, after all, not we who hope, but God who hopes in us; and because it is God who has the hope, that hope is sure."[59] Amen and Amen.   O

Notes

Chapter one

1. Roland Bainton, *Christian Attitudes Toward War and Peace*, chapter 1.

2. These two contrasting emphases have been identified in the scholarly literature with the terms "negative peace" and "positive peace." Johann Galtung, in the *International Encyclopedia of the Social Sciences* (Vol. II, pp. 487-496) defines negative peace as the absence of overt personal violence and positive peace as the presence of social justice.

A similar distinction is used by Paul Wehr, who refers to positive peace "as a set of social, economic and political conditions which insure nonviolent, non-exploitative, equitable and just relationships between individuals, groups and nations" (Paul Wehr, "Developing the Study of Peace and Conflict," paper presented at the joint meetings of the Society for Applied Anthropology, the American Ethnological Society, and the Council on Anthropology and Education, Montreal, 1972, p. 7). Adam Curle says that, in general, books dealing with peace or its opposite are concerned with hostilities between nations, groups, or individuals, and the ways in which they may be curbed or prevented (Adam Curle, *Making Peace*, p. 2). I, however, take the view of Galtung, who maintains that "violence exists whenever an individual's potential development, mental or physical, is held back by the conditions of a relationship."

3. See the book by Ralph Potter, *The Moral Logic of War*, for a brief description of the just war theory. In Christian thought the theory goes back to Ambrose and Augustine. The concept of *shalom* is an eschatological concept for the Hebrew prophets, the hope for a future in which righteousness and justice will reign on earth. Since humans know of no situation in which there is peace with justice in a complete sense, and in fact most human situations are very far from the realization of shalom, a growing pessimism about the possibilities of peace on earth developed. The church developed as its dominant position a theory of just war which was resigned to the permanence of evil in the world and war as an unfortunate but necessary institution due to humanity's evil. Since war is inevitable under conditions of sin, the church sought to give ethical guidelines establishing conditions under which violent force could be used to preserve peace and order.

4. For an excellent description of the Calvinist theocratic vision see Michael Walzer's book, *The Revolution of the Saints*.

5. See these books on nonviolent defense: Anders Boserup, and Andrew Mark, *War Without Weapons: Nonviolence in National Defense*; Robin Remington, ed., *Winter in Prague: Documents on Czechoslovakia Communism in Crisis*; Olar Riste, and Berit Nokleby, *Norway: 1940-1945: The Resistance Movement*; Adam Roberts, *Civilian Resistance as a National Defense*; Yuri Suhl, ed., *They Fought Back: The Story of Jewish Resistance in Nazi Europe*; Werner Warmbrunn, *The Dutch Under German Occupation 1940-45*; Philip Windsor, and Adam Roberts, *Czechoslovakia 1968: Reform, Repression and Resistance*. Also for a short description of the idea see Gene Sharp, *Making the Abolition of War a Realistic Goal*, available from the Institute for World Order.

6. Kenneth Boulding, *The Meaning of the 20th Century*, p. 90.

7. See the book of essays in honor of James L. Adams, edited by D. B. Robertson, *Voluntary Associations, A Study of Groups in Free Societies*.

8. Gene Sharp, *The Politics of Nonviolent Action*, and George Lakey, *Strategy for a Living Revolution*.

Chapter Two

1. Quincy Wright, *A Study of War* (abridged edition), p. 124.
2. Ibid.
3. Robert O. Keohane and Joseph Nye, *Power and Interdependence*, p. 27. See also the book edited by them, *Transnational Relations and World Politics*.
4. One of the most important issues in international relations theory is what model can best account for international behavior. In a book, *Globalism Versus Realism: International Relations Third Debate*, editors Ray Maghroori and Bennett Ramberg state: "Although realists and globalists disagree on the essential character of the international system, they both accept one point: models do count. They argue that 'one's assumptions about world politics profoundly affect what one sees and how one constructs theories to explain events' " (Keohane and Nye, op. cit., p. 23). Even more important, they believe that "the model we impose on the world affects directly the policies we prescribe" (Michael P. Sullivan, "Competing Frameworks and the Study of Contemporary International Studies," *Millennium: Journal of International Studies* [Autumn 1978], p. 73).
5. Richard Barnet, *The Giants: Russia and America*, p. 145. Copyright © 1977 by Richard J. Barnet. Reprinted by permission of Simon & Schuster, Inc.
6. Edwin O. Reischauer, *Toward the 21st Century: Education for a Changing World*, p. 43.
7. Ibid., p. 52.
8. Russett's view as summarized by Charles R. Beitz and Theodore Herman, ed., in *Peace and War*, p. 214. W. H. Freeman and Company. Copyright © 1973.
9. Richard Barnet and Ronald Muller, *Global Reach: The Power of Multinational Corporations*, pp. 14-19. Copyright © 1974 by Richard J. Barnet and Ronald E. Muller. Reprinted by permission of Simon & Schuster, Inc.
10. Karl Deutsch, *The Analysis of International Relations*, pp. 17-18.
11. Gene Sharp, *The Politics of Nonviolent Action*, pp. 8-9.
12. Kenneth Boulding, *The Meaning of the 20th Century*, p. 87.
13. Paul Ramsey, "A Political Ethics Context for Strategic Thinking," in *Strategic Thinking and Its Moral Implications*, ed. by Morton A. Kaplan, p. 104.
14. Quoted by Peter A. Corning, "Human Violence: Some Causes and Implications," in *Peace and War*, ed. by Charles R. Beitz and Theodore Herman, p. 120.
15. Ibid., p. 120.
16. Ibid., p. 120.
17. Paul Wehr, *Conflict Regulation*, pp. 15-16. Several additional points can be made about the "human nature" theories. Biological theories explaining war in terms of the human instinct of territoriality and aggression have serious empirical problems. One question is whether it is legitimate to generalize from animal behavior to human behavior. It is clear that humans are fundamentally different from animals in their expression of aggression by engaging in organized group intraspecific mass killing. Aggression in the animal kingdom is designed for purposes of survival of the species by protecting certain territories for purposes of mating, raising the young, and providing food. Usually animals of the same species are warned against infringing upon the territory of another animal by some kind of signaling system. When an infringement is made and there is a fight between the animals, seldom, if ever, is the result the killing of one animal by the other. The usual response is flight. Another problem with the aggression theory is that this theory does not sufficiently take into account the existence of other factors such as cooperativeness in the human genetic inheritance. Certainly in order for human beings to have survived this long, it has been necessary for them to develop deeply ingrained traits of cooperativeness. This is especially the case with humans because the rearing of the young is such a long process. Cooperativeness has also been operative in the development of technology, the passing of information of one generation to another, in hunting and the secur-

ing of food, and is absolutely essential to a highly differentiated technological society in which we depend upon each other for our survival. For an excellent critique of the "aggression theories" of Lorenz and others see Ashley Montague, *The Nature of Human Aggression*.

18. John C. Bennett and Harvey Seifert, *U.S. Foreign Policy and Christian Ethics*, pp. 17-18.

19. Ramsey, op. cit., p. 104.

Chapter three

1. One of the most helpful books on the role of the Bible in ethics is by Larry Rasmussen and Bruce C. Birch, *The Bible and Ethics in the Christian Life*. I agree with their view that a Christian ethic, when it makes use of the Bible, cannot be arbitrarily selective, but must take seriously the entire canon.

2. The misuse of the Bible in giving guidance to the church today can be seen in the discussion of male-female roles. A direct literal application of Paul would seem to support the subordination of women to men. Yet if we see the New Testament view of women in the context of the culture of the time, women have remarkable degrees of freedom and responsibility as compared to the surrounding culture. These new roles stood in such sharp contrast to the surrounding culture that evidently the new patterns became somewhat of a scandal and embarrassment to the church. It is in this context that Paul urges on women some of the old Jewish patterns. Paul's prescriptions are clearly formulated for the setting of the church in the ancient world. Our setting is different from Paul's. It would be a mistake to apply Paul's prescriptions for his setting and to his time so as to inhibit the process of transformation of female-male roles in our setting and our time. The question we have to ask is how does the message of the gospel of Christ, in which there is "neither male or female," apply to our setting? Books which struggle with the issue of how one interprets the Bible on this issue are Krister Stendahl's *The Bible and the Role of Women* and Paul Jewett's *Man as Male and Female*. Also see Willard Swartley's *Slavery, Sabbath, War, and Women* for a thorough discussion of the methods of biblical interpretation used in this issue.

3. The organization of my thinking into these four areas has been influenced by the helpful book by Richard Mouw, *Politics and the Biblical Drama*.

4. John H. Yoder, *The Politics of Jesus*, p. 143. Yoder draws heavily upon Hendrik Berkhof's work, *Christ and the Powers*. See other references in Yoder's book, p. 142.

5. There has been a great deal of speculation in theological thinking about what is the meaning of God's image in humanity. Most theological views have attempted either to define this image in terms of human reason, or the spiritual or religious dimension of humanity. These attempts are problematic because they are forced to posit some "divine" spark in people, as if there were a special property in humans that is not finite but divine. The debate has then been over whether this image remains in people in any respect after the Fall. The link between the divine image and human sociality which makes humans creators of culture suggests an approach which avoids these problems of a "divine" spark. Gordon Kaufman develops this approach with his view of the "imago dei as man's historicity." "Man is preeminently a historical being because he is both made by his history and he himself makes history (p. 333). In all our relations with others they create us and we them . . . . Selves are not independent and isolated atoms, but relational realities gaining the form and substance of their being through the relations in which they stand" (p. 334). People create culture because of this fact that they are social creatures with the capacity of language and social interaction. In this creative capacity, human beings "image" God in themselves through the dynamic process of social and cultural transformation.

This approach avoids the problem of whether God's image is effaced by the Fall. For in this view, human beings in their fundamental capacity as humans (i.e., as historical beings) express the divine image. We are not forced to the view either that this image disappears nor are we forced to conclude that human beings in some way possess a special divine spark, which in some way makes us less than the finite creatures that we are. Gordon Kaufman, *Systematic Theology: A Historicist Perspective*, pp. 329f. See also other theologians who link human sociality and the "imago dei": Karl Barth, *Church Dogmatics III/1*, p. 192; Richard Mouw, *Politics and the Biblical Drama*, pp. 24f.; Paul Jewett, *Man as Male and Female*, pp. 32f.

6. I am indebted to many for this social view of humans. I was particularly influenced by my graduate school adviser at Harvard Divinity School, James L. Adams, and by my subsequent dissertation research on the work of Ernst Troeltsch. This social view of the self is reflected in many works in the social sciences, but I particularly point to the work of George H. Mead, *Mind, Self and Society*. I'm also heavily influenced by my own past as a Mennonite where social-communal forces have been very strong in shaping my own values and perspective on theology.

7. Ashly Montagu, *The Nature of Human Aggression*, pp. 160-161.

8. Karl Deutsch, *An Analysis of International Relations*, p. 17.

9. Kaufman, op. cit., pp. 336-337.

10. Ibid., p. 343.

11. See the classic statement of this problem in Reinhold Neibuhr's book, *Moral Man and Immoral Society*. Niebuhr argues quite persuasively that when human beings operate in collectives as groups they tend to operate according to principles of self-interest. Moralistic appeals to conscience—as if the groups were individuals who are altruistic—are thus unrealistic and ineffective.

12. For a helpful description of the nature of social reality as understood from the standpoint of the New Testament language of "principalities" "powers" and "cosmos" see Stephen Mott's *Biblical Ethics and Social Change*, p. 10f. Mott characterizes social life in the following ways: one, its formal elements are much older than the individuals who constitute it; two, it goes on with relatively little dependence upon conscious individual decision making or responsibility; three, it often consists of complex problems for which there seem to be no solutions.

13. John H. Yoder, *The Politics of Jesus*, p. 143.

14. Erich Fromm, *Escape to Freedom*, p. 50.

15. See Mouw's critique of Fromm, op. cit., pp. 39-41. This misunderstanding partly arises in Western thought out of the dichotomy between pure and practical reason in Kant. Within the realm of pure reason humanity is totally determined, but within practical reason action is a totally autonomous act, a self-initiated act unaffected by empirical reality. Kant's understanding of freedom lies in back of much modern existentialist thought.

16. Mouw, op. cit., p. 41.

17. The link of salvation to social structures is seen in a number of theological works, ranging from Walter Rauschenbush's *Theology for a Social Gospel* to Gustavo Gutierrez's *A Theology of Liberation*. This emphasis upon the structural or social nature of evil is evident in New Testament studies in the discussion of the "principalities and powers." But this emphasis was also already present in the religious socialists and the social gospel movement. In my own past experience the failure of the church to understand the social nature of evil was evident in the way in which texts like Isaiah 1:18 ("Though your sins are scarlet, they may become white as snow", NEB) were lifted out of their social context (the sins referred to in the context of Isaiah are injustice and oppression) and in the situation of a revival service applied to individual sin and conversion of the individual to God. See Mott, op. cit., p. 17.

18. The Tower of Babel story in Genesis 11:1-9 appears to support the view that the pluralism of human cultures and languages itself is a result of human sinfulness. The sin of the Tower of Babel project is not pluralism, however, but just the opposite. The story symbolizes a corporate effort expressing the human desire to be as God ("a tower with its top in the heavens" Gen. 11:4). The main point of this text in the Genesis narrative is to point to the general pattern of human sin (the Tower of Babel story is preceded by the Flood story) which

sets the stage for God's redemptive intervention in human history to create a special people from the seed of Abraham.

19. I have been influenced very much in this section by the ideas of H. R. Niebuhr, particularly his distinction between radical monotheism and henotheism. See his *Radical Monotheism and Western Culture*. This idolatry is expressed also in piety and prayer life. Take the example of a prayer by a bomber pilot for God to protect him while he delivers a load of bombs upon a city whose inhabitants are also praying for protection. Can this be regarded as anything but a prayer to an idol, to the henotheistic god of "my" people, rather than a prayer to the Lord who cares for all being?

20. Jacques Ellul, *Violence*, pp. 94, 98. See also John Swomley's analysis of the continuity of means and ends in his study of specific revolutionary movements in his book *Liberation Ethics*.

CHAPTER FOUR

1. Gerhard von Rad, "Shalom in the Old Testament," *Theological Dictionary of the New Testament*, ed. by Gerhard Kittel, Vol. II, p. 402. For a very helpful statement of the biblical view of shalom, see *Living Toward a Vision: Biblical Reflections on Shalom*, by Walter Brueggemann.

2. Ibid., p. 406.

3. Ibid., p. 403.

4. George E. Mendenhall, *Law and Covenant in Israel and the Ancient Near East*.

5. Ibid., p. 25.

6. John Bright, *A History of Israel*, p. 135.

7. Mendenhall, op. cit., p. 19. See Millard Lind's *Yahweh Is a Warrior: The Theology of Warfare in Ancient Israel* for an analysis of the tension with traditional views of kingship, especially pp. 114f.

8. In the Babylonian New Year ritual celebrating the triumph of Marduk over Tiamat, the Babylonians simultaneously declared their loyalty to the king, Marduk's representative, and to Marduk. The religious symbol system did not differentiate between the king and the god in such a way as to allow for the prophetic judgment of the king in the name of the god. Mircea Eliade, *The Sacred and the Profane*, pp. 77f.

9. Abraham Heschel, *The Prophets*, Vol. I, pp. 135f.

10. Gustavo Gutierrez, *A Theology of Liberation*, p. 157.

11. Mendenhall, op. cit., p. 19.

12. Karl Barth used this text in writing to Christians in East Germany in the early days under a Marxist regime.

13. Gutierrez, op. cit., p. 161.

14. Ibid., p. 161.

15. Norman Perrin, *The Kingdom of God in the Teaching of Jesus*, p. 158. This is a very helpful survey of the entire sweep of scholarly discussion on the subject going back to Schleiermacher and Ritschl.

16. Ibid., p. 159.

17. C. H. Dodd, *Coming of Christ*, pp. 15f. This position is stated in a similar way by Rudolf Schnackenburg, *God's Rule and Kingdom*.

18. See this emphasis in the work of Oscar Cullmann, *Christ and Time*, and that of Werner Kummel, *Promise and Fulfillment*.

19. Perrin, op. cit., p. 159.

20. Amos Wilder, *Eschatology and Ethics in the Teaching of Jesus*, p. 145.

21. Ibid., p. 160.

22. Ibid., p. 163.

23. John H. Yoder, *The Politics of Jesus*, p. 28.

24. Ibid., p. 34.

Some New Testament scholars have interpreted Jesus' message as an announcement of the Jubilee year as described in Leviticus 25 (Yoder, pp. 36f., and 64f.). The basic idea of Jubilee included four prescriptions: (1) leaving the soil fallow, (2) the remission of debts, (3) the liberation of slaves, (4) the return to each individual of his family's property.

One of the problems with a strict application of the Jubilee is that as the sabbatical year approached, the wealthy hesitated to loan to the poor for fear of losing their capital. The Pharisee Hillel found a solution to this problem in what was called the "prosboul," "which is Greek for 'an action formalized before the tribunal.' According to the treatise *Gittin* of the Mishnah, Hillel in this way authorized a creditor to transfer to a court the right to recover in his name a debt which the sabbatical year otherwise might have cancelled" (Yoder, p. 69). According to Yoder, the very existence of the "prosboul" proves that the provision of the Jubilee remission of debts was still regarded as applicable at the time of Jesus.

Jesus came into conflict with the authorities precisely in his strict adherence to the humanitarian prescriptions of the law of Moses. When Jesus said, " 'God made the sabbath for man,' he meant God had liberated the Jews by taking them out of Egypt. The sabbatical year, like the day of sabbath, must be practiced. Both are meant to liberate men, and not to enslave them. This is why the *prosboul*, like all the other human traditions, which were added to the law in order to attenuate its revolutionary and liberating character, called forth Jesus' indignation" (Yoder, p. 71).

25. Gutierrez, op. cit., pp. 298-299.

26. For an excellent summary of the attitude of Jesus toward women, see Paul Jewett, *Man as Male and Female*, pp. 94-105.

27. Werner Foerster, *Theological Dictionary of the New Testament*, pp. 408, 411.

28. Ibid., pp. 401, 411.

29. Ibid., p. 412.

30. This dualism leads Gerardo Zampaglione, *The Idea of Peace in Antiquity*, to distort the meaning of peace in the New Testament. Though he acknowledges that the word "peace" corresponds in many passages to the fundamental content of the Hebrew word "shalom" (p. 210), he says of the early Christians that "their aims and hopes were concentrated solely on the values of the spirit and not on the organization of the world" (p. 208). "The Christians were called to embrace a happiness separated from things human, sustained by faith and the practice of virtue. . . . Mainly concerned with a supernatural world" (p. 209). What Zampaglione is doing is using a very old principle of interpretation in how to relate the Old and New Testaments, i.e., the "spiritualizing influence which the New Testament has on the Old." Gustavo Gutierrez has an excellent critique of this approach, op. cit., pp. 165f.

31. Foerster, op. cit., p. 413.

32. Ibid., p. 409.

33. Ibid., p. 419.

34. See Gerhard von Rad's study, *Der Heilige Krieg im alten Israel*. I'm also dependent on materials from Millard Lind, professor of Old Testament, Associated Mennonite Biblical Seminaries, Elkhart, Indiana. See the interview with him in *Lordship as Servanthood*, by William Keeney, p. 84f. For a more thorough and scholarly treatment of Lind's position see his book, *Yahweh Is a Warrior: The Theology of Warfare in Ancient Israel*.

35. Bright, op. cit., pp. 275-276.

36. Keeney, op. cit., p. 89. In this context of holy war, the question of the moral justification—the rightness or wrongness—of war is not the primary question. This is a modern question imported into the text, a question which was not the focus in a historical context where war came under the category of religious ritual. To use the texts as moral justification for war in a modern context is mistaken for two reasons: (1) The moral justification of violence for the sake of a political cause is not considered in the text. That kind of thinking belongs to a much later period—not until the post-Constantine period when Ambrose and Augustine began to

wonder whether it was morally justifiable for Christians to participate in war. (2) The modern moral justification of war requires one to support standing armies, weapons systems, a huge bureaucracy which can organize people for war, a governmental system which is linked with industry which provides the necessary weapons systems and a citizenry willing to pay huge sums of taxes for the support of military systems. This world is far removed from the holy war tradition of the Old Testament, where the emphasis is upon trust in Yahweh and in a charismatic leader who will arise at the moment of crisis.

37. Yoder, op. cit., pp. 87-88. It is in the context of this "trusting" attitude toward Yahweh that Jesus' view of liberation and victory over the powers and principalities is to be understood. It is in this context that we are to understand Jesus' action as a servant and the ethic he calls his disciples to follow.

38. This issue can best be seen against the background of Jesus' relationship to the Zealot movement. In his book *The State in the New Testament*, Oscar Cullmann describes how closely Jesus' ministry is related to the Zealot cause. There is considerable evidence in the Gospel accounts that the disciples expected Jesus to lead in a violent overthrow of the Roman occupation in the Zealot tradition. The disciples certainly did not seem to understand Jesus when he began to talk about going up to Jerusalem to suffer and die. Their discussions about who would be the greatest in Jesus' kingdom and the place they would have in leadership may well be tied to their traditional Zealot expectations.

Stephen Mott (op. cit.) argues that Jesus' views are not to be interpreted in the context of the Zealot option because a fully organized Zealot party did not yet exist in Jesus' time. It seems to me, however, that there did not have to be a fully organized party of Zealots to sustain the argument of Cullmann and Yoder that the Zealot tendency toward armed rebellion was a live option in Jesus' time (which Mott admits) over against which Jesus defined his position.

39. Yoder, op. cit., p. 52. Yoder argues that the three temptations of Jesus all reflect traditional ways of achieving political power. In Luke's report the testing begins with the economic option. "The option here, suggested or reinforced by Jesus' own renewed sensitivity to the pangs of hunger, was that his messianity would be expressed by providing a banquet for his followers" (p. 31).

Yoder interprets the third temptation to throw himself from the pinnacle of the temple as "Jesus contemplating the role of religious reformer, heavenly messenger, appearing unheralded from above to set things right" (p. 31). Rudolf Schnackenburg (quoted by Yoder) asks the question: "Would such a descent from such a symbolic place mark the signal for a religious-political freedom fight, making Jesus ultimately the Triumphator, in the way sought after by those pseudo-messianic pretenders, of whom the New Testament and Josephus report examples enough in this period?" (p. 34).

In response to these temptations Luke gives no evidence at all that Jesus tells his disciples that the salvation he brings is really "spiritual," that they have misunderstood the gospel as laden with sociopolitical import. He continues to teach, to heal, and to confront the powers that be with the ethic of the new order right up to the end. Neither is there evidence that Jesus counseled his disciples to withdraw to the desert to purify themselves in order to hasten the messianic age (the Essene alternative), or to work out an accommodation or compromise with the political authorities (the Pharisee and Sadducee alternatives).

That Jesus was seen in political terms is evident in the trap question put to Jesus whether "we are permitted to pay taxes to the emperor." If Jesus says "no" to paying taxes to Caesar, he can be accused of being a revolutionary: if he says "yes," a compromiser with the Roman occupation army (Luke 20:20-25). Yoder says: "It is hard to see how the denarius question could have been thought by those who put it to be a serious trap, unless Jesus' repudiation of the Roman occupation were taken for granted, so that he could be expected to give an answer which would enable them to denounce him . . . . The 'spiritualizers' picture of a Jesus whose only concern about politics was to clarify that he was not concerned about politics is refuted by the fact that this question could arise. In the context of his answer 'the things that are God's' most normally would not mean 'spiritual things'; the attribution 'to Caesar Caesar's things and to God God's things' points rather to demands or prerogatives which somehow overlap or compete, needing to be disentangled." The whole point here is not a distinction between a religious and a political realm, but rather two claims for competing loyalty—both having political dimensions. The kingdom of God was a message of liberation from oppression which is not apolitical, though it is political in a way that is different from the revolutionary violence of the Zealots.

40. See Richard Mouw's discussion of the meaning of the Zacchaeus episode in *Politics and the Biblical Drama*, p. 72.

41. Yoder says that the Authorized Version of Matthew 5:48 ("be perfect as your Father is perfect") has for years been made the key to the whole Sermon on the Mount. Perfectionist preachers saw there the promise of an accessible sinlessness; mainstream ethicists turned it around as the proof that the sermon's intent is not at all to be obeyed but to prepare men for grace by crushing them under the demand of an unattainable Godlikeness. Both extremes are wrong because they import a modern concept of "perfection" where it has no place. We are to understand the meaning of Luke as unconditional or indiscriminate. Op. cit., pp. 119-120.

42. The meaning of the kingdom of God for faith and for social ethics is to be understood in the context of the concrete Jesus of history who lived and taught about justice and righteousness in such a way as to end up being crucified by the powers that be. It is crucial that we know something about this concrete Jesus of history in order to understand how his message of the kingdom relates to human institutional life. We have no way to penetrate "behind" these sources to construct a life of Jesus. At the same time, the "faith" of the early church is that it is in and through the concrete historical Jesus, a Jew who lived and died in Palestine, that God's revelation comes. What, if anything, can be said about the concrete and particular historical memory of the Jesus of history that is relevant to the early church's view of Jesus as the Christ? One extreme view, which we must reject, is that of Kierkegaard, who held that all we need for faith is to be able to affirm that God revealed himself in concrete form in history. The content of faith is also integrally tied with the concrete form in which that historical revelation occurred. We agree here with John H. Yoder, in *Politics of Jesus*, where he argues that it is precisely his *historical* memory of the concrete Jesus who as a servant suffered and died on the cross who is also the Christ of faith. We are not attempting to go behind the sources to construct a life of Jesus. Rather, the sources themselves and our knowledge of the historical context enable us to see an important connection between history and faith precisely at the point of Jesus' proclamation of the kingdom and his clash with human institutions which led to his death on the cross.

I also have theological reasons for my position. Ever since Lessing and Kant (since the rise of historical thinking), theologians have been struggling with the problems created by the historical, the contingent. Since the historical is by definition contingent and therefore a changing reality, attempts have been made to ground theology in the universal and necessary. So Kant tried to build a theology on the basis of a universal moral reason, Schleiermacher on the general religious feeling of absolute dependence, and Paul Tillich in the common ontological structure of being and nonbeing. Even in those theologies such as Barth's which claim to be grounded in Christology, the distinction between "Historie" and "Geschichte" enables Barth to think of Christ primarily as the Revealer of God, as the Word, a Word (Logos), which in its cosmic dimensions is not connected adequately with the concrete and particular historical Jesus of history who was a Jew who lived in Palestine and died somewhere around A.D. 30. The attempt to avoid the shifting sands of contingency has in my view caused theology to err in the direction of the docetic heresy. Despite all the assertions that Jesus was fully man, the threat of the historical and the contingent has led theology to give insufficient attention to the concrete and historical Jesus. I want to claim that Jesus is normative theologically precisely in his concreteness as servant who in that servanthood is exalted to lordship (Philippians 2).

43. Yoder, op. cit., p. 118f. outlines the basic themes and lists the texts which call upon us

to follow Christ's way of life. Despite the concern in the Old Testament to protect the transcendence of God, the Old Testament also presupposes the notion that persons somehow correspond to God's own being. Not only is this reflected in the creation story, but this correspondence is the basis for ethical exhortation to be toward others as God has been toward his people. Walter Eichrodt, in his *Theology of the Old Testament*, characterizes the basic theme of the holiness code, "the forming of human nature after the pattern of the divine" (Vol. II, p. 373). This ties into what we said earlier about the close connection between one's image or view of God and self-knowledge or self-perception (see Yoder, pp. 116-117).

44. Over the past 25 years scholars have invested a great deal of energy in seeking to interpret the meaning of terms like "principalities," "powers," "thrones," and "dominions." We cannot in this book even summarize that debate, much less exegete the texts where the language occurs. For my purposes, sufficient progress has been made in understanding these terms as references to sociopolitical structures to utilize this understanding in my interpretation. See Richard Mouw's summary (op. cit., pp. 85-116) of this discussion and the issues that are still under debate. See also Yoder's discussion of the same topic, op. cit., pp. 135-162, and Stephen Mott, op. cit.

45. It seems to me that the discussion of the "powers," while it may have contributed to a better understanding of the New Testament, is implicit in perceptive social analysts who did not benefit from this recent exegesis. For example, Walter Rauschenbusch recognizes in *A Theology for the Social Gospel* the sociostructural nature of evil. For Rauschenbusch, Jesus was crucified not just by individuals but by such "constitutional forces in the kingdom of evil" as "religious bigotry, the combination of graft and political power, the corruption of justice, the mob spirit, militarism, and class contempt" (p. 257f.).

46. Karl W. Deutsch, *The Analysis of International Relations*, second edition, p. 19.

47. Gene Sharp, *The Politics of Nonviolent Action*, p. 8f. The possibility of nonviolent resistance was not an impossibility in Jesus' time. Josephus reports a very interesting episode of nonviolent resistance by the Jews to Pilate's introduction of images of Caesar. The Jews persisted to entreat Pilate to remove the images to the point that "they threw themselves upon the ground and laid their necks bare and said they would take their death very willingly rather than that the wisdom of their law should be transgressed; upon which Pilate was deeply affected with their firm resolution to keep their laws inviolable, and presently commanded the images to be carried back from Jerusalem to Caesarea." From Josephus, *Antiquities*, xviii, 3.

48. Karl Barth, *How to Serve God in a Marxist Land*. See also Charles West, *Communism and the Theologians*.

49. A brief digression into the history of the Mennonite church illustrates this point. Originally the Anabaptists were very aggressive in trying to change the institutions (mainly the church) of the sixteenth century. They hoped, originally as followers of Zwingli, that the church at Zurich would reform itself. They initiated and engaged in vigorous dialogue, especially with Reformed theologians. They engaged in active missionary work. They had a great deal of empathy with the plight of the peasants. When severe persecution came, they were forced underground, or else they escaped to remote mountain valleys or to geographical enclaves where they were tolerated. The Schleitheim Confession of Faith (1527), which speaks of a sharp church-world dualism of those "within the perfection of Christ" and "those outside the perfection of Christ," reflects the Anabaptist experience of intense suffering for the faith. It reflects the experience of being pushed by both the Catholic and Protestant churches into a small separated group which was forced either to go underground or escape to relatively safe geographical regions. The church-world dualistic theology thus grows initially out of an intense activism in the world. Once Mennonites became a separated minority no longer in a position to press for change in the world, the theology became supportive of a stance of withdrawal from the world. As Mennonites became basically a rural-ethnic community, the church-world theology served to justify a permanently withdrawn sociological group.

One can understand and empathize with the "withdrawal" psychology and sociology that results from minority status as a result of severe persecution. Yet we must emphasize that the cross of Jesus Christ grew out of a clash with the powers because of his compassion for his fellow Jews and their institutions. He healed, taught, preached, and acted politically in the midst of the polis. The voluntary cross accepted by Jesus grows out of the clash of two value systems.

50. For a fuller elaboration of this theme and an analysis of the various interpretations of the text from Revelation, see Mouw, op. cit., pp. 117-139.

51. We must be careful here to distinguish between "self-righteousness" and legitimate prophetic criticism. It is a ploy of some Christians (who do not like to be called to repentance) to accuse a person or group of self-righteousness whenever judgment is pronounced on the human condition and repentance is called for. Self-righteousness arises out of pride in one's own superior righteousness, not out of the prophetic stance itself which may be the manner in which God communicates his will to his people. Otherwise, how could we understand the action of the Old Testament prophets?

52. In Niebuhr's view sin has its roots precisely in what makes humans unique in creation—in human freedom which allows persons to transcend themselves and choose objects of loyalty and devotion which become the center of their interest. However, since persons are both free to transcend themselves and yet cannot escape their finitude, this produces anxiety. Though this anxiety can only be resolved by trust in God, human beings express their freedom by giving unconditional loyalty to themselves or their own limited collectivities which leads them to attitudes of selfishness and acts of domination over others.

53. My critique of Niebuhr is a quite common criticism of his position among theologians. Daniel Day Williams, in *God's Grace and Man's Hope*, criticizes Niebuhr and other neo-orthodox theologians for emphasizing sin so much that they cut the "nerve of hope." A. J. Muste in his essay, "Pacifism and Perfectionism," criticizes Niebuhr for the same reason (*The Essays of A. J. Muste*, ed. by Nat Hentoff, p. 312f.). John H. Yoder makes a similar critique in his essay, *Reinhold Niebuhr and Christian Pacifism*. The point is also made in a Yale dissertation (1975) by Laurence Alan Letts, *Peace and the Gospel: A Comparative Study of the Theological and Ethical Foundations of A. J. Muste's Radical Pacifism and Reinhold Niebuhr's "Christian Realism."* Letts believes Niebuhr even misunderstands the Reformers, Luther and Calvin, who gave a much stronger role to the transformed life of faith (p. 89). Letts cites other theologians such as Paul Lehmann, Daniel Day Williams, Abraham Heschel, and Georg Hermann Dellbruger, who believe that Niebuhr has departed from mainline Reformation views.

54. Abraham Heschel, who otherwise has a deep appreciation of Niebuhr, criticizes him for similar reasons. I am in agreement with Heschel's assessment of Niebuhr. Heschel agrees that Niebuhr rightly points to the presence and mystery of evil which permeates modern history and culture. Second, he agrees with Niebuhr that the freedom of the self which expresses itself in evil is radical and is not easily brought under the control of reason. Third, he agrees with Niebuhr in viewing the problem not as good and evil, but the "evil within the good, or more accurately the confusion of good and evil" (p. 134). But he disagrees with Niebuhr where Niebuhr goes on to speak of "evil as an inevitable fact of human existence. Now if every good action is liable to corruption, what would be the worth and relevance to the worship and service of God? Does not the grace of God consist precisely in its guarding the sacred acts from being vitiated by evil? It is profoundly true that goodness may turn to cruelty, piety to fanaticism, faith to arrogance. Yet this, we believe, is a perpetual possibility rather than a necessity, a threat rather than an inevitable result. . . . Biblical history bears witness to the constant corruption of man; it does not, however, teach the inevitable corruptibility of the ultimate in the temporal process. . . . There are good moments in history that no subsequent evil may obliterate" (pp. 142-143). The commands of God at Sinai are superimposed upon human fallenness, and this, according to Heschel, points to the possibility to do God's will. The carrying out of the sacred deed (mitzvah) is given to persons as a constant opportunity. From *The Insecurity of Freedom.*

CHAPTER FIVE

1. There has been an ongoing attempt to bridge the gap between the community of faith and the political arena. Though I do not use the language, I am sympathetic with the intent of those who used the language of "middle axioms" as an attempt to relate the Christian gospel to the broader community consisting of a plurality of faiths. The term "middle axioms" originated in the ecumenical movement with the Oxford Conference on Life and Work in 1937. John Bennett, in particular, picked up the terminology and attempted to give it more precision. See the brief summary of Bennett's efforts in J. Philip Wogaman, *A Christian Method of Moral Judgment*, pp. 21f.

2. See particularly chapter 1, "From System to Story: An Alternative Pattern for Rationality in Ethics," in *Truthfulness and Tragedy* and his more complete statement of his position in *The Peaceable Kingdom: A Primer in Christian Ethics*. Roman Catholic moral teaching has been dominated by natural law thinking. Though natural law has not been rejected by the church, it has come under increasing criticism. The criticism has centered around the tendency of the church in the past to define natural law statically as a system of principles which underlie the central institutions of society—family, property, and the state. Joseph Gremillion reports that since Pope John XXIII Catholic social teaching has emphasized increasingly less a static view of human nature to place more of an emphasis on "human rights and fulfillment of human capacities, promoted by man's innate worth. . . . Also Vatican II focused more deeply on the human person as known through and in Christ. It also stressed the recent scientific knowledge of man (the new anthropology) and the experience of human community in today's technological society," *The Gospel of Peace and Justice: Catholic Social Teaching Since Pope John*, p. 8. I find myself sympathetic with the direction in which Roman Catholic social teaching is going, as I think it harmonizes with a biblical perspective. Much more could be said about the rich resources from Roman Catholicism in dealing with these issues. I refer the reader particularly to the statement of the 1968 Medellin Conference (Second General Conference of Latin American Bishops). See Gremillion, pp. 445f.

3. For a discussion of the importance of concern with structures and causes, not just individuals and effects, see John Swomley, *Liberation Ethics*, especially chapter 3, "Oppression and the Structures of Violence"; John Galtung, "Social Structure, Religious Structure and the Fight for Peace," in *Peace: Research, Education, Action; Essays in Peace Research*, Vol. 1, pp. 348f.; and Stephen Mott, *Biblical Ethics and Social Change*, pp. 3-21.

4. John Rawls, *A Theory of Justice*, see especially pp. 17f.

5. Ibid., p. 60.

6. Ibid., p. 83.

7. This principle was also implied by the sixteenth-century Radical Reformation which critiqued both the Catholic and mainline Reformation alliance of church and state. The radicals held that freedom of conscience and freedom of choice in matters of religion could not be upheld in a state allied with and supportive of a particular religious perspective. The conditions of citizenship could not be dependent upon adopting the religion of a particular territory, because equal liberty could not be granted to those with alternative positions. The reason why infant baptism versus adult baptism became such a point of contention in the sixteenth century was that infant baptism symbolized one's entry into the religion of the territory, and thus was simultaneously a rite of entry into citizenship in the state. It was by attacking the assumption that everyone should automatically be baptized as infants that the radicals sought to make room for an alternative religious choice based upon freedom of conscience. I think that many persons have falsely labeled major segments of the Radical Reformation as apolitical. This label arises from the fact that many of them refused to use the instruments of violence which was regarded as the essence of political authority. The position of this entire paper is that ways to be political exist without using violence, a point demonstrated by the Radical Reformation. The radicals, in fact, had a profound influence upon the structure of society, for eventually

their views about freedom of religion were incorporated into the constitutions of many governments.

8. Rawls, op. cit., pp. 14-15.

9. Stanley Hauerwas, *Truthfulness and Tragedy*. See especially his critique on pp. 16f. Preston Williams argues that human beings are embedded in communities, and that one cannot put oneself in an original position of impartiality with respect to both one's racial and gender identity. See *The Annual of the Society of Christian Ethics*, 1983, pp. 147f.

10. Mott, op. cit., p. 67.

11. Ibid., pp. 79-80.

12. David Wills, "Racial Justice and the Limits of American Liberalism," *The Journal of Religious Ethics*, Fall 1978, p. 188.

13. Ibid., pp. 191-92.

14. Ibid., p. 194.

15. Ibid., p. 197.

16. Reported by J. Philip Wogaman in his book, *The Great Economic Debate: An Ethical Analysis*, p. 133. Wogaman's book gives a very helpful analysis and evaluation of five different types of economic systems. Wogaman himself argues that democratic socialism is most near to the Christian view of social justice. One could here also cite the numerous liberation theologians who have found kinship between the Christian faith and Marxist and socialist views. Earlier in the third chapter I drew heavily upon the thought of Gustavo Gutierrez which indicates the influence of liberation theology on my thinking. My problem with liberation theology is not its view of justice, but the readiness by some to adopt the use of violence to change systems. Also sometimes liberation theologians do not sufficiently emphasize the church as the primary locus of God's action in the world.

17. My discussion of the different levels of human rights draws upon a speech given in the 1978-79 "Peace Lecture Series" at Bethel College by Burns Weston, Professor of International Law, University of Iowa.

18. Mott, op. cit., pp. 51-53.

19. This is how Paul Ramsey argues in his discussion of the difficulties faced by a public committee at the Swedish Hospital in Seattle when it deliberated in the 1960s about who should get kidney machines when they were not available for all, in *The Patient as Person*, p. 256. See also the discussion of these issues in Gene Outka's article, "Social Justice and Equal Access to Health Care," *The Journal of Religious Ethics*, Spring, 1974, pp. 11-32.

20. See the article "The Tragedy of the Commons," in the appendix (pp. 250f.) of the book by Garrett Harden, *Exploring New Ethics for Survival: The Voyage of the Spaceship Beagle*.

21. William K. Tabb calls Reagan's philosophy "reactionary" because it seeks to revive the classical economic philosophy of Adam Smith in a world that is fundamentally different from the world in which Adam Smith developed his views. Smith assumes a relatively large number of small entrepreneurs in a free competitive market. Reagan and others of similar persuasion blame government interference as the reason why the market cannot function properly. According to Tabb, "It is the unregulated nature of the capitalist expansion, not Big Government, which causes the contemporary economic crisis" (p. 192). "In classical economic theory, a firm seeks out a low-cost location for its plant, using criteria based on transportation, energy, labor and material costs, markets, local taxes and services. The classical theory also assumes atomistic competition in which no single firm can influence markets by itself. Involuntary unemployment is not possible in this model. The real world of today features high unemployment and interjurisdictional competition. Under these conditions rather than passively accepting the best of given opportunities, companies negotiate and pressure to create terms they want." The market does not operate freely not because of government interference but because "a few large transnational corporations can play workers and taxing units against each other. The new competition takes place in the context of semi-permanent high levels of unem-

ployment and fiscal crisis brought on by the increased mobility of capital and the private control of technology" (pp. 198-199). The rationale for Reaganomics is that by allowing business a freer reign and by giving business tax incentives the benefit will eventually "trickle down" to the masses. The long-term effect, however, is to further enhance the power of large transnational corporations and further increase the gap between the wealthy few and the larger masses who have increasingly less control over their economic future. See the "Social, Political and Ethical Meaning of the Reagan Revolution" in *The Annual of the Society of Christian Ethics*, 1983, pp. 185-216.

22. The classical utilitarian position has been formulated by Jeremy Bentham and John Stuart Mill. One of the most recent statements of this position is by Henry Sidgwick, *Methods of Ethics*. John Rawls has developed in his book, *A Theory of Justice*, a position growing out of the contract tradition of Locke and Kant that stands in contrast to the utilitarian view.

23. Rawls, op. cit. p. 378.

24. One of the rather popular ethical notions current today relating justice to international life is the idea of "triage" and Garrett Harden's "Lifeboat Ethic." For a discussion surrounding the ethical evaluation of these concepts see the book edited by Thomas Ogletree and George Lucas, *Lifeboat Ethics: The Moral Dilemmas of World Hunger.* "Triage" is an idea that grows out of the battlefield setting in which one can imagine a situation of scarce medical resources to take care of all the injuries from battle. In this setting there are three types of persons: those who will not survive even with help, those who will survive without help, and those who will survive only if they receive help. Since resources are scarce, it is the obligation of those with medical aid to help those who will survive only if they receive help, to ignore those who will survive anyway, and to let die those who are helpless. This image has been applied to the international situation. Some countries can be helped and will survive. Other countries will survive without help. A third set of countries cannot survive even if they are helped, and therefore they should be allowed to go under.

As an ethical concept triage is ambiguous. Does the situation mean that one ought to save life (as one acts in the battlefield situation to save those that can be saved) because all life is of intrinsic worth? Or, does triage mean a commitment to the greatest good for the greatest number? Since all cannot survive, we then act to preserve as many as possible, even if that means the sacrifice of the few for the sake of the many. If we take this latter interpretation, then the notion of triage is a violation of the principles of justice we established earlier. Triage interpreted in a utilitarian way does not view all human beings as ends in and of themselves, but is willing to sacrifice the few for the sake of the greater number. It seems to me that in a battlefield situation where we clearly know that we can only save some lives, the triage notion can function as a principle in harmony with justice, but when it is applied to the community of nations, where there are grave doubts about who and on what terms nations can survive, it functions more likely as a utilitarian principle which legitimates injustice.

The "Lifeboat Ethic" of Garrett Harden is based upon the image of a lifeboat that is already swamped with people and with many more people clamoring to get on. If, of course, everyone is allowed to get on the boat, the boat will sink and everyone will drown. Harden applies this image to the global environmental situation. The richer nations are already in the lifeboat, and the poorer nations who are struggling to survive are also trying to get in. Presumably, if we try to save everyone, we will all perish.

Is the global survival problem due to the desire of poor nations wanting to survive, or is it due to the excessive consumption of those who are rich? Harden does not raise the question of distributive justice. Harden's image serves to support a utilitarian ethic of the greatest sum of satisfaction for the few or the wealthy nations. Harden is willing to sacrifice some nations for the sake of the good of others. This violates the principles of justice we have set out.

25. In their book, *Global Reach: The Power of Multinational Corporations*, Richard Barnet and Ronald Mueller argue that multinational corporations work against the benefits of the poor, whereas representatives of these corporations would argue that they have improved

the lot of the poor by the jobs they have created all over the world.

26. For an excellent discussion of the role of technological and factual expertise in moral judgment see J. Philip Wogaman, *A Christian Method of Moral Judgment*, especially pp. 170f. Wogaman carries on a debate with Paul Ramsey who questioned the tendency of church bodies to make judgments that are too specific on political and social questions. See Paul Ramsey, *Who Speaks for the Church?* Wogaman argues that "when the church abandons the field of specificity in moral teaching it really abandons the field of moral teaching altogether" (p. 173).

27. Richard Barnet, *The Lean Years*, pp. 97-98.

28. Peter Berger, *Pyramids of Sacrifice*, pp. 47-48.

29. Barnet, op. cit., p. 230.

30. Ibid., p. 260.

31. Berger, op. cit., p. 72.

32. For an excellent account of the way modern technology has transformed the traditional nation-state system see the book by Lester Brown, *World Without Borders*.

33. I am dependent upon Barrington Moore, Jr., for my definition of exploitation. See his *Reflections on the Causes of Human Misery and upon Certain Proposals to Eliminate Them*, p. 53.

34. Barnet, op. cit., pp. 122f.

35. Ibid., pp. 139f.

36. Quoted by Barnet, ibid., pp. 141-142.

37. Bennett and Seifert, op. cit., pp. 203f.

38. See the book edited by Charles Powers, *People/Profits: The Ethics of Investment*, and the book by Oliver Williams and John W. Houck, *Full Value: Cases in Christian Business Ethics*.

39. Bennett and Seifert, op. cit., p. 204.

40. For an excellent summary of world social and military expenditures since 1960, see the series of books, published on an annual basis, by Ruth Sivard, *World Military and Social Expenditures*. The data comes from the 1983 edition. Copyright © 1983 by World Priorities.

41. Sivard, Ibid., p. 7.

42. Sivard, *World Military and Social Expenditures*, 1978. Copyright © 1978 by World Priorities.

43. Ibid., p. 12.

44. Ibid., p. 14.

45. Ibid., p. 13.

46. Data provided by SANE, 514 C St., N.E., Washington, DC 20002.

47. For an analysis of how military spending has affected the U.S. economy see the article by Lloyd Dumas, "Economic Conversion, Productive Efficiency and Social Welfare," *Journal of Social Welfare*, Jan./March 1977, pp. 567-596.

48. Quoted by Barnet, op. cit., p. 229.

49. Dumas, op. cit., p. 570.

50. In the past decade a great deal has been written about how to "convert" the U.S. economy from dependency on government spending for military purposes. For an update on current research and resources on this issue, persons can contact SANE, 318 Mass. Ave., N.E., Washington, DC 20002.

51. Edgar Stoesz, *Thoughts on Development*," (Akron, Pa.: Mennonite Central Committee Development Monograph Series, No. 1), p. 2.

52. Merrill Ewert, *Humanization and Development*, (Akron, Pa.: Mennonite Central Committee Development Monograph Series, No. 2), p. 32.

53. Some examples of the type of development I am advocating are as follows:

In April 1975 the Mennonite Central Committee program in Bangladesh received the President's Gold Award for Agriculture for introducing and promoting new crops that include vegetables, soybeans, sunflowers, and grains in the Noakhali district of Bangladesh. The crops are raised during the winter months when the soil is too dry to grow rice. The program also included a four-person team that traveled through the district demonstrating for farmers, village women, and schools how these new crops could be used, relying only on equipment and ingredients available in the average home, to prepare both new and common foods with a higher nutritional and protein value. *The Mennonite*, May 6, 1975, p. 289. Mennonite Central Committee News Service, April 4, 1975.

Family Farms of the United Church of Canada has been successful working with fishermen in the southern province of Zambia. The fishing occupation of these people had led to a nomadic lifestyle and a reputation of unreliability, and to living without adequate medical or educational facilities. Family Farms gave the fishermen basic training in economics and fish technology, and helped the fishermen secure loans to improve their nets and put motors on their boats. The results have been the establishment of eight permanent village sites allowing for numerous improvements, and a tripling of fish production. "Family Farms," *Z Magazine*, April 1974, pp. 6-11.

Other resources on development are: Paulo Freire, *Pedagogy of the Oppressed;* Denis Goulet, *A New Moral Order;* Lester Brown, *By Bread Alone;* Joseph Collins and Frances Moore Lappé, *Food First;* Uma Lele, *The Design of Rural Development;* E. F. Schumacher, *Small Is Beautiful;* Mennonite Central Committee Development Monograph Series, Akron, Pa.; in this series, see especially Edgar Stoesz, *Beyond Good Intentions.*

CHAPTER SIX

1. For a definition of and the various dimensions of the term "violence" see the article by Johann Galtung, "Violence, Peace, and Peace Research," *Journal of Peace Research*, 1969 (No. 3), pp. 167-191. He uses the term "structural violence" in a way that is equivalent to my term "injustice." The same equation of "structural violence" and injustice is found in Robert McAfee Brown's book *Religion and Violence*. He refers to Dom Helder Camara, the Roman Catholic bishop of Recife, Brazil, who "feels that the basic form of violence, which he calls Violence No. 1, is injustice." Brown describes this as "the subtle, institutionalized destruction of human possibilities that is around us all the time, but is often not apparent to those who are comfortably situated" (p. 9). This same notion is in the 1973 World Council of Churches study document, "Violence, Nonviolence and the Struggle for Social Justice." The document states that "the ecumenical encounter, especially since the World Conference on Church and Society (Geneva 1966), has sharpened our awareness of the *violence* [emphasis mine] which is built into many of the world's existing social, political and economic structures." *The Ecumenical Review*, Vol. XXV, No. 4, Oct. 1973, par. 5.

2. The problem with the term "structural violence" is that it muddles together a number of factors, particularly a number of ethical components inherent in the term "violence." Alice's exchange with Humpty Dumpty expresses my sentiment. "That's a great deal to make one word mean," Alice said in a thoughtful tone. "When I make a word do a lot of work like that," said Humpty Dumpty, "I always pay it extra." Rather than paying one word extra, I suggest we use a variety of terms to describe and assess a relationship. The terms "justice" and "injustice" describe what persons are getting at with the concept of "structural violence."

3. Martin L. King, *Stride Toward Freedom*, pp. 103-104.

4. Ibid.

5. For an argument that love may be expressed in violent acts see Wogaman, *A Christian Method of Moral Judgment*, p. 129.

6. The word comes from the Middle English "power," from the Old French "poeir" and from the Vulgate Latin "potere," which is rooted in the Latin verb "posse, potesse," which means "to be able."

7. Bernard M. Loomer, "Two Kinds of Power," *Criterion*, Vol. 15, No. 1, Winter 1976,

pp. 11f. This is the inaugural lecture of the D. R. Sharpe Lectureship on Social Ethics given at the Divinity School of the University of Chicago, October 29, 1975. This view of power is also reflected in several essays of James L. Adams, *On Being Human Religiously.*

8. This view of power fits in with my theological assumptions in two respects. With respect to the doctrine of God, God is both a transforming power in the universe and also one who is responsive to human need to the extent that his power is expressed in such depth of love that he takes evil into himself in the cross. With respect to the doctrine of man, man is both a being who is affected by God and finds his meaning in response to the divine action upon him and at the same time is an active creative agent in history. This view of power is reflected in H. R. Niebuhr's *The Responsible Self*, where Christian ethics is seen primarily in terms of the "fitting," answering or responding to what God is doing. It is reflected in the Quaker concept of listening to the Spirit or the Anabaptist notion of discernment as the context within which "doing" is to be interpreted.

9. Hans Morgenthau, *Politics Among the Nations*, p. 26. See Berenice Carroll's critique of this view of power, a view of power she says has also inappropriately dominated the perspective of many peace researchers (*Journal of Conflict Resolution*, Vol. 16, No. 4, Dec. 1972). Carroll argues that peace researchers, in accepting this definition of power, have identified with institutions and groups and persons concerned to be powerful.

The same problem is evident in mainline Protestant social ethics. Ecumenical social strategy tends to be focused upon how to change those at the center of power. Ecumenical conversation since 1948 has been based on the "assumption that the forces which really determine the march of history are in the hands of the leaders of the armies and markets, in such measure that if Christians are to contribute to the renewal of society they will need to seek, like everyone else—in fact in competition with everyone else—to become in their turn the lords of the state and of the economy, so as to use that power toward the ends they consider desirable" (John H. Yoder, *The Politics of Jesus*, p. 156). Those in the realist school following Reinhold Niebuhr do the same. John Swomley says: "The whole power analysis of the realist needs to be called into question. Power to the realist . . . is not the ability to induce change, but the ability to impose one's will on others. A good illustration of the realist position is the oft-repeated slogan that if you must negotiate, you should 'negotiate from strength.' However, if the agreement that flows from such negotiations is to be lasting, it should be mutually satisfactory. It should be negotiated so as to be in the national interest of all parties to the agreement rather than in the interest only of the stronger power" (*American Empire: The Political Ethics of Twentieth Century Conquest*, p. 21).

Kenneth Boulding's analysis helps us to distinguish between three types of power and also helps to show why the notion of power as "dominance over" is so inadequate. One form of power is "threat power" where "you do something nice to me or I will do something nasty to you." This is a negative sum notion. In order for the threat to be perceived as a threat, the threatener must be able to create a perception of credibility, i.e., he must be *capable* and *willing* to carry out the threat. Boulding says four possible responses to this are: (a) submission, (b) defiance, (c) counter threat or deterrence, (d) integrative response. The integrative response is one that tends to produce some sense of community between the threatener and threatened by producing common values and a common interest. Submission out of the desire to survive or to avoid mutual annihilation, or nonviolent resistance which may undermine the morale of the threatener, may both lead to some kind of integration. Counterthreat or deterrence, however, is the most unstable. It tends to divide because it is based on demonstrating both one's *capability* and *will* to carry out the threat. At some point it is likely that one side will feel a need to demonstrate the capability of the threat, if it is to be viable. The other side will need to defy the threat if its credibility is to be maintained, so the likelihood is war.

A second type of power is "exchange power" where "you do something nice to me and I'll do something nice to you." This is a positive sum notion, and generally functions in the realm of economics. Boulding argues that because of the lack of viability of threat power (nation-states lack unconditional viability because of technology of nuclear age—i.e. they *cannot* carry out their threats because of obvious mutual disadvantage), the tendency is for power to shift to the exchange notion of power, and his third view of power, integrative power.

Integrative power is that power which results from the meeting of minds, where the power is the capacity to respond to other groups and situations so as to cooperate together to fulfill common needs and objectives. In the kind of world we live in today, says Boulding, power has much less to do with threat and much more to do with knowledge and technological capacity, economic viability, and diplomatic negotiation so as to prevent war and devise policies for mutual advantage. See Kenneth Boulding, "Toward a Pure Theory of Threat Systems," in Roderich Bell, David V. Edwards and R. Harrison Wagner, ed.; *Political Power: A Reader in Theory and Research.* See also his book, *Conflict and Defense.*

In a similar kind of argument Silviu Brucan argues that recent changes in world politics have changed the dynamics of power itself in that the relative weight of the military component of power has been reduced in favor of the economic, technological, and political— diplomatic components. A new kind of "systemic" power is able to cause disturbances within a relatively integrated system of interdependent nations because of three factors: the decentralization of power with so many political units now in the world, the interdependence of nations in the world market and international monetary system, and the change in the dynamics of power (relative less weight to military power). Silviu Brucan, "The Systemic Power," *Journal of Peace Research* 121 (1975), pp. 63-70.

10. Karl Deutsch, *The Analysis of International Relations*, pp. 17-18.

11. This definition comes largely from Berenice Carroll, op. cit.

12. Gene Sharp, *The Politics of Nonviolent Action*, p. 8.

13. Gene Sharp, who has done more than any other scholar to describe and analyze this history in his *Politics of Nonviolent Action*, says:

That there is a rich lode of material awaiting the analyst and actionist is abundantly clear. Even at the present early stage of investigation, he who looks can find numerous examples, ranging from ancient Rome to the civil rights struggle in the United States and the resistance of the Czechs and Slovaks to the Russian invasion of 1968. By searching diligently through scattered sources, he can find mention of plebeian protests against Rome as far back as the fifth century B.C.; he can trace the resistance of the Netherlands to Spanish rule in mid-sixteenth century Europe. But the history of nonviolent struggle in these centuries still remains to be written. What we have now are only brief glimpses.

In more modern times, however, the picture becomes more crowded. Important examples of nonviolent action and struggle occur in extremely varied settings. For example, to an extent which has on the whole been ignored, the American colonists used nonviolent resistance in their struggle against Britain, refusing to pay taxes and debts, refusing to import, refusing to obey laws they considered unjust, using independent political institutions, and severing social and economic contact with both the British and pro-British colonists.

Later, especially in the late nineteenth and early twentieth centuries, working people in many countries used noncooperation in the form of strikes and economic boycotts to improve conditions and to gain greater power. The Russian Revolution of 1905 is full of nonviolent responses to the events of "Bloody Sunday": paralyzing strikes, refusal to obey censorship regulations, establishment of "parallel" organs of government—these were only some of the pressures which led the tsar's government to the promise of a more liberal governmental system. When the collapse of the tsarist system came in 1917 it was because it had disintegrated in face of an overwhelmingly nonviolent revolution—months before the Bolsheviks seized control in October. Nor does nonviolent pressure always have to be "against"; it can also be "for," as was made clear in Berlin in 1920, when the bureaucracy and population, who remained loyal to the existing Ebert government, brought down the militarist Kapp Putsch by refusing to cooperate with it.

Gandhi, who was the outstanding strategist of nonviolent action, regarded nonviolent struggle as a means of matching forces, one which had the greatest capacity for bringing real freedom and justice. The classic national Gandhian struggle was the 1930-31 campaign, which began with the famous Salt March as a prelude to civil disobedience against the British monopoly. A year-long nonviolent campaign followed. It shook British power in India and ended with negotiations between equals.

Despite highly unfavorable circumstances, nonviolent resistance sometimes also produced political tremors in certain Nazi-occupied countries during World War II. Occasionally—as in Norway—where Quisling's effort to set up a corporative state was thwarted by nonviolent resistance—it won some battles. Covert noncooperation and, very rarely, nonviolent defiance even helped save the lives of Jews. During the same period, on the other side of the world, popular nonviolent action was being used successfully to dissolve the power of two Central American dictators. Communist systems, too, have felt the power of nonviolent action in the East German Rising in 1953, in strikes in Soviet prison camps, and in the nonviolent phase of the 1956 Hungarian Revolution. In the United States nonviolent action has played a major role in the struggles of Afro-Americans from the Montgomery bus boycott on. And in 1968, one of the most remarkable demonstrations of unprepared nonviolent resistance for national defense purposes took place in Czechoslovakia after the Russian invasion. The struggle was not successful, but the Czechs and Slovaks were able to hold out far longer—from August to April—than they could have with military resistance (pp. 4-6). Reprinted with permission from: *The Politics of Nonviolent Action* by Gene Sharp in three volumes: Part 1, *Power and Struggle;* Part 2, *The Methods of Nonviolent Action;* and Part 3, *The Dynamics of Nonviolent Action.* Published by Porter Sargent Publishers, 11 Beacon Street, Boston, MA 02108. Copyright by Gene Sharp.

14. Martin L. King, *Why We Can't Wait*, p. 80.

15. Sharp, op. cit., pp. 109-110.

16. Sharp classifies the methods of nonviolent action under the following categories:
    A. The Methods of Nonviolent Protest and Persuasion
    B. The Methods of Social Noncooperation
    C. The Methods of Economic Noncooperation
       1. Economic Boycotts
       2. The Strike
    D. The Methods of Political Noncooperation
    E. The Methods of Nonviolent Intervention

He compiles a list of 198 methods of change and resistance that have been used by nonviolent activists. See *Politics of Nonviolent Action*, pp. 117-435.

17. William Miller, *Nonviolence: A Christian Interpretation*, p. 34.

18. Reinhold Niebuhr, *Love and Justice*, p. 250.

19. The ambiguity in Niebuhr arises out of the contrast he makes between love and nonviolent social change. When Niebuhr talks about love as a passive nonresistant agape of self-abnegation or withdrawal from the world, then love stands in sharp conflict to any use of force. He then tends to equate nonviolent and violent force. On the other hand, when Niebuhr speaks of love as a redemptive process in the world (much closer to my understanding of love, and, I think, much closer to the New Testament perspective), then he views violent force and nonviolent force as opposites, the latter being much more congruent with redemptive love than violent force.

20. There have been a number of different classifications of types of nonviolence. William Miller distinguishes between nonresistance, passive resistance, and nonviolent direct action. The problem with Miller's classification is that at one level the distinction between nonresistance and the other two types of nonviolence is defined as a theological or philosophical difference. At another level the distinction between passive resistance and nonviolent direct action is more a difference in strategy of action. The latter two tend to merge into each other as groups readily move from one level to the other. C. J. Cadoux has a much better

classification with his distinction between noncoercive and coercive types of actions, with the coercive types broken down into two types: noninjurious and injurious. His classification does not take into account the philosophical differences, and also he fails to consider the possible injurious nature of noncoercive actions. His classification is not as helpful in elaborating the various types of nonviolent coercive action. More descriptive of the techniques of nonviolent action is the classification of the sociologist, Clarence Marsh Case, who distinguishes between various kinds of persuasion, nonviolent coercion and violent coercion. (See Miller, op. cit., pp. 46f; C. J. Cadoux, *Christian Pacifism Re-examined*, p. 45; C. M. Case, *Non-Violent Coercion*, p. 397).

More recently Gene Sharp has classified nonviolent action in terms of the political methods (see footnote 16). In reflecting upon what means of classification is best we need to be careful to distinguish the variable we are trying to keep in mind when making our classification. Classifications like Miller's are most confusing, since they mix variables and are inconsistent in the use of variables, while Sharp's classification is most clear, though it is one-dimensional. I think at least four key variables are operative as we seek to distinguish types: 1. The religious or philosophical orientation, 2. the continuum from persuasion to coercion, 3. the continuum from nonviolence to violence, and 4. the methods of nonviolent action. At the religious level, there are many types of nonviolence as John H. Yoder has pointed out in his book, *Nevertheless: The Varieties of Religious Pacifism*, which describes 18 different types. I do not want to venture any kind of classification here except to counter the assumption that there are primarily two types: a pure religious pacifism of Christianity which is nonresistant and a nonviolent social action which is pragmatic. This is Reinhold Niebuhr's typology, a typology which did not permit him to see and describe clearly an active nonviolence that is principled and rooted in the gospel (as in Martin L. King, and also in his contemporary, A. J. Muste—see Alan Letts' dissertation comparing Niebuhr and Muste), a pacifism which is not simply pragmatic or based on the liberal optimistic assumptions of progress, but also which does not withdraw from the world into a political isolationism as does nonresistance as Niebuhr described it.

21. My argument should not be interpreted to mean that one ought to intervene and physically prevent all persons from killing themselves. For example, the Buddhist monk who burned himself in a symbolic protest over the Vietnam War really killed himself out of the principle of life affirmation, in that his action was an extreme form of speech seeking to sensitize persons to violations of life. His act may well have been a conscientious act of self-sacrifice for the sake of the community and therefore not really an act of suicide. To have prevented him physically from carrying out his action might therefore have been a denial of his freedom to speak as he conscientiously viewed that, and thus would have been a violation of his dignity as a person.

22. The incident in the New Testament when Jesus cleanses the temple has often been an embarrassment to pacifists. Here we see Jesus using force, driving the animals out with a whip, dumping the money tables upside down, and denouncing the money changers as robbers. To those who see love in the New Testament primarily as nonresistant, as a passive and noncoercive withdrawal from conflict, this incident poses a serious problem. For myself, the incident illustrates exactly the point that I have been trying to make in this chapter, that there is a way to exercize power and force that is nonviolent and potentially redemptive. In this incident Jesus exposes evil dramatically. He announces judgment. Though Jesus' action negatively affects the livelihood of the money changers, he opens up to them the possibility of repentance and a more humane vocation that does not depend upon exploitation and manipulation. The outcome is potentially redemptive, though the incident may have contributed to Jesus' crucifixion. Powerful vested interests do resist and the cross is the symbol of that resistance. For an illuminating discussion of Jesus' relationship to power see the chapter, "Christ and Power," in Ronald Sider's book, *Christ and Violence*.

23. Yoder, *Politics of Jesus*, p. 234.

24. Ibid., p. 234.

25. Ibid., p. 235.

26. Ibid., p. 238.

27. Martin L. King, *Stride Toward Freedom*, p. 92.

28. Abraham Heschel, *The Insecurity of Freedom*, pp. 145-146.

29. W. D. Ross, *The Right and the Good*.

30. This methodology of doing ethics has been developed most recently by J. Philip Wogaman, *A Christian Method of Moral Judgment*. He develops the concept of "methodological presumption," the notion that something is to be regarded as true or right unless other overwhelming evidence leads one to conclude otherwise.

31. One of the criticisms of pacifism has been its failure to recognize the plurality of moral claims upon the person and its absolutizing of one principle, nonviolence. For example, Ralph Potter says of pacifists:

> Pacifists . . . profess to know ahead of time that a believer can never participate in the use of violence. The need for subtle forms of ethical reasoning is foreclosed by the conviction that the issues are not subtle. Doing violence in any form is incompatible with Christian discipleship. These affirmations constitute simple, forthright replies to two basic questions: When may I, in good conscience, participate in the use of force? Never. What forms of violence may I employ? None. (*War and Moral Discourse*, p. 51.)

Ted Koontz (himself a pacifist) has argued that pacifists should be consistent in their use of moral reasoning. If, for example, they are willing to consider various moral claims of mother and fetus on the issue of abortion, then why should they be unwilling to weigh the complexity of claims on the issue of war and peace? If abortion is sometimes justified as a result of reasoning out of the complexity of moral claims, then why is war also not sometimes justified? Ted Koontz, "Hard Choices: Abortion and War," *The Mennonite*, Feb. 28, 1978, pp. 132-134.

In general I am sympathetic to Potter's and Koontz's viewpoints. We do need to recognize the complexity by recognizing the claims of both justice and nonviolence upon us. I also find a legalistic ethic impossible, one which says in advance of any particular situation exactly what is right or wrong. Countless pacifists have felt the same way. For example, Dietrich Bonhoeffer, who considered himself a pacifist during the 1930s, before he became a participant in the resistance against Hitler, when asked in a private inquiry what he would do in a future war, refused to say exactly what he would do. Rather he replied that he hoped God would grant him the power to refuse weapons.

Larry Rasmussen, and other interpreters of Bonhoeffer, have thus tended to qualify Bonhoeffer's pacifism as relative, conditional, or provisional. But these adjectives, as applied to his pacifism, arise, says Dale Brown, out of a caricature and stereotype of pacifism as a commitment to absolute principle. Brown says two factors mitigate against a sharp contrast between a Bonhoeffer type of "provisional" pacifism and a pacifism of absolute principle. The noncreedal orientation of the historic peace churches have appropriated existentially the Reformed admonition "to let new light break forth from the Word," and therefore have resisted absolute certainty for every case. Second, Bonhoeffer's reply about what he would do in a future war "resonates with the replies of countless of pacifists before draft boards who have stated that they are not able to state absolutely what they might do in hypothetical situations, but they do pray that they might be faithful to their Lord." (Dale Brown, "Bonhoeffer and Pacifism," p. 11. A paper prepared for the Bonhoeffer Consultation of the American Academy of Religion, St. Louis, Oct. 29, 1976.) Potter's description above is of one type of pacifism, certainly not a view held by many other pacifists who prefer to recognize moral complexities and are more tentative and open about the future.

32. Emil Brunner, *The Divine Imperative*, pp. 470-471.

33. For a brief and clear description of these principles see Ralph Potter's book, *The Moral Logic of War*.

34. Christians have justified theologically the use of armed force in a variety of ways. Some have sought to support their position with biblical texts, others from natural law position,

still others arguing that the general principle of love requires the use of force sometimes to defend an innocent third party who is under attack from an unjust aggressor. Ernst Troeltsch and later Reinhold Niebuhr agree with pacifists that Jesus advocated a pacifist ethic, but they believe it was defined in a more simple world of one-on-one relationships and does not take account of the more complex, modern, political world. In a more complex situation, therefore, pacifism is not workable, and the simple pacifist ethic of Jesus must be supplemented with other norms.

Stephen Mott (op. cit., pp. 167f.) has recently made a very similar argument. He distinguishes between bilateral (one-on-one) and multilateral relationships (defending the cause of a third party). He argues that Jesus' pacifism is defined in relationship to bilateral relationships, but is not developed by Jesus to speak to multilateral or political situations. Thus to say that Jesus is a pacifist with respect to multilateral situation is to argue from silence. Jesus just does not speak to these situations. Crucial to Mott's case is that he demonstrates that Jesus' pacifism was not developed at all to counter the Zealot political option. For if Jesus' pacifism was at all an alternative response to Zealots who believed in the use of violence for the sake of a just cause, then it cannot be said that Jesus was silent about multilateral situations. In fact, the opposite case can be made. It is precisely over against the Zealots that Jesus developed his pacifism. We already discussed the weakness of Mott's case (see footnote 38, chapter 4). If Mott's argument does not hold up, then he must argue that Jesus is simply not our authority on this issue. But if he does that, then he has a more difficult theological problem on the nature of biblical authority. For some theologians that would not be a problem, but it is for Mott given his evangelical theological orientation.

35. James T. Johnson, "Just War Theory: What's the Use?" *Worldview*, July-August, 1976, p. 42.

36. Ibid., p. 42.

37. Ibid., p. 43.

38. This is the subtitle of Ramsey's first major book on war, *War and the Christian Conscience*. Charles Curran is critical of Ramsey's position because of his essential reduction of just war theory to the *jus in bello*. *Politics, Medicine and Christian Ethics: A Dialogue with Paul Ramsey*, pp. 75-76.

39. Michael Walzer, *Just and Unjust Wars*, p. 53.

40. Paul Ramsey, *The Just War*, p. 143.

41. I am indebted for some of these ideas to John Yoder, "What Would You Do If . . . ," *Journal of Religious Ethics*, Fall, 1974, pp. 81f.

42. John Swomley, *American Empire*, op. cit., pp. 84f.

43. Yoder, "What Would You Do If . . ." p. 89.

44. Walzer, op. cit., pp. 151f.

45. Ramsey, *The Just War*, p. 235.

46. Curran, op. cit., p. 94. The dilemmas of applying just war criteria to political reality are reflected in Roman Catholic teaching on deterrence. In *The Challenge of Peace: God's Promise and Our Response*, the May 3, 1983, Pastoral Letter on War and Peace of the National Conference of Catholic Bishops, the bishops say use of nuclear weapons is not permitted because such use would violate the principles of discrimination (killing vast numbers of innocent civilians and noncombatants) and proportionality (the massive destruction that would result would be far greater than the good to be gained). Thus "no use of nuclear weapons which would violate the principles of discrimination or proportionality may be intended in a strategy of deterrence" (iii). Yet, given the nature of the world we live in where "peace of a sort" is obtained by maintaining a minimal balance of deterrence among the superpowers, the bishops allow for deterrence as a transitional strategy "only in conjunction with resolute determination to pursue arms control and disarmament" (iv.). For a detailed justification of this argument see pages 51f. of the letter.

The problem that is still not resolved is how one can simultaneously say that nuclear weapons cannot be used and still maintain the credibility of deterrence. Deterrence is credible only if the other side believes that nuclear weapons will be used. Some might say that simply having the weapons is a credible deterrent because they *might* be used. However, the credibility of this "might" is undermined the more the church teaches that nuclear weapons cannot be used. Since the bishops say that the use of these weapons violates the principles of discrimination and proportionality, the only way out of this dilemma is if one can make the enemy believe that one will use the weapons, even though one's own side is taught not to use them. But how can one teach one's own side that it is morally illicit to use the weapons and still have the other side believe that they will be used if necessary?

47. Alan Newcombe and James Wert, *An Inter-nation Tensiometer for the Prediction of War*, p. 23.

48. Ibid., p. 1.

49. Johnson, op. cit., p. 44. Incidently, there are all kinds of nonviolent means of defense against propaganda, spying, and covert activities (see Sharp, op. cit.). Johnson seems to suggest that these kinds of actions by another nation might constitute a legitimate resort to war. In my judgment these kinds of actions would not by any means constitute a legitimate resort to war since we have other ways to defend against such actions short of war.

50. Ramsey, *The Just War*, p. 195.

51. Curran, op. cit., pp. 82-83.

52. The only guidance I can find in Wogaman is that objectively good ends must be brought about by the violence, and that any violent action undertaken must be interpreted to one's opponent as not motivated by hate but by goodwill (p. 129). The latter suggestion seems to me to be completely unrealistic, especially in the case of war. I am not clear on the first suggestion how one would *know* what possible good ends could be brought about through the use of violence which would outweigh the evil done by the violence. See J. Philip Wogaman, *A Christian Method of Moral Judgment*, especially pp. 117f.

Chapter seven

1. Kenneth Boulding, *Stable Peace*, pp. 31f., 47f.

2. The word "strength" does not mean any particular kind of strength, such as military power. We mean more the stability of a social system to maintain itself in a situation of stable peace. What produces that situation is yet to be described.

3. Margaret Mead, "Warfare Is Only an Invention—Not a Biological Necessity," in *Peace and War*, ed. by Charles K. Beitz and Theodore Herman, p. 117.

4. Quoted by John Swomley, *American Empire: The Political Ethics of Twentieth Century Conquest*, pp. 165-166.

5. John C. Bennett and Harvey Seifert, *U.S. Foreign Policy and Christian Ethics*, pp. 17-18.

6. Lewis Coser, *Functions of Social Conflict*, pp. 48ff. The "behaviorist" approach is another name for the study of international relations as primarily consisting of unrealistic conflict. Robert North and Herbert Kelman are representative scholars of international relations who have used behaviorist approaches. David Halberstam's book, *The Best and the Brightest*, describes the process by which the United States became involved in Vietnam as a series of miscalculations, misperceptions, and blunders.

"Behavioral conflict researchers focus upon the various person-actors in conflict—decision-making styles of national leaders, variables influencing the decision-making process, perceptions of and communication between conflict parties, values and attitudes influencing conflictual behavior, personality variables and their determinants which make for peace- or war-proneness" (Paul Wehr, *Conflict Regulation*, pp. 15-16).

7. Adam Curle, *Making Peace*, pp. 3f.

8. A basic orientation and summary of basic literature on the nature and function of intervenors in conflict is described by Paul Wehr in his book, *Conflict Regulation*. The negotia-

tion for the release of the United States hostages from Iran is an interesting case study of the significance of third-party intervenors in helping resolve that crisis. This process was described in a three-hour ABC news program. A transcript of this program is available from ABC News.

9. Curle, op. cit., p. 261.

10. Pope John XXIII, *Pacem in Terris—Peace on Earth*, par. 127.

11. John Bennett and Harvey Seifert, *U.S. Foreign Policy and Christian Ethics*, p. 99. See also the book by John Bennett, *The Radical Imperative*, pp. 183-184.

12. Margaret Mead, "Warfare Is Only an Invention—Not a Biological Necessity," in *Peace and War*, ed. by Charles R. Beitz and Theodore Herman, p. 113.

13. Melko, Matthew, *Fifty-two Peaceful Societies*.

14. Mead, op. cit., p. 113.

15. Werner Levi, "The Causes of War and Peace," in the four-volume series, *The Strategy of World Order*, edited by Richard A. Falk and Saul H. Mendlovitz, Vol. I, p. 151.

16. Ibid., p. 153.

17. Ibid., p. 154.

18. In his book, *War and Moral Discourse*, Ralph Potter argues that pacifism is responsible for the excesses of war because pacifism fails to provide the proper restraints upon the conduct of war that is provided by just war theory. This argument has two problems. One problem is that he assumes that war is inevitable and therefore believes that a system of restraint upon war is more realistic than the attempt to prevent and abolish war altogether. This is itself a legitimation of war that furthers the likelihood of war. The other problem is that his case can hardly be sustained by empirical observation. The unrestrained nature of war can hardly be blamed upon pacifism, a group of people that has always been a very small minority, even in times like between the world wars when pacifism was relatively popular. War has broken out with such intensity because nations have never abandoned the preparation for war, and that preparation has always adopted the most advanced forms of technology available. To hope to restrain war by moral thought is an illusion. Once a war begins, nations will use, as they have in the past, the technology available to them. A much more realistic approach would be to prevent war in the first place by working at the levels of the problem we are describing in this chapter.

19. John Swomley, *Liberation Ethics*, p. 147f.

20. Lloyd Dumas, "National Insecurity in the Nuclear Age," *Bulletin of the Atomic Scientists*, May 1976.

21. Ibid., p. 24.

22. Ibid., p. 27. Reprinted by permission of *The Bulletin of the Atomic Scientists*, a magazine of science and world affairs. Copyright © 1976 by the Educational Foundation for Nuclear Science, Chicago, IL 60637.

23. Ibid., pp. 28-29.

24. *Wichita Eagle-Beacon*, Nov. 10, 1979.

25. Dumas, op. cit., p. 31.

26. Ibid., p. 31.

27. Ibid., p. 32.

28. Ibid., p. 49.

29. Kenneth Boulding, *The Meaning of the Twentieth Century*, p. 87.

30. John Cox, *Overkill: Weapons of the Nuclear Age*, p. 45.

31. Ibid., p. 80.

32. For an excellent analysis of the SALT process see the pamphlet by Alan Geyer, *Arms Limits and SALT Limits: The Superpowers' Role in Nuclear Disarmament*. Published by the Center for Theology and Public Policy.

33. Michael Novak, *The Christian Century*, Feb. 21, 1979, p. 172f.

34. Robert Kaiser, "The Nuclear Arms Race: A Soviet View," *The Washington Post*, Feb. 21, 1977.

35. Randall Forsberg, "A Bilateral Nuclear Freeze," *Scientific American*, Nov. 1982, pp. 9-10.

36. Kaiser, op. cit.

37. See Reinhold Niebuhr's critique of world government, "The Illusion of World Government," in a collection of his essays, *Christian Realism and Political Problems*.

38. Betty Reardon and Saul H. Mendlovitz, "World Law and Models of World Order," in Beitz and Herman, op. cit., p. 159. Their position draws heavily on Greenville Clark and Louis B. Sohn, *World Peace Through World Law*.

39. Kenneth Boulding, *Stable Peace*, p. 117.

CHAPTER EIGHT

1. A vast number of new resources are coming out in the area of peace education. The best place to write for information about these resources is the Consortium for Peace Research, Education and Development (COPRED), University of Illinois, Urbana, IL. Several books I have found particularly helpful are: Susan Carpenter, *A Repertoire of Peacemaking Skills* (available from COPRED); Paul Wehr and Michael Washburn, *Peace and World Order Systems: Teaching and Research*; Charles Beitz and Michael Washburn, *Creating the Future*; Paul Wehr, *Conflict Regulation*; Roger Fisher, *International Conflict for Beginners*; Barbara Stanford, ed., *Peacemaking*; Adam Curle, *Making Peace*; Stephanie Judson, *A Manual on Nonviolence and Children; To End War* (World Without War Council); and many others. Carpenter's book gives a list of books and organizations that one might consult for further information.

2. Billy Graham, for example, at the height of the Vietnam War appeared on the same platform with President Lyndon Johnson at a support America rally. Though Graham claimed at the time that he had no political position in his mind, most Americans probably interpreted his actions as indicating basic support for the U.S. position in Vietnam. To his credit, Graham has changed his views considerably in recent years. He is now very critical of the arms race, and also looks back to his own past attitudes and actions quite critically. See the interview with Graham, *Sojourners*, August 1979.

3. Dallas Lee, *The Cotton Patch Evidence*. The Clarence Jordan family and several friends began Koinonia Farm near Americus, Georgia, in 1942. The group began introducing scientific farming methods in the area and was quite successful. However, in early 1956, because the farm included both blacks and whites and supported desegregation, the farm's products were almost totally boycotted, business services were refused in Americus, the farm's roadside stand was bombed twice, and shots were fired into farm buildings.

4. South African churchman John deGruchy reports that the churches belonging to the South African Council of Churches have been opposed to apartheid, at least in principle, since 1948. The goal of the church is reconciliation. The goal of the government is separation. The two obviously clash, and the clash creates conflict along the whole spectrum of social life. In that situation it becomes important for blacks and whites to share communion and worship together. That visible sign of reconciliation strengthens the people involved and gives hope of overcoming the problems. John deGruchy, *The Church Struggle in South Africa*.

5. Religion provided the dominating influence for establishing hospitals through the Middle Ages. From a decree of Constantine issued in A.D. 335 Christian hospitals developed at Rome, Constantinople, Ephesus, and other parts of the Roman Empire. Monks and various religious orders gave themselves to the care of the sick. Monasteries had an infirmatorium, which provided a model for the laity, where sick were taken for treatment, and which frequently possessed a pharmacy and garden with medicinal plants. Many Mennonite young men who were conscientious objectors in World War II worked in mental health institutions. Partly out of this experience Mennonites developed a number of mental hospitals, introducing some of the most innovative mental health care in the country. See *If We Can Love: The*

Mennonite Mental Health Story, by Vernon Neufeld.

6. James Luther Adams, in "The Political Responsibility of the Man of Culture" (Venice, Italy: Comprendre, Société Européenne de Culture, No. 16, 1956), contends that nonconformity by religious groups has decisively contributed to the concept of freedom of association and the development of modern democracy. Where nonconformity has been feeble or suppressed, democracy and freedom of association have been slow to develop. Early Christian sects, the Anabaptists of the left wing of the Reformation, and other religious groups which directly challenged the monolithic society of their time are the prototypes of modern voluntary associations. Their actions built the base for a pluralistic society that allows for many free associations of people around causes of social reform and cultural interest. See also D. B. Robertson, ed., *Voluntary Associations: A Study in Free Socieities.*

7. See *The Victim Offender Reconciliation Program* by Howard Zehr. (Available from the Mennonite Central Committee, Akron, Pa.) The Movement for a New Society (MNS), 4722 Baltimore, Philadelphia, PA 19143, is perhaps one of the best examples of setting up alternative institutions. In Philadelphia members have worked at an alternative method of crime control by trying to build a sense of community in neighborhoods, and break the mentality of having to lock everything up tight and be suspicious. As part of the program 24 blocks have been organized with captains and monthly meetings. Teams of residents walk the streets during peak crime times armed only with pocket-sized freon horns. Members of MNS are also involved in food co-ops, clinics, worker-controlled industries, etc. See also George Lakey, *Strategy for a Living Revolution.*

8. John P. Adams, *At the Heart of the Whirlwind.* In March 1973 Indians from the American Indian Movement took over the town of Wounded Knee, South Dakota. The federal government responded by sending troops to the area. Adams served as go-between for the two groups. Each side trusted him enough to let him pass back and forth across the embattled lines. He kept communication open by carrying messages from one side to the other, and he arranged for food and supplies to be brought in for the Indians.

9. In Asheville, North Carolina, the residents of a public housing project were the victims of housing conditions that were in various states of disrepair. Carl Johnson, one of the residents in the project, served as a third party *activist* by helping the tenants organize a rent strike. As an activist he made only suggestions, not decisions. The strike lasted almost a year, but the tenants were able to get the necessary repairs, and a more favorable lease. St. Louis: Washington University, *Crisis and Change,* Vol. 2, No. 4, Aug. 1972, pp. 6-7.

In St. Louis a community group concerned with the inadequate enforcement of city housing codes hired Henry Freund as an *activist* to support their cause. Freund researched city records, advised on legal technicalities, and helped the community group document their claims and get a hearing with city aldermen. The results of the effort led to the replacement of the Housing Court judge by two judges who had worked for effective housing code enforcement, and thus more confidence in the court and better code enforcement. St. Louis: Washington University, *Crisis and Change,* Vol. 2, No. 2, Spring 1972.

10. In Juneau, Alaska, several complaints were filed against the Juneau school administration for their handling of disciplinary actions involving minority students. A *mediator* entered the dispute and conducted talks between representatives of the citizens groups and the school board. The talks resulted in several recommendations—review of disciplinary policy, strengthening of the school counseling program, staff training in human relations and cultural awareness, and input from parents on the student handbook. *Southeast Alaska Empire,* Juneau, Alaska, January 26, 1977.

11. St. Louis: Washington University, *Crisis and Change,* Vol. 3, No. 3, Fall 1973.

12. In the past few years the Mennonite Central Committee has developed an institution called Mennonite Conciliation Service. This institution provides consultation and resources to persons and groups who are experiencing conflict and need help in resolving their disputes peacefully.

13. The Quakers have been more active at the international level than any other Christian group. A description and analysis of Quaker efforts at international conciliation can be found in the book by C. H. Mike Yarrow, *Quaker Experiences in International Conciliation.*

14. See Michael Walzer, *Political Action: A Practical Guide to Movement Politics,* for useful pointers on organizing campaigns and various political actions, and for a discussion of the use of electoral politics as a way to politicize the constituency, raise important issues, and put pressure on other candidates.

15. John Adams, *The Growing Church Lobby in Washington.* For many the Civil Rights Act of 1964 presented a clear choice of right and wrong and thus was able to generate widespread support for its passage. The National Council of Churches, working with various denominations, developed a four-pronged approach: 1) working with the Leadership Conference on Civil Rights, which was a coalition of 75 groups; 2) forming alliances among denominations; 3) bringing religious leaders to Washington to meet with legislators; and 4) sending out teams to generate support. Beyond these more formal measures many church members participated in demonstrations, urged congressmen to vote favorably, etc. In the summer of 1964, the Senate, for the first time and under pressure from a strong church lobby, voted to end a Southern filibuster against civil rights, and later that summer both houses passed the act.

16. The Mennonite Central Committee Peace Section, 21 S. 12th St., Akron, PA 17501, or 100 Maryland Ave. NE, Washington, D.C. 20002, maintains offices in Washington and Ottawa, publishes a *Memo* to keep church constituents up-to-date on current legislation and government action, and carries on a variety of peace-related projects around the world.

The Friends Committee on National Legislation, 245 2nd St. NE, Washington, DC 20002, is a registered Washington lobby, and a working committee of Friends that attempts to translate Quaker beliefs into action by actively influencing congressional members, and by publishing a regular newsletter and other materials related to the electoral and legislative process.

17. See Paul Ramsey's book, *Who Speaks for the Church,* where he raises a number of important questions about the church's credibility when it speaks on public issues.

In a March 1978 meeting with National Council of Churches' leaders, President Carter commented in response to some of their criticisms: "The government has done a great deal to eliminate segregation, one of the afflictions of our society. The churches have done much less. . . . I recognize we have a long way to go in the government, but on balance the government has done a better job than the churches. I say this as a member of both" *Christian Century,* March 15, 1978, p. 264.

18. James Luther Adams stresses the idea that humans are to be understood in terms of their associations, and that voluntary association can be a potent element in society. D. B. Robertson, ed., *Voluntary Associations: A Study of Groups in Free Societies,* is a collection of writings on voluntary associations in honor of James Luther Adams and includes a bibliography of Adams' writings.

19. Karl Holl, "A History of the Word Vocation," presents an extensive analysis of the history and development of the concept of vocation, especially within a Christian context.

20. For further discussion on this issue see Michael Washburn and Paul Wehr, *Peace and World Order Systems,* pp. 101-117.

21. Roger Fisher, *International Conflict for Beginners,* underscores the necessity for politicians and governments to calculate constructively their actions when trying to influence another nation or group in a certain direction. He sets up a schematic map (see next page) on which the different features of an influence problem can be thought through and action calculated by answering each of the questions, and also estimating how the presumed adversary would answer them.

See also the final chapter in J. Philip Wogaman's book, *A Christian Method of Moral Judgment,* for a discussion of strategy issues.

22. In 1962 as the Southern Christian Leadership Conference was taking its campaign to

	DEMAND The decision desired by us	OFFER The consequences of making the decision	THREAT The consequences of not making the decision
WHO?	Who is to make the decision?	Who benefits if the decision is made?	Who gets hurt if the decision is not made?
WHAT?	Exactly what decision is desired?	If the decision is made, what benefits can be expected? —what costs?	If the decision is not made, —what risks? —what potential benefits?
WHEN?	By what time does the decision have to be made?	When, if ever, will the benefits of making the decision occur?	How soon will the consequences of not making the decision be felt?
WHY?	What makes this a right, proper, and lawful decision?	What makes these consequences fair and legitimate?	What makes these consequences fair and legitimate?

Birmingham, King reflected back on the recent actions in Albany, "We had been so involved in attacking segregation in general that we had failed to direct our protest effectively at any one major facet." That analysis led the SCLC to develop a strategy of much more intensive, sustained effort, focused on a limited number of objectives. William R. Miller, *Martin Luther King, Jr.*, p. 132.

During the civil rights struggle the SCLC held off its intended nonviolent campaign in Birmingham for almost six months pending the outcome of a run-off election for mayor on April 2, 1963, between Bull Conner and more moderate Albert Boutwell. William R. Miller, *Martin Luther King, Jr.*, p. 133.

During 1924-1925 Gandhi led a campaign specifically to gain the right for untouchables to use the road that passed a temple. In 1928 the objective of action was to persuade the government to launch an impartial inquiry into the enhancement of the land revenue assessment in the area of Bardoli. In 1930-1931 the immediate objective of Gandhi's action was the removal of the Salt Acts imposed by the British. Joan Bondurant, *Conquest of Violence: The Gandhian Philosophy of Conflict*, pp. 45-104.

23. Muzafer Sherif, *In Common Predicament: Social Psychology of Intergroup Conflict and Cooperation.*

24. Tom Stonier has made extensive proposals for approaching two world problems—eliminating air pollution and food production in deserts—as superordinate goals to both solve the problems and promote cooperation among nations. Part of his proposals are printed in "A Proposal for Global Cooperation," *Bulletin of the Atomic Scientists*, May 1972, pp. 31-34. See also Gene Keyes and Scott Seymour, "The Sahara Forest and Other Superordinate Goals," *Peace Research Reviews*, Vol. 6, No. 3, Jan. 1975.

25. Dietrich Bonhoeffer, *Letters and Papers from Prison*, pp. 3-4.

26. John Fox, William Forbush, ed., *Fox's Book of Martyrs: A History of the Lives, Sufferings, and Triumphant Deaths of the Early Christian and Protestant Martyrs;* Thieleman Jansz van Braght, *The Bloody Theater or Martyrs Mirror;* Geoffrey Nuttall, *Christian Pacifism in History.*

CHAPTER NINE

1. W. Somerset Maugham, *The Razor's Edge*, quoted by Jack Canfield and Harold Wells, *100 Ways to Enhance Self-Concept in the Classroom*, p. 29.

2. Romain Rolland, *Gandhi*, p. 40.

3. M. L. King, *Stride Toward Freedom*, "Pilgrimage to Nonviolence," chapter VI.

4. Henri Nouwen, *Pray to Live*, p. 63.

5. Marjorie Hope and James Young, *The Struggle for Humanity*, p. 73.

6. Dietrich Bonhoeffer, *The Cost of Discipleship*, p. 84.

7. James Douglass, *Resistance and Contemplation*, p. 145.

8. King, op. cit., pp. 102-107.

9. Hope and Young, op. cit., pp. 105-106.

10. Malcolm Little, *Autobiography*, pp. 340-341.

11. It would be inappropriate to catalogue in this chapter the wide spectrum of religious experience. For further reading on the subject see William James, *Varieties of Religious Experience*.

12. William James, *The Varieties of Religious Experience*, pp. 188-258.

13. See Erik Erikson's book, *Identity: Youth and Crisis*. James Fowler has shown how the stages of psycho-social development relate very closely to the developmental stages of faith. *Stages of Faith*.

14. Peace education manuals for teachers (and parents) of children often begin with exercises designed to affirm and increase the individual's self-esteem through creative self-expression in an open, supportive atmosphere. In sequence, the focus is then directed to relationship with others, outlining activities which encourage cooperation, appreciation of diversity, and peaceful methods of conflict resolution. (See Canfield and Wells, op. cit.; Stephanie Judson, *A Manual on Nonviolence and Children;* Grace Abrams and Fran Schmidt, *Peace Is in Our Hands.)* The order of emphasis is not without significance. For love of others follows from love of self, and appreciation of the worth of others follows from recognition of one's own self-worth.

15. Douglass, op. cit., p. 149.

16. Ibid., p. 25.

17. Ibid., p. 10.

18. Ibid., p. 77.

19. Ibid., p. 91.

20. Hope and Young, op. cit., p. 76.

21. See Simone Weil's books, *Waiting for God, The Need for Roots, Gravity and Grace, Seventy Letters, and Selected Essays.*

22. Simone Weil, *Gravity and Grace*, p. 11.

23. Ibid., p. 10.

24. Thich Nhat Honh has also coauthored, with Daniel Berrigan, *The Raft Is Not the Shore*, a dialogue on Christian-Buddhist awareness.

25. Thomas Merton, *Asian Journal*, p. 306.

26. Nouwen, op. cit., p. 24.

27. Desmond Doig, *Mother Teresa*, pp. 155, 166.

28. Dag Hammarskjöld, *Markings*. tr. by Leif Sjöberg and W. H. Auden (New York: Alfred A. Knopf, 1964; London: Faber and Faber, 1964), pp. 214-215. Reprinted by permission of publishers.

29. John Alexander, "Rediscovering the Spiritual," *The Other Side*, Oct. 1977, p. 20.

30. See the book by Mina C. and H. Arthur Klein, *Käthe Kollwitz: Life in Art*.

31. Leonard Bernstein, "Introduction," in *Sing, Children, Sing*, edited by Carl S. Miller, U.S. Committee for UNICEF, 1972.

32. For further elaboration of the idea of "story," and the notion of "story as autobiography," see Michael Novak's *Ascent of the Mountain, Flight of the Dove*. For

thoughts on the relationship between story and ethics, see Stan Hauerwas's *Vision and Virtue*.

33. Novak, op. cit., p. 109.

34. Annis Duff, *Bequest of Wings*, p. 135.

35. The following description of the shalom-church incorporates many of the Anabaptist views of church and discipleship, as portrayed in Guy F. Hershberger's *Recovery of the Anabaptist Vision;* Franklin H. Littell's *Anabaptist View of the Church;* and J. Lawrence Burkholder's "The Peace Churches as Communities of Discernment," which appeared in the Sept. 4, 1963 issue of *Christian Century.*

36. Harold S. Bender, "The Anabaptist Vision," in *Recovery of the Anabaptist Vision*, edited by Guy Hershberger, p. 50.

37. Abraham Heschel, *The Sabbath*.

38. Littell, op. cit., p. 10.

39. Dietrich Bonhoeffer, *Life Together*, p. 122.

40. Dorothy Day, *Loaves and Fishes*, p. 122.

41. Dorothy Day, *On Pilgrimage*, p. 86.

42. Doig, op. cit., p. 165.

43. Robert Cooney and Helen Michalowoki, eds., *The Power of the People: Active Nonviolence in the United States*, pp. 85-87.

44. Day, *On Pilgrimage*, p. 8.

45. Cooney and Michalowoki, op. cit., p. 131.

46. King, op. cit., chapter IV, pp. 53-89.

47. Ibid., pp. 153-157.

48. Rolland, op. cit., p. 95.

49. George Lakey, *Strategy for a Living Revolution*, p. 102.

50. Douglass, op. cit., p. 40.

51. Ibid., p. 39.

52. James Cone, *The Spirituals and the Blues*.

53. Rolland, op. cit., p. 96.

54. Mary Harris Jones, "How the Women Sang Themselves Out of Jail," in *Peacemaking*, edited by Barbara Stanford.

55. Day, *On Pilgrimage*, p. 60.

56. Day, *Loaves and Fishes*, p. 69.

57. Ibid., p. 210.

58. Anna Juhnke, speaking to the Mennonite World Conference, Wichita, Kansas, 1978. Quoted in *Which Way Women?* Dorothy Yoder Nyce, ed., p. 156.

59. James H. Forest, "Astonishing Hope," *Sojourners*, Feb. 18, 1980.

BIBLIOGRAPHY
OF SOURCES CITED

Abrams, Grace and Fran Schmidt, *Peace Is in Our Hands*. Philadelphia: Jane Addams Peace Association, 1974.

Adams, James, *The Growing Church Lobby in Washington*. Grand Rapids: Eerdmans, 1970.

Adams, James Luther, *On Being Human Religiously*. Boston: Beacon Press, 1976.

Adams, James Luther, "The Political Responsibility of the Man of Culture." Venice, Italy: Comprendre, Société Européene de Culture (No. 16, 1956) 11-25.

Adams, John P., *At the Heart of the Whirlwind*. New York: Harper and Row, 1976.

Alexander, John, "Rediscovering the Spiritual." *The Other Side* (Oct. 1977), 20.

Bainton, Roland, *Christian Attitudes Toward War and Peace*. Nashville: Abingdon, 1960.

Barnet, Richard, *The Giants: Russia and America*. New York: Simon and Schuster, 1977.

Barnet, Richard and Ronald Mueller, *Global Reach: The Power of Multinational Corporations*. New York: Simon and Schuster, 1974.

Barnet, Richard, *The Lean Years*. New York: Simon and Schuster, 1980.

Barth, Karl, *Church Dogmatics III/1*. Edinburgh: T. and T. Clark, 1961.

Barth, Karl and Johannes Hamel, *How to Serve God in a Marxist Land*. New York: Association Press, 1959.

Beitz, Charles and Michael Washburn, *Creating the Future*. New York: Bantam Books, 1974.

Beitz, Charles R., and Theodore Herman, eds., *Peace and War*. San Francisco: W. H. Freeman and Co., 1973.

Bender, Harold S., "The Anabaptist Vision," in *Recovery of the Anabaptist Vision*. Ed., Guy Hershberger, Scottdale, Pa.: Herald Press, 1957.

Bennett, John, *The Radical Imperative: From Theology to Social Ethics*. Philadelphia: Westminster Press, 1975.

Bennett, John C. and Harvey Seifert, *U.S. Foreign Policy and Christian Ethics*. Philadelphia: Westminster Press, 1977.

Berger, Peter, *Pyramids of Sacrifice*. Garden City, New York: Anchor Books, 1976.

Berkhof, Hendrik, *Christ and the Powers*. Scottdale, Pa.: Herald Press, 1977.

Bernstein, Leonard, "Introduction," in *Sing, Children, Sing*. Ed., Carl S. Miller, U.S. Committee for UNICEF, 1972.

Bondurant, Joan, *Conquest of Violence: The Gandhian Philosophy of Conflict*. Revised edition. Berkeley: University of California Press, 1965.

Bonhoeffer, Dietrich, *Letters and Papers from Prison*. London: S.C.M. Press, 1953.

Bonhoeffer, Dietrich, *Life Together*. London: S.C.M. Press LTD, 1954.

Bonhoeffer, Dietrich, *The Cost of Discipleship*. New York: Macmillan Company, 1959.

Boserup, Anders and Andrew Mack, *War Without Weapons: Nonviolence in National Defense*. New York: Schocken, 1975.

Boulding, Kenneth, *Conflict and Defense*. New York: Harper & Row, 1962.

Boulding, Kenneth, *The Meaning of the 20th Century*. New York: Harper & Row, 1964.

Boulding, Kenneth, *Stable Peace*. Austin: University of Texas Press, 1978.

Boulding, Kenneth, "Toward a Pure Theory of Threat Systems," in *Political Power: A Reader in Theory and Research.* Eds., Roderich Bell, David V. Edwards, and R. Harrison Wagner, New York: Free Press, 1969.

Braght, Thieleman Jansz van, *The Bloody Theater or Martyrs Mirror of the Defenseless Christians.* Scottdale, Pa.: Herald Press, 1972.

Bright, John, *A History of Israel.* Philadelphia: Westminster Press, 1959.

Brown, Dale, "Bonhoeffer and Pacifism." A paper prepared for the Bonhoeffer Consultation of the American Academy of Religion, St. Louis (Oct. 29, 1976).

Brown, Lester, *By Bread Alone.* New York: Praeger, 1974.

Brown, Lester, *World Without Borders.* New York: Vintage Books, 1972.

Brown, Robert McAfee, *Religion and Violence.* Philadelphia: Westminster Press, 1973.

Brucan, Silviu, "The Systemic Power." *Journal of Peace Research,* 121 (1975) 63-70.

Brueggeman, Walter, *Living Toward a Vision: Biblical Reflections on Shalom.* Philadelphia: United Church Press, 1976.

Brunner, Emil, *The Divine Imperative.* Philadelphia: Westminster Press, 1979.

Burkholder, J. Lawrence, "The Peace Churches as Communities of Discernment." *Christian Century* (Sept. 4, 1963), 1072-1075.

Cadoux, C. J., *Christian Pacifism Reexamined.* New York: Garland Pub., 1940.

Canfield, Jack, and Harold Wells, *100 Ways to Enhance Self-Concept in the Classroom.* Englewood Cliffs, N.J.: Prentice-Hall, 1976.

Carpenter, Susan, *A Repertoire of Peacemaking Skills.* Consortium on Peace Research, Education and Development and the Institute for World Order, 1977.

Carroll, Berenice, "Peace Research: The Cult of Power." *Conflict Resolution,* Vol. 16, No. 4 (Dec. 1972), 585-619.

Case, C. M., *Non-Violent Coercion: A Study in Methods of Social Pressure.* New York: Century Co., 1923.

The Challenge of Peace: God's Promise and Our Response, Pastoral Letter on War and Peace of the National Conference of Catholic Bishops (May 3, 1983). Washington, D.C.: United States Catholic Conference, 1983.

Christian Century. "NCC Leaders Meet with President" (March 15, 1978), 264.

Clark, Greenville, and Louis B. Sohn, *World Peace Through World Law.* Cambridge: Harvard University Press, 1966.

Collins, Joseph, and Francis Moore Lappe, *Food First: Beyond the Myth of Scarcity.* Boston: Houghton-Mifflin, 1977.

Cooney, Robert, and Helen Michalowoki, eds., *The Power of the People: Active Nonviolence in the United States.* Culver City, Calif.: Peace Press, Inc., 1977.

Cone, James, *The Spirituals and the Blues.* New York: Seabury Press, 1972.

Corning, Peter A., "Human Violence: Some Causes and Implications," in *Peace and War.* Eds., Charles R. Beitz and Theodore Herman, San Francisco: W. H. Freeman and Co., 1973.

Coser, Lewis, *Functions of Social Conflict.* New York: Free Press, 1956.

Cox, John, *Overkill: Weapons of the Nuclear Age.* New York: Crowell, 1978.

Crisis and Change. Vol. 2, No. 2, St. Louis: Washington Univ., Spring, 1972.

Crisis and Change. Vol. 2, No. 4, St. Louis: Washington Univ., Aug., 1972.

Crisis and Change. Vol. 3, No. 3, St. Louis: Washington Univ., Fall, 1973.

Cullmann, Oscar, *Christ and Time.* Philadelphia: Westminster Press, 1950.

Cullmann, Oscar, *The State in the New Testament.* New York: Charles Scribner's Sons, 1956.

Curle, Adam, *Making Peace.* London: Tavistock Publications, 1971.

Curran, Charles, *Politics, Medicine and Christian Ethics: A Dialogue with Paul Ramsey.* Philadelphia: Fortress Press, 1973.

Day, Dorothy, *Loaves and Fishes.* San Francisco: Harper & Row, 1963.

Day, Dorothy, *On Pilgrimage.* New York: Curtis Books, 1972.

deGruchy, John, *The Church Struggle in South Africa.* Grand Rapids: Eerdmans, 1979.

Deutsch, Karl, *The Analysis of International Relations,* Second Edition. Englewood, Cliffs, N.J.: Prentice-Hall, 1978.

Dodd, C. H., *The Coming of Christ.* Cambridge (England): University Press, 1951.

Doig, Desmond, *Mother Teresa, Her People and Her Work.* New York: Harper & Row, 1976.

Douglass, James, *Resistance and Contemplation: The Way of Liberation.* Garden City, N.J.: Doubleday, 1972.

Duff, Annis, *Bequest of Wings, A Family's Pleasures with Books.* New York: Viking Press, 1944.

Dumas, Lloyd, "Economic Conversion, Productive Efficiency and Social Welfare." *Journal of Social Welfare,* (Jan./March 1977), 567-596.

Dumas, Lloyd, "National Insecurity in the Nuclear Age." *Bulletin of Atomic Scientists* (May 1976), 24-35.

Eichrodt, Walther, *Theology of the Old Testament.* Philadelphia: Westminster Press, 1961.

Eliade, Mircea, *The Sacred and the Profane.* New York: Harcourt, Brace, and World, Inc., 1959.

Ellul, Jacques, *Violence.* New York: Seabury Press, 1969.

Erikson, Erik, *Identity: Youth and Crisis.* New York: W. W. Norton & Co., Inc., 1968.

Ewert, Merrill, *Humanization and Development.* Akron, Pa.: Mennonite Central Committee Development Monograph Series, No. 2.

"Family Farms." *Z Magazine* (April 1974) 6-11.

Fisher, Roger, *International Conflict for Beginners.* New York: Harper & Row, 1969.

Foerster, Werner, "Eirene in the New Testament." *Theological Dictionary of the New Testament.* Ed., Gerhard Kittel, Vol. II, Grand Rapids: Eerdmans, 1964, 411-420.

Forest, James H., "Astonishing Hope." *Sojourners* (Feb. 18, 1980), 16-19.

Forsberg, Randall, "A Bilateral Nuclear Freeze." *Scientific American* (Nov. 1982), 9-10.

Fowler, James, *Stages of Faith.* San Francisco: Harper & Row, 1976.

Fox, John, and William Forbush, eds., *Fox's Book of Martyrs: A History of the Lives, Sufferings, and Triumphant Deaths of the Early Christian and Protestant Martyrs.* Philadelphia: Schaefer & Koradi, 18??.

Friere, Paulo, *Pedagogy of the Oppressed.* New York: Herder and Herder, 1970.

Fromm, Erich, *Escape from Freedom.* New York: Farrar & Rinehart, Inc., 1941.

Galtung, Johann, "Peace." *International Encyclopedia of the Social Sciences.* Vol. II, Crowell, Collier, and Macmillan, Inc., 1968, 487-496.

Galtung, Johann, "Social Structure, Religious Structure, and the Fight for Peace," *Peace: Research, Education, Action. Essays in Peace Research.* Vol. 1, Copenhagen: Christian Ejlers, 1975.

Galtung, Johann, "Violence, Peace, and Peace Research." *Journal of Peace Research,* No. 3 (1969), 167-191.

Geyer, Alan, *Arms Limits and SALT Limits: The Superpowers' Role in Nuclear Disarmament.* Washington, D.C., Center for Theology and Public Policy, 1979.

Goulet, Denis, *A New Moral Order: Studies in Development Ethics and Liberation Theology.* Maryknoll, N.Y.: Orbis Books, 1974.

Gremillion, Joseph, *The Gospel of Peace and Justice: Catholic Social Teaching Since Pope John.* Maryknoll, N.Y.: Orbis Books, 1976.

Gutierrez, Gustavo, *A Theology of Liberation.* Maryknoll, N.Y.: Orbis Books, 1973.

Halberstam, David, *The Best and the Brightest.* Greenwich, Conn.: Fawcett Publications, Inc., 1969.

Haley, Alex, and Malcom X, *The Autobiography of Malcolm X.* New York: Grove Press, Inc., 1964.

Hanh, Thich Nhat, and Daniel Berrigan, *The Raft Is Not the Shore.* Boston: Beacon Press, 1975.

Hammarskjöld, Dag, *Markings.* New York: Alfred A. Knopf, 1964. London: Faber and Faber, Ltd., 1964.

Harden, Garrett, "Lifeboat Ethics: The Case Against Helping the Poor." *Psychology Today* (Sept., 1974).

Harden, Garrett, "The Tragedy of the Commons," in *Exploring New Ethics for Survival: The Voyage of the Spaceship Beagle*. New York: Viking Press, 1968, 250-264.

Hauerwas, Stanley, "From System to Story: An Alternative Pattern for Rationality in Ethics," in *Truthfulness and Tragedy*. Notre Dame: University of Notre Dame Press, 1977, 15-39.

Hauerwas, Stanley, *The Peaceable Kingdom: A Primer in Christian Ethics*. Notre Dame: University of Notre Dame Press, 1983.

Hauerwas, Stanley, *Truthfulness and Tragedy*. Notre Dame: University of Notre Dame Press, 1977.

Hauerwas, Stanley, *Vision and Virtue*. Notre Dame: Fides Publishers, Inc., 1974.

Hershberger, Guy F., *Recovery of the Anabaptist Vision*. Scottdale, Pa.: Herald Press, 1957.

Heschel, Abraham, *The Insecurity of Freedom: Essays on Human Existence*. New York: Farrar, Straus & Giroux, 1966.

Heschel, Abraham, *The Prophets*. New York: Harper & Row, 1962.

Heschel, Abraham, *The Sabbath*. New York: Noonday Press, 1951.

Holl, Karl, "A History of the Word Vocation." Translation by Heber F. Peacock unpublished. *Gesammelte Aufsatze zur Kirchengeschichte*. Vol. III, Darmstadt: J. C. B. Mohr, 1965, 189-219.

Hope, Marjorie, and James Young, *The Struggle for Humanity: Agents of Nonviolent Change in a Violent World*. Maryknoll, N.Y.: Orbis Books, 1977.

James, William, *Varieties of Religious Experience*. New York: New American Library, 1958.

Jewett, Paul, *Man as Male and Female*. Grand Rapids: Eerdmans, 1975.

Johnson, James T., "Just War Theory: What's the Use?" *Worldview*, (July-August, 1976), 42.

Josephus, *Complete Works*. Grand Rapids: Kregel Publications, 1960.

Jones, Mary Harris, "How the Women Sang Themselves Out of Jail," in *Peacemaking*. Ed., Barbara Stanford, New York: Bantam Books, 1976.

Judson, Stephanie, *A Manual on Nonviolence and Children*. Philadelphia: Nonviolence & Children Program, Friends Peace Committee, 1977.

Kaiser, Robert, "The Nuclear Arms Race: A Soviet View." *The Washington Post* (Feb. 21, 1977).

Kaufman, Gordon, *Systematic Theology: A Historicist Perspective*. New York: Charles Scribner's Sons, 1968.

Keeney, William, *Lordship as Servanthood*. Newton, Kans.: Faith and Life Press, 1975.

Keohane, Robert O., and Joseph Nye, *Power and Interdependence: World Politics in Transition*. Boston: Little, Brown, 1977.

Keohane, Robert O., and Joseph Nye, eds., *Transnational Relations and World Politics*. Cambridge Mass.: Harvard University Press, 1972.

Keyes, Gene, and Scott Seymour, "The Sahara Forest and Other Superordinate Goals." *Peace Research Reviews*, Vol. 6, No. 3 (Jan. 1975).

King, Martin L., *Stride Toward Freedom*. New York: Harper & Brothers, Publishers, 1958.

King, Martin L., *Why We Can't Wait*. New York: New American Library, 1963.

Klein, Mina C., and H. Arthur Klein, *Käthe Kollwitz: Life in Art*. New York: Holt, Rinehart, and Winston, 1972.

Koontz, Ted, "Hard Choices: Abortion and War." *The Mennonite* (Feb. 28, 1978), 132-134.

Kummel, Werner, *Promise and Fulfillment, The Eschatological Message of Jesus*. Napervill, Ill.: A. R. Allenson, 1957.

Lakey, George, *Strategy for a Living Revolution*. San Francisco: W. H. Freeman and Company, 1968.

Lee, Dallas, *The Cotton Patch Evidence*. New York: Harper & Row, 1971.

Lele, Uma, *The Design of Rural Development: Lessons from Africa*. Baltimore: Johns Hopkins University Press, 1975.

Letts, Laurence Alan, *Peace and the Gospel: A Comparative Study of the Theological and Ethical Foundations of A. J. Muste's Radical Pacifism and Reinhold Niebuhr's Christian Realism*. A doctoral dissertation. Yale University, 1975.

Levi, Werner, "The Causes of War and Peace," in *The Strategy of World Order*, Vol. I, eds., Richard A. Falk and Saul H. Mendlovitz. New York: World Law Fund, 1966.

Lind, Millard, *Yahweh Is a Warrior: The Theology of Warfare in Ancient Israel.* Scottdale, Pa.: Herald Press, 1980.

Littell, Franklin H., *Anabaptist View of the Church.* Boston: Starr King Press, 1958.

Loomer, Bernard M., "Two Kinds of Power." *Criterion*, Vol. 15, No. 1 (Winter 1976), 11f.

Maghroori, Ray and Bennett Ramberg, *Globalism Versus Realism: International Relations Third Debate.* Boulder, Colo.: Westview Press, 1982.

Maugham, W. Somerset, *The Razor's Edge.* Garden City, New York: Doubleday, Doran & Co., Inc., 1944.

Mead, George H., *Mind, Self and Society from the Standpoint of a Social Behaviorist.* Chicago, Ill.: University of Chicago Press, 1934.

Mead, Margaret, "Warfare Is Only an Invention—Not a Biological Necessity," in *Peace and War*, eds., Charles K. Beitz and Theodore Herman. San Francisco: W. H. Freeman and Company, 1973.

Melko, Matthew, *Fifty-two Peaceful Societies.* Ontario, Canada: Oakville, 1973.

Mendenhall, George E., *Law and the Covenant in Israel and the Ancient Near East.* Pittsburgh, Pa.: The Presbyterian Board of Colportage of Western Pennsylvania, 1955.

Merton, Thomas, *The Asian Journal of Thomas Merton.* New York: New Directions Publishing Corporation, 1968.

Michaelson, Wes and Jim Wallis, "A Change of Heart: Billy Graham on the Nuclear Arms Race." *Sojourners*, (August 1979), 12-14.

Miller, William, *Nonviolence: A Christian Interpretation.* New York: Schocken Books, 1964.

Miller, William R., *Martin Luther King, Jr.: His Life, Martyrdom, and Meaning for the World.* New York: Weybright and Talley, 1968.

Montagu, Ashley, *The Nature of Human Aggression.* New York: Oxford University Press, 1976.

Moore, Jr., Barrington, *Reflections on the Causes of Human Misery and Upon Certain Proposals to Eliminate Them.* Boston: Beacon Press, 1970.

Morgenthau, Hans, *Politics Among the Nations: The Struggle for Power and Peace.* New York: A. A. Knopf, 1948.

Mott, Stephen, *Biblical Ethics and Social Change.* New York: Oxford University Press, 1982.

Mouw, Richard, *Politics and the Biblical Drama.* Grand Rapids: William B. Eerdmans Publishing Company, 1976.

Muste, A. J., "Pacifism and Perfectionsism." in *The Essays of A. J. Muste*, Ed. Nat Hentoff, New York: Simon and Schuster, 1967.

Neufeld, Vernon, ed., *If We Can Love: The Mennonite Mental Health Story.* Newton, Kans.: Faith and Life Press, 1983.

Newcombe, Alan and James Wert, *An Internation Tensiometer for the Prediction of War.* Oakville, Ontario: Canadian Peace Research Institute, 1972.

Niebuhr, H. R., *Radical Monotheism and Western Culture.* New York: Harper & Row, 1943.

Niebuhr, H. R., *The Responsible Self.* New York: Harper & Row, 1963.

Niebuhr, Reinhold, "The Illusion of World Government." in *Christian Realism and Political Problems*, New York: Charles Scribner's Sons, 1953.

Niebuhr, Reinhold, *Love and Justice.* Selections from the Shorter Writings of Reinhold Niebuhr, ed. by D. B. Robertson. Cleveland: World Publishing Company, 1957.

Niebuhr, Reinhold, *Moral Man and Immoral Society.* New York: Charles Scribner's Sons, 1932.

Nouwen, Henri, *Pray to Live, Thomas Merton: A Contemplative Critic.* Notre Dame: Fides Publishers, 1972.

Novak, Michael, *Ascent of the Mountain, Flight of the Dove.* New York: Harper & Row, 1971.

Novak, Michael, *The Christian Century.* (Feb. 21, 1979), 172f.

Nuttall, Geoffrey, *Christian Pacifism in History.* Berkeley, Calif.: World Without War Council, 1958.

Nyce, Dorothy Yoder, ed., *Which Way Women?* Akron, Pa.: Mennonite Central Committee Peace Section, 1980.

Ogletree, Thomas, and George Lucas, eds., *Lifeboat Ethics: The Moral Dilemmas of World Hunger.* New York: Harper & Row, 1976.

Osgood, Charles. *An Alternative to War or Surrender.* Urbana: University of Illinois Press, 1962.

Outka, Gene, "Social Justice and Equal Access to Health Care." *The Journal of Religious Ethics* (Spring 1974), 11-32.

Perrin, Norman, *The Kingdom of God in the Teaching of Jesus.* Philadelphia: Westminster Press, 1963.

Pope John XXIII, *Pacem in Terris*, 1963.

Potter, Ralph, *War and Moral Discourse.* Richmond, Va.: John Knox Press, 1969.

Potter, Ralph, *The Moral Logic of War.* Richmond: John Knox Press, 1969.

Powers, Charles, ed., *People/Profits: The Ethics of Investment.* New York: Council on Religion and International Affairs, 1972.

Rad, Gerhard von, *Der Heilige Krieg im alten Israel.* Zurich: Zwingli Verlag, 1951.

Rad, Gerhard von, "Shalom in the Old Testament." *Theological Dictionary of the New Testament*, ed. Gerhard Kittel, Vol. II. Grand Rapids: Eerdmans Publishing Company, 1964, 402-406.

Ramsey, Paul, "A Political Ethics Context for Strategic Thinking," in *Strategic Thinking and Its Moral Implications.* Ed., Morton A. Kaplan. University of Chicago, 1973.

Ramsey, Paul, *The Just War.* New York: Charles Scribner's Sons, 1968.

Ramsey, Paul, *The Patient as Person.* New Haven: Yale University Press, 1970.

Ramsey, Paul, *War and the Christian Conscience.* Durham, N.C.: Duke University Press, 1961.

Ramsey, Paul, *Who Speaks for the Church?* Nashville: Abingdon Press, 1967.

Rasmussen, Larry, and Bruce C. Birch, *The Bible and Ethics in the Christian Life.* Minneapolis: Augsburg Publishing House, 1976.

Rauschenbusch, Walter, *Theology for a Social Gospel.* Nashville: Abingdon Press, 1945.

Rawls, John, *A Theory of Justice.* Cambridge: Harvard University Press, 1971.

Reardon, Betty and Saul H. Mendlovitz, "World Law and Models of World Order," in *Peace and War.* Eds., Charles Beitz and Theodore Herman. San Francisco: W. H. Freeman and Company, 1973.

Reischauer, Edwin O., *Toward the 21st Century: Education for a Changing World.* New York: Vintage Books, 1974.

Remington, Robin, ed., *Winter in Prague: Documents on Czechoslovakia, Communism in Crisis.* Cambridge: M.I.T. Press, 1969.

Riste, Olav and Berit Nokleby, *Norway: 1940-1945: The Resistance Movement.* Oslo: Tanum, 1970.

Roberson, D. B., ed., *Voluntary Associations, A Study of Groups in Free Societies.* Richmond, Va.: John Knox Press, 1966.

Roberts, Adam, *Civilian Resistance as a National Defense.* Harrisburg, Pa.: Stackpole Books, 1968.

Rolland, Romain, *Mahatma Gandhi: The Man Who Became One with the Universal Being.* New York: Garland Publishing Co., 1973.

Ross, W. D., *The Right and the Good.* London: Oxford University Press, 1930.

Schnackenburg, Rudolf, *God's Rule and Kingdom.* New York: Herder and Herder, 1968.

Schumacher, E. F., *Small Is Beautiful.* New York: Harper and Row, 1973.

Sharp, Gene, *Making the Abolition of War a Realistic Goal.* Copyright by Gene Sharp, 1980.

Sharp, Gene, *The Politics of Nonviolent Action.* Boston: Porter Sargent, Publisher, 1973.

Sherif, Muzafer, *In Common Predicament: Social Psychology of Intergroup Conflict and Cooperation.* London: Routledge & K. Paul, 1967.

Sider, Ronald, *Christ and Violence.* Scottdale, Pa.: Herald Press, 1979.

Sidgwick, Henry, *The Methods of Ethics.* Chicago: University of Chicago Press, 1962.

Sivard, Ruth, *World Military and Social Expenditures.* Leesburg, Va.: World Priorities, 1978 and 1983 editions.

Southeast Alaska Empire. Juneau, Alaska (Jan. 26, 1977).

Stanford, Barbara, ed., *Peacemaking*. New York: Bantam Books, Inc., 1976.

Stendahl, Krister, *The Bible and the Role of Women*. Philadelphia: Fortress Press, 1966.

Stoesz, Edgar, *Beyond Good Intentions*. Newton, Kans.: United Printing Inc., 1972.

Stoesz, Edgar, *Thoughts on Development*. Akron, Pa.: Mennonite Central Committee Development Monograph Series, No. 1.

Stonier, Tom, "A Proposal for Global Cooperation." *Bulletin of the Atomic Scientists* (May 1972), 31-34.

Suhl, Yuri, ed., *They Fought Back: The Story of Jewish Resistance in Nazi Europe*. New York: Schocken Books, 1967.

Sullivan, Michael P., "Competing Frameworks and the Study of Contemporary International Studies." *Millennium: Journal of International Studies* (Autumn 1978), 73.

Swartley, Willard, *Slavery, Sabbath, War, and Women*. Scottdale, Pa.: Herald Press, 1983.

Swomley, John, *American Empire: The Political Ethics of Twentieth Century Conquest*. New York: Macmillan Company, 1970.

Swomley, John, *Liberation Ethics*. New York: Macmillan Company, 1972.

Tabb, William K., "Social, Political, and Ethical Meaning of the Reagan Revolution." *The Annual of the Society of Christian Ethics*, 1983, 185-216.

The Mennonite (May 6, 1975), 289.

Walzer, Michael, *Just and Unjust Wars*. New York: Basic Books, 1977.

Walzer, Michael, *Political Action: A Practical Guide to Movement Politics*. Chicago: Quadrangle Books, 1971.

Walzer, Michael, *The Revolution of the Saints*. New York: Atheneum, 1972.

Warmbrunn, Werner, *The Dutch Under German Occupation, 1940-45*. Stanford, Calif.: Stanford University Press, 1972.

Washburn, Michael, and Paul Wehr, *Peace and World Order Systems*. Beverly Hills, Calif.: Sage Publications, Inc., 1976.

Wehr, Paul, *Conflict Regulation*. Boulder, Colo.: Westview Press, 1979.

Wehr, Paul, "Developing the Study of Peace and Conflict." Unpublished paper delivered at the joint meetings of Society for Applied Anthropology, The American Ethnological Society, and the Council on Anthropology and Education, Montreal, 1972.

Weil, Simone, *Gravity and Grace*. London: Routledge and Kegan Paul, 1963.

Weil, Simone, *The Need for Roots*. New York: Octagon, 1979.

Weil, Simone, *Selected Essays*. New York: Oxford University Press, 1962.

Weil, Simone, *Seventy Letters*. London: Oxford University Press, 1965.

Weil, Simone, *Waiting for God*. New York: Harper and Row, 1973.

West, Charles, *Communism and the Theologians*. New York: Macmillan Company, 1958.

Weston, Burns, "Human Rights and the World Order." Lecture delivered at Bethel College, Peace Lecture Series, March 1, 1979. Available in Mennonite Library and Archives, Bethel College, North Newton, KS 67117.

Wichita Eagle (Nov. 10, 1979).

Wilder, Amos, *Eschatology and Ethics in the Teaching of Jesus*. New York and London: Harper and Brothers, 1939.

Williams, Daniel Day, *God's Grace and Man's Hope*. New York: Harper & Row, 1949.

Williams, Oliver, and John W. Houck, *Full Value: Cases in Christian Business Ethics*. San Francisco: Harper & Row, 1978.

Williams, Preston, "Impartiality, Racism and Sexism" *The Annual of the Society of Christian Ethics*, 1983, 147f.

Wills, David, "Racial Justice and the Limits of American Liberalism." *The Journal of Religious Ethics* (Fall 1978), 187-220.

Windsor, Philip, and Adam Roberts, *Czechoslovakia 1968: Reform, Repression and Resistance*. New York: Columbia University Press, for the Institute of Strategic Studies, London, 1969.

Wogaman, J. Philip, *A Christian Method of Moral Judgment*. Philadelphia: Westminster Press, 1976.

Wogaman, J. Philip, *The Great Economic Debate: An Ethical Analysis.* Philadelphia: Westminster Press, 1977.

World Council of Churches, "Violence, Non-violence and the Struggle for Social Justice." *The Ecumenical Review*, Vol. XXV, No. 4 (Oct. 1973).

Wright, Quincy, *A Study of War*, abridged edition. Chicago: University of Chicago Press, 1964.

Yarrow, C. H. Mike, *Quaker Experiences in International Conciliation.* New Haven, Conn.: Yale University Press, 1978.

Yoder, John H., *Nevertheless: The Varieties of Religious Pacifism.* Scottdale, Pa.: Herald Press, 1971.

Yoder, John, *Reinhold Niebuhr and Christian Pacifism*, A Concern Reprint. Scottdale, Pa.: Herald Press. Reproduced with no modification from the *Mennonite Quarterly Review* (Vol. XXIX) 101f.

Yoder, John H., *The Politics of Jesus.* Grand Rapids: Eerdmans, 1972.

Yoder, John, "What Would You Do If . . ." *Journal of Religious Ethics* (Fall 1974), 81f.

Zampaglione, Gerardo, *The Idea of Peace in Antiquity.* Notre Dame: University of Notre Dame Press, 1973.

Zehr, Howard, *Victim Offender Reconciliation Program: Organizers Manual.* Akron, Pa.: Mennonite Central Committee, Office of Criminal Justice, 1982.

INDEX OF SCRIPTURES

293

Index of Persons

Subject Index

THE CHRISTIAN PEACE SHELF

The Christian Peace Shelf is a selection of Herald Press books and pamphlets devoted to the promotion of Christian peace principles and their applications. The editor (appointed by the Mennonite Central Committee Peace Section) and an inter-Mennonite editorial board represent the historic concern for peace within these constituencies.

FOR SERIOUS STUDY

Durland, William R. *No King but Caesar?* (1975). A Catholic lawyer looks at Christian violence.

Enz, Jacob J. *The Christian and Warfare* (1972). The roots of pacifism in the Old Testament.

Friesen, Duane K. *Christian Peacemaking and International Conflict* (1986). Realistic pacifism in the context of international conflict.

Hershberger, Guy F. *War, Peace, and Nonresistance* (Third Edition, 1969). A classic comprehensive work on nonresistance in faith and history.

Hornus, Jean-Michel. *It Is Not Lawful for Me to Fight* (1980). Early Christian attitudes toward war, violence, and the state.

Kaufman, Donald D. *What Belongs to Caesar?* (1969). Basic arguments against voluntary payment of war taxes.

Lasserre, Jean. *War and the Gospel* (1962). An analysis of Scriptures related to the ethical problem of war.

Lind, Millard C. *Yahweh Is a Warrior* (1980). The theology of warfare in ancient Israel.

Ramseyer, Robert L. *Mission and the Peace Witness* (1979). Implications of the biblical peace testimony for the evangelizing mission of the church.

Trocmé, André. *Jesus and the Nonviolent Revolution* (1975). The social and political implications of the year of Jubilee in the teachings of Jesus.

Yoder, John H. *The Original Revolution* (1972). Essays on Christian pacifism.

_____. *Nevertheless* (1971). The varieties and shortcomings of religious pacifism.

FOR EASY READING

Beachey, Duane. *Faith in a Nuclear Age* (1983). A Christian response to war.

Drescher, John M. *Why I Am a Conscientious Objector* (1982). A personal summary of basic issues for every Christian facing military involvements.

Eller, Vernard. *War and Peace from Genesis to Revelation* (1981). Explores peace as a consistent theme developing throughout the Old and New Testaments.

Kaufman, Donald D. *The Tax Dilemma: Praying for Peace, Paying for War* (1978). Biblical, historical, and practical considerations on the war tax issue.

Kraybill, Donald B. *Facing Nuclear War* (1982). Relates Christian faith to the chief moral issue of our time.

_____. *The Upside-Down Kingdom* (1978). A fresh study of the synoptic Gospels on affluence, war-making, status-seeking, and religious exclusivism.

McSorley, Richard. *New Testament Basis of Peacemaking* (1985). A Jesuit makes the case for biblical pacifism.

Miller, John W. *The Christian Way* (1969). A guide to the Christian life based on the Sermon on the Mount.

Miller, Melissa, and Phil M. Shenk. *The Path of Most Resistance* (1982). Stories of Mennonite conscientious objectors who did not cooperate with the Vietnam draft.

Sider, Ronald J. *Christ and Violence* (1979). A sweeping reappraisal of the church's teaching on violence.

Steiner, Susan Clemmer. *Joining the Army That Sheds No Blood* (1982). The case for biblical pacifism written for teens.

Wenger, J. C. *The Way of Peace* (1977). A brief treatment on Christ's teachings and the way of peace through the centuries.

Yoder, John H. *He Came Preaching Peace* (1985). Bible lectures addressed to persons already involved in the Christian peace movement.

_____. *What Would You Do?* (1983). A serious answer to a standard question.

FOR CHILDREN

Bauman, Elizabeth Hershberger. *Coals of Fire* (1954). Stories of people who returned good for evil.

Lenski, Lois, and Clyde Robert Bulla. *Sing for Peace* (1985). Simple hymns on the theme of living with others.

Moore, Ruth Nulton. *Peace Treaty* (1977). A historical novel involving the efforts of Moravian missionary Christian Frederick Post to bring peace to the Ohio Valley in 1758.

Smucker, Barbara Claassen. *Henry's Red Sea* (1955). The dramatic escape of 1,000 Russian Mennonites from Berlin following World War II.

ABOUT THE AUTHOR

Duane K. Friesen was born in 1940 and raised on a farm near American Falls, Idaho. He graduated from Bethel College in North Newton, Kansas, in 1962 with majors in English and philosophy. From 1962 to 1965 he attended the Associated Mennonite Biblical Seminaries in Elkhart, Indiana, graduating with a B.D. degree in 1965. After studying for one year in Berlin, Germany, at the Freie Universität and the Kirchliche Hochschule, he attended Harvard Divinity School from 1966 to 1970. He received the Th.D. degree in social ethics from Harvard Divinity School in 1972. His dissertation focused on Ernst Troeltsch's *Social Teachings of the Christian Churches*.

He has taught at Bethel College (Kansas) since 1970. Currently he is professor of Bible and Religion and chairman of the department. While at Bethel College he was responsible for developing a program in peace studies. He has been active in the Consortium of Peace Research, Education and Development (COPRED), having served on the executive committee of the organization for several years. In 1976-77 he spent a sabbatical at the Institute for Ecumenical and Cultural Research, Collegeville, Minnesota, where work on this book was begun. He has also traveled and studied on several occasions in the Middle East, having been a fellow at the Institute for Advanced Theological Research Ethics and the American Academy of Religion.

He is a member of the General Conference Mennonite Church. He has been active on various committees, including an abortion committee which prepared a statement on abortion that was adopted by the General Conference in 1980. To help congregations study the issue of abortion he wrote the book *Moral Issues in the Control of Birth* (1974). He is a member of the Board of the Great Plains Seminary Extension Program and is chairman of the Peace and Social Concerns Committee of the Western District Conference of the General Conference Mennonite Church.

He is married to Elizabeth Voth Friesen and has two daughters, Anne and Sara.